DUMBARTON OAKS
MEDIEVAL LIBRARY

Jan M. Ziolkowski, General Editor

OLD ENGLISH SHORTER POEMS

VOLUME II

DOML 32

Old English Shorter Poems

VOLUME II
WISDOM AND LYRIC

Edited and Translated by

ROBERT E. BJORK

DUMBARTON OAKS
MEDIEVAL LIBRARY

HARVARD UNIVERSITY PRESS
CAMBRIDGE, MASSACHUSETTS
LONDON, ENGLAND
2014

Library of Congress Cataloging-in-Publication Data
Old English Shorter Poems. Volume II, Wisdom and Lyric / edited and translated by Robert E. Bjork.
   pages cm. — (Dumbarton Oaks Medieval Library ; 32)
   Includes bibliographical references and index.
   ISBN 978-0-674-05306-9 (alk. paper)
   1. English poetry—Old English, ca. 450–1100 —Translations into English. I. Bjork, Robert E., 1949– II. Title: Wisdom and Lyric.
   PR1508.O553 2014
   829′.1 — dc23   2013034086

Contents

Introduction

From suffering comes wisdom, and the Anglo-Saxons—like every other people on earth—had an abundance of both. For the mundane afflictions and tribulations of everyday life, they had their remedies. If someone had a stabbing pain, if someone was troubled by a cyst, if a dwarf was plaguing someone's sleep with nightmares or witch-riding or fever, the Anglo-Saxons had well-tested charms to ameliorate the situation. For more complicated conundrums, such as loss of fortune or position or being exiled from everything held dear, they had their solutions, too, from the stoic, matter-of-fact observation in *Maxims II* about the indifference of the universe to human suffering ("Woe is wondrously clinging; clouds glide," l. 13) to the Boethian philosophical musings in a poem such as *The Wanderer* about the ephemerality and unreliability of all earthly things. Poetry thus becomes therapy, and the Anglo-Saxons seem to have known even better than Wallace Stevens did that it "is a purging of the world's poverty and change and evil and death. It is a present perfecting, a satisfaction in the irremediable poverty of life."[1]

Many of the poems collected in this volume are the most famous and most read of the corpus outside of *Beowulf,* such as *The Wanderer* and *The Seafarer.* Others are obscure and seldom referred to at all, such as *A Proverb from Win-*

frid's Time, arguably the earliest Old English verse on record (perhaps the early seventh century). All, however, have been assembled in two edited volumes from the Anglo-Saxon Poetic Records (ASPR) titled *The Exeter Book* and *The Anglo-Saxon Minor Poems.* For ease of reference, all twenty-four poems and twelve metrical charms are reproduced here in the order in which they appear in those two books. For ease of discussion, however, I will introduce them in four groups into which, from our modern perspective, they seem to cluster. These groups (again from our modern perspective) move from the least to the most sophisticated and complex, from the most utilitarian and concrete to the most abstract and cerebral: (1) metrical charms (printed last in the present volume), (2) gnomic and proverbial poems, (3) wisdom poems, and (4) lyrical and elegiac poems. Examples of the last three are scattered throughout this entire book. The Anglo-Saxons themselves undoubtedly would not have made such fine distinctions among genres if they made any at all, and you will quickly see that wisdom and lyricism and the elegiac infuse just about every poem translated here. And you will see, too, that they all testify to the Anglo-Saxon belief in the value and power of words.[2]

1. THE METRICAL CHARMS

We begin with the twelve metrical charms for three reasons: first, they may contain the oldest, pre-Christian material in the Old English corpus (their irregular Old English meter perhaps indicates that they rely on a period of oral tradition older than that of classical Old English poetry); second, they represent a relatively simple manifestation of wisdom, namely, how to cope with the mundane realities of living (cattle theft, for example, or miscarriage, or a cyst);[3] and third, they affirm the power of poetry. In fact, the Old English word for charm, incantation, or spell is *galdor,* which derives from the verb *galan* (to sing) and which indicates that singing or chanting is central to the charm tradition. The charms, therefore, offer a fine starting place for beginning to appreciate the other poetry, the other sounds and songs and rhythmic and spiritual ruminations, of the Anglo-Saxons.

The metrical charms are dispersed throughout five different manuscripts ranging in date from the tenth to the late eleventh century.[4] The charms themselves cannot be dated with any certainty,[5] but they have been used regularly as a means for elucidating Anglo-Saxon culture, particularly pre-Christian Anglo-Saxon culture. The possible reference to the heathen fertility goddess Erce in Charm 1, the mention of the pagan god Woden in Charm 2, the appearance of the dwarf in Charm 4 and of the elves in Charms 4 and 7 have garnered most attention for that enterprise. Yet most of the charms display a syncretic blend of pagan and Christian, and all were recorded during the Christian period. At least two questions, then, naturally arise: Were these ritual utterances written down because they worked? And if so, how were they performed?

We do not know the answer to the first question. We can comfortably surmise, however, that the charms merited transcription because they did work—or at least were perceived to work well enough to be passed down to posterity. Given their content and nature, that statement seems ludicrous to us in the twenty-first century, when a wen or harmless sebaceous cyst (Charm 12) is best dealt with by a dermatologist wielding needle and syringe or scalpel, not by a chant commanding it to disappear. We simply do not believe in charms any more. The Anglo-Saxons, on the other hand, did, and we should not dismiss their versions of them as mere quaint relics of an ignorant past. Faith and belief, after all, have been accepted as powerful agents for healing even in our own day, as a cursory search of the MEDLINE online health and medicine databases reveals.[6] The metrical charms could have been effective in their own way for the people who believed in them and chanted them on appropriate occasions.

We also do not know by whom or how these charms were performed on those occasions, so the second question above has to go unanswered as well. The speakers could, of course, have been those most directly affected by the problems posed, regardless of their learning, such as the man or boy faced with plowing an unfertile field in Charm 1 or the woman experiencing a difficult childbirth or miscarriage in Charm 6. Or the speakers could have been witches[7] or others specially trained for the purpose, such as herbalists (Charm 2)[8] or priest-poets, who would lead sacral dances,[9] or tribal shamans, who would function as mediums between this world and the spirit world.[10] Similarly, these speakers could have chanted the charms with much animation and dance, as the instructions in Charms 1 and 4 seem to imply, or they could have done so with little; and they could have accomplished their task in a loud voice (what Charm 4 seems to call for) or a mumbling or soft one (as seems required by Charm 8 for settling a swarm of bees). The performative aspects of the charms are forever lost to us, unfortunately.[11] Their intrinsic interest and mystery, however, are not. They still cast their spells.

2. GNOMIC AND PROVERBIAL POETRY AND *WIDSITH*

Gnomic and proverbial poetry—pithy sayings or observations about fundamental truths—also still cast their spells, and they possess some of the same virtues as the charms. They seem ancient and fairly practical in articulating both what is ("Winter is coldest," *Maxims II*, l. 5) and what ought to be ("One must be true to a friend on each path," *Maxims I*, l. 144); and they seem to reflect the values of the culture that produced them. *A Proverb from Winfrid's Time*, for example, reflects the immense value the Anglo-Saxons and other Germanic peoples placed on courage; the lack of it may allow you to live longer, but you will die friendless. Gnomic poetry thus seems to function as the repository of the wisdom of the tribe as it relates to the natural world, the preoccupations of the social world, and the verities and lasting realities of the Christian world.

Gnomic poetry is ubiquitous in Old English and other old Germanic poetry,[12] but in Old English it is mainly concentrated in two heterogeneous collections of aphorisms, now titled *Maxims I* in *The Exeter Book* and *Maxims II* in the manuscript Cotton Tiberius B.1 housed in the British Library. Neither collection can be dated with any certainty, although the conversion period has had its strong proponents.[13] The latest dates would be the times of composition of *The Exeter Book* (second half of the tenth century) and Cotton Tiberius B.1 (mid-eleventh century). We do not know who wrote or compiled these poems, either, although in the case of *Maxims I,* one scholar has plausibly argued that it could have been a woman.[14] And we do not know the purpose of either poem, although naturally there have been speculations. Among those are that they may have been used in schools for instruction in values and poetic composition.[15] In expressing basic components of the Anglo-Saxon worldview, they clearly had didactic import, and that could well have extended beyond the confines of school, however.[16] Through these simple catalogs of common wisdom—on things ranging from the temperature of hail to drinking customs, funerary practices, and marriage settlements—we get a strong sense of the need for past experience to establish a current order in society. And when individual maxims appear in other poems, they lend credence to those poems by anchoring them in a venerable and ancient tradition. To use Stanley Greenfield's term for the narrator in *Beowulf,* they supply the poems with an authenticating voice.[17]

The bearer of that voice is the Anglo-Saxon poet, who, in a predominantly oral society, is also the bearer of cultural memory, legend, and wisdom. The poem *Widsith,* another very early composition, probably from the seventh century,[18] illustrates how crucial the poet was for the Anglo-Saxons. Widsith (meaning "far traveler") describes just how far afield his audiences have been, ranging over three centuries and a number of peoples from the Medes, Romans, and Greeks to the Saracens, Persians, Egyptians, and Hebrews to the continental Germans, who dominate the list.[19] The poem may have functioned as a mnemonic device for remembering major themes and tribes and periods of history that should be incorporated into the present worldview. The speaker in it then becomes the symbol for all poets, the far travelers who gather wisdom through vast expanses of time and space for the betterment of their people.

3. WISDOM POETRY

Having talked about charms and maxims, we have already been talking about wisdom poetry, for they both embody the accumulated knowledge of the Anglo-Saxons on certain subjects. They are, at the core, sagacious poems, wise poems. Generally speaking, in fact, all poetry can be considered an expression of wisdom, because every poem instructs us in some way. The lyric and elegiac poems in this volume do, and epic poems, such as *Beowulf,* do as well. In talking about Old English poetry, however, scholars have narrowed the definition of "wisdom poetry" to those poems already discussed plus some ten or so others "that have certain affinities with near-eastern wisdom texts best exemplified by the Old Testament books of Proverbs and Ecclesiastes."[20] They tend to be nonnarrative treatments of general and universal truths that reveal the wisdom and learning of the speaker.

Three of these poems are catalog poems, *The Gifts of Mortals, The Fortunes of Mortals,* and *The Rune Poem.* The first two appear in *The Exeter Book* and, like the vast majority of Old English poetry, cannot be dated with certainty, although meter and language may point to a date in the late eighth or early ninth century.[21] The third poem exists only in an early eighteenth-century printed version of a transcription and—unsurprisingly—cannot be dated with any precision at all. Somewhere between the seventh and the tenth centuries has been suggested as a possible date, with a later one currently having the most scholarly support.[22]

The Gifts of Mortals, which has its classical[23] and biblical antecedents[24] as well as a close parallel in Cynewulf's *Christ II,*[25] lists a large number of talents with which human beings have been endowed. It thereby reveals a good deal about what the Anglo-Saxons valued. Running, hunting, playing at tables, playing the harp, building sturdy halls, singing songs, giving good counsel, knowing the law, steering a ship, being witty at a banquet—all these virtues and more are lauded by their presence in this poem. And most of them point to the prominence of the life of the mind in Anglo-Saxon culture. The poem emphasizes intellectual skills, arts and crafts, which by their nature tend toward abstraction. *The Fortunes of Mortals,* while it does emphasize some of the things *The Gifts of Mortals* does, stands in stark contrast to that poem. The tone and atmosphere derive from quotidian, violent and hard, reality, and the poem is fixated on death.[26] We witness a youth devoured by a wolf, for example, another plunge to his death from a tree, and a man's corpse hanging by the neck while a raven plucks out its eyes. *The Fortunes of Men* makes clear by its focus why the life of the mind is a better thing to cling to than this mortal life. The mutability and instability of the world encourage us to move beyond it and eventually to the absolute in God.

The third catalog wisdom poem, *The Rune Poem,*[27] likewise tends toward Christian didacticism or at least toward the subordination of whatever may have originally been pagan in it to a Christian purpose. The runic alphabet, or futhark, was created by the Germanic peoples in the centuries after the birth of Christ.[28] The Old English poem about it offers us the twenty-nine letters themselves, followed by their names (e.g., ᚠ, the first rune, indicates both the sound "f" and the word *feoh,* "wealth"). The rune's name is the first word of a stanza describing what it stands for as a symbol. The poem can be classified with the maxims (e.g., "Ice is very cold," l. 29) and has some riddling qualities (e.g., a play on the Old English words for "tree" and "faith" [*treow* and *treo*], l. 80).[29] And it ends on a decidedly elegiac note with the ineluctable fate of all human beings: "Earth is horrible for everyone when inexorably the flesh, the corpse, begins to cool, the pallid one to choose soil as a bedfellow; fruits fail, joys depart, pledges cease" (ll. 90–94).

The last four poems in this "wisdom" category have largely been greeted in our day with audible yawns. As with the metrical charms, however, we should be quick to listen to what these poems may tell us, not to scoff at their content. Elaine Tuttle Hansen says, our "'modern' views of what is platitudinous and what is poetic are of little use in interpreting the parts of the extant Old English canon that give us the most difficulty."[30]

Precepts, perhaps the earliest of the four,[31] is an admonition of father to son akin in spirit to Hrothgar's "sermon" to Beowulf in the poem of that name, lines 1700–84. Most critics have been merciless in their condemnation of this piece. One memorably describes it as belonging to "the debris or spoil heaps of the monastic tradition."[32] But a few scholars have found merit in it. Hansen, for example, puts the work in the context of the ancient Near Eastern and

Old Irish "instruction genre,"[33] and Michael Drout details how the poem reflects major societal changes occasioned by the tenth-century Benedictine reform.[34] You, on the other hand, may simply find interesting the ways, by means of the dramatic scene the poem creates, that it may partially answer our question about how *Maxims I* and *Maxims II* and other proverbial lore were used by the Anglo-Saxons. A wise man or father figure could have passed on to others proverbs and maxims that were biblical in import ("Love your father and mother with your heart," l. 9 [one of the Ten Commandments]) or more generally gnomic ("you should never be deceitful to your friend," l. 31 [compare *Maxims I*, l. 144]). The same observation can be made about *Vainglory* and *The Order of the World* (sometimes called *The Wonders of Creation*), which become more compelling when understood in the context of Old English gnomic and proverbial literature. Both contain the wisdom of the tribe as well as the wisdom of books.

The last of the wisdom poems, *Solomon and Saturn*, is a combination of two poetic fragments and one prose fragment. Only the poetic fragments are translated here.[35] Dating these fragments has proved to be impossible, and guesses at fixing a date have ranged from the early eighth to the late tenth centuries.[36] Deliberately obscure, the dialogues present the god Saturn questioning King Solomon about the nature and power of the Pater Noster in the first and about a range of topics, such as the power of books and what free will is, in the second. The dialogues emphasize learning and erudition as a guide to living—Saturn begins the first by saying that he has "eaten the books of all islands" (ll. 1–2)—which moves toward the reflective elegiac mode.

4. LYRIC AND ELEGY

Charms, gnomic poetry, the catalog wisdom poems mentioned above—especially *The Fortunes of Mortals*—are all closely connected to the elegy. Elegy, like charm, uses language to ameliorate a bad situation.[37] Gnomic and catalog poems like elegies contain within them a kind of nostalgia, since they are memorial verse. In the lists of common wisdom and common fates, we get a strong sense of the need for a past to establish a current order and a wish that that past (in the case of gnomic poetry) could live again. The *ubi sunt* (where are they now) theme or theme of lost glory and prosperity used to such great effect in *The Wanderer,* lines 92 ff., reinforces that wish.[38] All the rest of the Old English elegies are nostalgic and implicitly make use of the *ubi sunt* theme and of the theme of exile that initially gives rise to the speaker's loss.[39]

Like the other terms for Old English genres, "elegy" is inadequate because it describes a wide variety of poems that are not entirely alike and do not conform to standard notions of what an elegy should be. Furthermore, an elegiac tone permeates virtually all of Old English poetry.[40] A generally accepted definition of the Old English elegy, however, is that it "is a relatively short reflective or dramatic poem embodying a contrasting pattern of loss *and* consolation, ostensibly based upon a specific personal experience or observation, and expressing an attitude towards that experience."[41] Nine poems have been accepted as fitting into that category.[42] All are contained in the tenth-century *Exeter Book;* none can be accurately dated.[43] Two are in the voice of a woman, and those two plus three others are extremely enigmatic compositions. *Deor, Wulf and Eadwacer, The Wife's Lament, The Husband's Message,* and *The Rhyming Poem* have all proved stubbornly resistant to interpretation.

In *Deor,* the poet-speaker deals with his own bad fortune by comparing it with the sometimes-horrific experiences of others both in the legendary Germanic past and in history.[44] It is an unusual poem in its having stanzaic form (as do *Wulf and Eadwacer* and *The Seasons for Fasting*) and a mysterious refrain, "that passed away; so can this," in which "that" refers to the woes depicted in the previous stanza and "this" to the poet's present trouble. The refrain seems fairly unambiguous in the beginning. It appears to change, however, as we move through the poem, so that bad and good fortune become one and the same. The poem ends, for example, with Deor identifying himself and specifying the source of his pain: he has been replaced as the poet of his people by another, the legendary Germanic bard Heorrenda. He has thus been deprived of his position but simultaneously elevated to the level of the other legendary and mythic figures in the poem. If there is consolation in this poem, it may come from that elevation.

Wulf and Eadwacer is even more mystifying than *Deor.* The female speaker has been violently separated from her husband, and she and he have been placed on different islands, but we do not know why. Cruel men want to kill her husband. Again, we do not know why. Someone perhaps named Eadwacer may have raped her, and there is a whelp, an offspring (of what nature, we can't be sure), of her union with either Wolf or Eadwacer, but we cannot be sure which. And the refrain ("It's different for us") is more elusive than the one in *Deor.* We cannot possibly tell what "it" refers to. In addition, lupine imagery seems basic to the poem (e.g., wolf, whelp, the word *bog,* which can mean the forequarters of an animal, all appear in it), but we are not sure why. Is the poem about a wolf pack, or is the wolf pack just an apt simile for the war-band bond in Anglo-Saxon society? To compound the interpretive problem, the poem ends with the utterly enigmatic statement that one cannot tear apart what was never joined, their song together.

The lack of a context is one major factor that makes *Wulf and Eadwacer* so frustratingly perplexing. So too with *The Wife's Lament,* a poem likewise spoken in a woman's voice. The details of her situation elude us, but her central dilemma is clear: she has been separated from her husband, his family has rejected her, she is in a cave lamenting her present misery. From these basic facts, a myriad of questions grow. Why did the husband go away? Why did his kin people turn against her? And who caused them to do so? Was it the husband himself? Where is the wife now, in voluntary exile, in her native country, in another country? Does her husband still love her? Or has he turned against her as well? Is the ending of the poem therefore a gnomic utterance extrapolated from personal experience or a curse on the husband beginning with a gnomic generalization?[45] We will undoubtedly never know the answers to such questions. We will, however, always be able to react to the dire mood of the poem and its major themes of exile, separation and loss, and earthly mutability. Pain does not need contextualization to be understood.

The Wife's Lament and *The Husband's Message* are often seen as complementary poems in *The Exeter Book,* but we have little assurance that the poems were meant to be read as companion pieces. Old English poetry is remarkably lacking in any "romantic" interest. Few women appear in it, so linking these two compositions is largely a fanciful venture, especially since we are not even sure if *The Husband's Message* constitutes a unified whole.[46] It is preceded in *The Exeter Book* by *Riddle 60,* which many feel constitutes the beginning of a sequence of four short poems (*The Husband's Message* as traditionally defined consists of three clearly discernible sections in the manuscript) in which a piece of wood bears a message from husband to wife assuring her of his love.[47] The elegiac elements of loss and consolation do not congeal as well in this piece as in the other elegies, which has moved one critic to label it the least elegiac of the group.[48]

The same cannot be said of *The Rhyming Poem,* which has a well-defined two-part structure juxtaposing the past joys and glory of the speaker in the mead hall with his present misery after having lost both. He finds his consolation in the Christian God. Despite that clear structure, however, this most mysterious and perplexing poem is almost impossible to understand at the lexical level. Anne Klinck says that "in its consistent use of both rhyme and alliteration throughout, it is unique in Old English, and worthy of attention for that reason alone, but the exigencies of the form compelled the author to use many rare words, perhaps nonce-words, making the poem obscure, and occasionally, when the problem is compounded by textual corruption, almost impenetrable."[49] If you keep two things in mind when reading it, however, it may become easier, or at least less frustrating, to grasp. The first is the Anglo-Saxon love of riddles and enigma. The original audience may have been perplexed, too, and were meant to be tantalized by its many complexities rather than moved to solve all of them. The second is the obvious prominence of aural effects in the poem. The pounding, rolling, rollicking rhyme forces the audience to focus on it more than anything else, so the sound of the poem perhaps contains more of its meaning than the narrative itself. A poem by Gerard Manley Hopkins offers an instructive analogue in this regard. *Inversnaid* begins,

> This darksome burn, horseback brown
> His rollrock highroad roaring down,
> In coop and in comb the fleece of his foam
> Flutes and low to the lake falls home.[50]

Sound supersedes sense in Hopkins's poem, as it does in the Old English, where the answer to the poem's riddle may be that life on earth is predictable and inevitable. The incessant rhyme, regular alliterative patterning, and regular stress patterns all intensify the poem's pace, thus reinforcing the sense of our inexorable rush toward loss and death and, if we make the right choices, toward heavenly reward in the afterlife.

Although none of the last four elegies poses such interpretive difficulties as the first five discussed here, they do have their challenges. The fragment here titled *Resignation (B): An Exile's Lament,* for example, was once thought to be the concluding part of *Resignation (A),* because one immediately follows the other in *The Exeter Book.*[51] Since 1976, however, the two have been generally accepted as separate fragments—the beginning of one poem and the conclusion of another. A leaf was lost at this point in the manuscript, which led to the deceptive appearance that the abutting fragments were a continuous poem, and they are printed as such in the ASPR under the title *Resignation*. Although some general thematic similarities contributed to the earlier editorial confusion, the first poem is a penitential prayer and the second an exile's lament.[52] *Resignation (B): An Exile's Lament,* in fact, may also be spoken by Jonah in his flight from God.[53] It may be a unique exploration in Old English of self-pity.[54] Alan Bliss and Allen Frantzen remind us that it is spoken, after all, "by a man who never succeeds in any of his enterprises, and who blames everyone but himself for his failure."[55]

The Ruin, too, seems relatively straightforward. It is a meditation on a decayed city, perhaps the Roman city of Bath, and is fruitfully read after reading *Durham,* an Old English *encomium urbis,*[56] or praise of a city, that brings to mind the country-house poems of the seventeenth century, such as Ben Jonson's *To Penshurst.* The scenes that *Durham* and *To Penshurst* evoke are splendid and idyllic, like the beautiful woman in her prime on one side of a *memento mori* painting, while the scenes that *The Ruin* evokes are like the skeletal image of the woman after death on the painting's other side. *The Ruin,* however, provides no explicit moral; that comes from the simple juxtaposition of a ruined city in the present with its time of vibrancy in the past. In one way at least, the poem is an extended maxim or gnome. Sorrow follows joy; silent ruin follows bustling life.

Ezra Pound famously translated *The Seafarer* into modern English, enraging some scholars with his infidelity to the text and delighting others with his keen ear for the poem's music:

May I for my own self song's truth reckon,
Journey's jargon, how I in harsh days
Hardship endured oft . . .[57]

Pound's translating the poem at all, however, testifies to
its power to engage, and because of that power it and *The
Wanderer* have become the most famous Old English poems
apart from *Beowulf.* Both explore the themes of exile from
the war band, both employ seascapes and the *ubi sunt* theme
to do so, and both are integrally Christian. The speaker of
The Seafarer initially details and laments the hardships and
suffering that he has endured on his sea journey but then
embraces them symbolically as necessary components of
the ascetic life Christians choose to live in this mutable
world. The sea therefore seems to take on a dual meaning
in the poem, reflecting both instability and permanence,
and the poem thus moves toward an eschatological vision
through the personal perspective of the poet.

In *The Wanderer,* however—and here we end with the
poem that begins this whole collection just as we began with
those that end it, *The Metrical Charms*—we get a vision that
is more Boethian in essence than eschatological. By system-
atically listing all the good things in life that he has lost in
his exile, the speaker comes to realize that earthly things
have no meaning. Earthly goods will not last, social custom
will not last, gnomic wisdom will not last, poetry will not
last. Nothing in the world, whether we perceive it as good or
as bad, can withstand time. Our only security, then, is in the
firm foundation of heaven, where we should invest all our
hope. So the wanderer, the "earth stepper" (l. 6), who waits

for God's favor at the beginning of the poem actively seeks it at the end (l. 114), as "the one wise in mind" sitting apart from the world and pondering its mutability.[58] The poem is psychological, not allegorical, and it teaches us perhaps more than any other in this volume how to deal with the vagaries and reversals and denials of life regardless of what our faith might be. It is an altogether fitting conclusion for the study of Old English wisdom and lyric poetry.

I would like to thank Arizona State University (ASU) for sabbatical leave during the fall of 2012, when I completed a great deal of work on this book, and I am grateful as well to the staff of Hayden Library at ASU for its superb help with securing all the interlibrary loans I needed for writing the introduction to and critical apparatus for this book. During the spring of 2013, three graduate students at ASU turned their attention to several of my translations and made them better through their penetrating observations: Kent Linthicum, Lakshami Mahajan, and Daniel Najork. And in the summer of 2013, Elizabeth Tyler and Christopher Jones of the DOML editorial board as well as the Old English Editor for the DOML, Daniel Donoghue, scrutinized what I thought was the final draft of this book and made numerous suggestions for improving it. I am greatly indebted to all of them.

Finally, I thank Shirley LaBarre, a woman of profound wisdom and constant lyricism, my high school English teacher nearly fifty years ago and adopted mother ever since. She knew and knows the way, and to her, I dedicate this volume.

NOTES

1 In *Opus Posthumous* (New York, 1989), p. 193. Compare Anlezark, *Solomon and Saturn,* ll. 238–42: "Books are renowned, often announcing a sure will to the one who thinks at all. They strengthen and establish steadfast thought, delight the heart of everyone against the painful pressure of this life." Compare also *Maxims I,* lines 1–7.

2 One indication of the value the Anglo-Saxons vested in words is the term they used for describing where words are stored, the "word hoard." Like treasures in safekeeping, words are stored up for eventual use by poets. For an exploration of the theme of the palpable, treasure-like quality of words for the Anglo-Saxons, see Robert E. Bjork, "Speech as Gift in *Beowulf," Speculum* 69 (1994): 993–1,022.

3 On the utilitarian nature of charms, see Olsan, "Inscription of Charms."

4 Briefly described in ASPR 6, cxxx–cxxxii. Charms 2, 3, 4, 5, and 6 are contained in the Old English text known as the *Lacnunga,* edited by Grattan and Singer, *Anglo-Saxon Magic and Medicine.* All the metrical charms have been edited by Grendon, *Anglo-Saxon Charms,* and Storms, *Anglo-Saxon Magic,* and again in ASPR 6.

5 ASPR 6, cxxxiii n. 1.

6 Take just one random example from this body of research: D. G. Hamilton, "Believing in Patients' Beliefs: Physician Attunement to the Spiritual Dimension as a Positive Factor in Patient Healing and Health," *The American Journal of Hospice & Palliative Care* 15.5 (1998): 276–79.

7 George Lyman Kittredge, *Witchcraft in Old and New England* (Cambridge, Mass., 1929), 191.

8 Andreas Heusler, *Die altgermanische Dichtung* (rev. ed. Darmstadt, 1957), 110.

9 Armin Rathe, "Tanzrunische Deutung altenglischer Strophformen," in *Festschrift für Karl Schneider,* eds. Ernst S. Dick and Kurt R. Janowsky (Amersterdam, 1982), 405–15.

10 Glosecki, *Shamanism.*

11 See Garner, "Charms in Performance."

12 See Cavill, *Maxims;* Deskis, *Proverb Tradition;* Howe, *Catalogue Poems;* and Williams, *Gnomic Poetry.* See also Larrington, *Store of Common Sense.*

13 E.g., Williams, *Gnomic Poetry,* 111–13.

14 Fred C. Robinson, "Old English Poetry: The Question of Authorship," *American Notes and Queries* NS 3 (1990): 59–64. Repr. in Fred C. Robinson, *The Tomb of Beowulf and Other Essays on Old English* (Oxford, 1993), 163–69.

15 Williams, *Gnomic Poetry,* 113.

16 On the social function of the maxims, see Cavill, *Maxims,* 106–17.

17 "The Authenticating Voice in *Beowulf,*" *Anglo-Saxon England* 5 (1976): 51–62.

18 Hill, *Minor Heroic Poems,* 15.

19 For a discussion of the Germanic legend in this poem and others, see Frank, "Germanic Legend."

20 DiNapoli, "Wisdom Literature," 484. For a discussion of the biblical and near-eastern wisdom tradition, see Hansen, *Solomon Complex,* 12–40.

21 ASPR 6, xlii.

22 Halsall, *Rune Poem,* 27–30.

23 Albert S. Cook, *The Christ of Cynewulf* (Boston, 1900), 136–37.

24 I Corinthians 12:8–10.

25 Lines 659–91. For a discussion of these and of the "gifts" theme, consult Earl R. Anderson, *Cynewulf: Style, Structure, and Theme in His Poetry* (London, 1983), 30–44.

26 See Jurasinski, "Caring for the Dead."

27 For full discussion, consult Halsall, *Rune Poem.*

28 For a discussion of the Anglo-Saxon use of runes, see Page, *Introduction to Old English Runes.*

29 For more on the poem's relationship to the riddles genre, see Sorrell, "Oaks, Ships."

30 *Solomon Complex,* 55.

31 Linguistics forms in the poem perhaps indicate a relatively early date, such as the eighth century. See Ashley Crandell Amos, *Linguistic Means of Determining the Dates of Old English Literary Texts* (Cambridge, Mass., 1980), 33–34.

32 Derek Pearsall, *Old English and Middle English Poetry* (London, 1977), 51.

33 *Solomon Complex,* 41–55.

34 Drout, *How Tradition Works,* 255–64.

35 For an edition and translation of all three fragments, see Anlezark, *Solomon and Saturn.*

36 Ibid., 49–57.

37 See, e.g., Champion, "From Plaint to Praise," and Fry, "A Wen Charm."

38 See Cross, "'Ubi Sunt' Passages."

39 See entry in Frantzen, *Keywords.*

40 See Harris, "Elegy."

41 Greenfield, "Old English Elegies," 143.

42 See Orchard, "Not What It Was," 104–8.

43 See discussion in Klinck, *Old English Elegies,* 13–21.

44 *Deor* concerns a poet and is therefore frequently discussed in conjunction with *Widsith;* it may not be an elegy at all. See Biggs, "*Deor*'s Threatened 'Blame Poem.'"

45 See Niles, "Problem of the Ending."

46 Howlett, "*The Wife's Lament* and *The Husband's Message,*" however, does link the two.

47 On the runic message in this poem, see Niles, "Trick of the Runes."

48 See Renoir, "Least Elegiac of the Elegies."

49 *Old English Elegies,* 40.

50 Gerard Manley Hopkins, *The Major Works,* ed. Catherine Phillips (Oxford, 2002).

51 For a translation of *Resignation A,* see Christopher A. Jones, ed. and trans., *Old English Shorter Poems,* vol. 1, *Religious and Didactic,* DOML 15 (Cambridge, Mass., 2012), 110–15.

52 See Bliss and Frantzen, "Integrity."

53 See Deskis, "Jonah and Genre."

54 Bliss and Frantzen, "Integrity," 400–402.

55 Ibid., 397.

56 See Schlauch, "An Old English 'Encomium Urbis.'"

57 Go to http://www.poetryfoundation.org/poem/174183, accessed June 6, 2013.

58 See Bjork, "*Sundor.*"

POEMS FROM
THE EXETER BOOK

The Wanderer

Oft him an-haga   are gebideð,
metudes miltse,   þeah þe he mod-cearig
geond lagu-lade   longe sceolde
hreran mid hondum   hrim-cealde sæ,
5   wadan wræc-lastas.   Wyrd bið ful aræd.
    Swa cwæð eard-stapa   earfeþa gemyndig,
wraþra wæl-sleahta   wine-mæga hryre:
    "Oft ic sceolde ana   uhtna gehwylce
mine ceare cwiþan.   Nis nu cwicra nan
10   þe ic him mod-sefan   minne durre
sweotule asecgan.   Ic to soþe wat
þæt biþ in eorle   indryhten þeaw
þæt he his ferð-locan   fæste binde,
healde his hord-cofan,   hycge swa he wille.
15   Ne mæg werig mod   wyrde wiðstondan,
ne se hreo hyge   helpe gefremman.
Forðon dom-georne   dreorigne oft
in hyra breost-cofan   bindað fæste.
    "Swa ic mod-sefan   minne sceolde,
20   oft earm-cearig,   eðle bidæled,
freo-mægum feor,   feterum sælan,
siþþan geara iu   gold-wine minne
hrusan heolstre biwrah,   ond ic hean þonan
wod winter-cearig   ofer waþuma gebind,
25   sohte sele-dreorig   sinces bryttan,

The Wanderer

Often the lone dweller awaits favor for himself,
the mercy of the creator, although heart-anxious
for a long time he had to stir with his hands
the rime-cold sea throughout the waterway,
to wander the paths of exile. Fate is fully fixed.   5
    Thus spoke the earth stepper, mindful of hardships,
of fierce slaughters, of the fall of kinsmen:
    "Often alone each daybreak I have had
to bewail my cares. No one is now living
to whom I might dare openly reveal   10
my heart. I know it's true
that it is a noble custom in a man
to bind fast his soul enclosure,
hold his treasure chamber, think as he will.
Nor can the weary heart alter fate,   15
nor the turbulent mind provide help.
Therefore those eager for fame often bind
mournful thoughts firmly in their breast coffers.
    "Thus often, wretched, deprived
of native land, far from kinsmen,   20
I have had to bind my heart with fetters,
since long ago the darkness of earth covered
my gold friend, and I downcast from there
traveled winter-sorrowful over the binding of the waves,
and sad for lack of a hall sought a giver of treasure,   25

3

hwær ic feor oþþe neah   findan meahte
þone þe in meodu-healle   mine wisse,
oþþe mec freondleasne   frefran wolde,
weman mid wynnum.   Wat se þe cunnað,
30 hu sliþen bið   sorg to geferan,
þam þe him lyt hafað   leofra geholena.
Warað hine wræc-last,   nales wunden gold,
ferð-loca freorig,   nalæs foldan blæd.
Gemon he sele-secgas   ond sinc-þege,
35 hu hine on geoguðe   his gold-wine
wenede to wiste.   Wyn eal gedreas.
   "Forþon wat se þe sceal   his wine-dryhtnes
leofes lar-cwidum   longe forþolian.
Ðonne sorg ond slæp   somod ætgædre
40 earmne an-hogan   oft gebindað.
Þinceð him on mode   þæt he his mon-dryhten
clyppe ond cysse,   ond on cneo lecge
honda ond heafod,   swa he hwilum ær
in gear-dagum   gief-stolas breac.
45 Ðonne onwæcneð eft   wineleas guma,
gesihð him biforan   fealwe wegas,
baþian brim-fuglas   brædan feþra,
hreosan hrim ond snaw,   hagle gemenged.
Þonne beoð þy hefigran   heortan benne,
50 sare æfter swæsne.   Sorg bið geniwad
þonne maga gemynd   mod geondhweorfeð;
greteð gliw-stafum,   georne geondsceawað
secga geseldan.   Swimmað eft onweg.
Fleotendra ferð   no þær fela bringeð
55 cuðra cwide-giedda.   Cearo bið geniwad

where I far or near could find the one
in the mead hall who might understand my feeling
and would comfort me friendless,
entertain me with joys. He understands, he who knows
how cruel sorrow is as a companion   30
for the one who has few loved confidants.
The exile track claims him, by no means twisted gold,
the frozen soul enclosure, not at all the splendor of earth.
He remembers hall warriors and receiving treasure,
how in youth his gold friend   35
accustomed him to feasting. All joy has vanished.
    "Therefore he understands, he who has had long
to do without the councils of his beloved lord-friend.
Then sorrow and sleep both together
often bind the wretched lone dweller.   40
It seems to him in his mind that he embraces and kisses
his lord and lays on his knee
hands and head, as he at times before
in days of old enjoyed the gift seats.
Then the lordless man awakes again,   45
sees the fallow waves before him,
the bathing sea birds spreading feathers,
frost and snow falling, mingled with hail.
Then the grievous wounds of the heart are the heavier
for the loved one. Sorrow is renewed   50
when the memory of kinsmen passes through his mind;
he greets joyfully, eagerly watches
the companions of men. They swim away again.
The spirit of the floating ones does not bring many
known utterances there. Care is renewed   55

þam þe sendan sceal   swiþe geneahhe
ofer waþuma gebind   werigne sefan.
    "Forþon ic geþencan ne mæg   geond þas woruld
forhwan mod-sefa   min ne gesweorce,
þonne ic eorla lif   eal geondþence,
hu hi færlice   flet ofgeafon,
modge magu-þegnas.   Swa þes middan-geard
ealra dogra gehwam   dreoseð ond fealleþ;
forþon ne mæg weorþan wis wer   ær he age wintra dæl
in woruld-rice.   Wita sceal geþyldig,
ne sceal no to hat-heort   ne to hræd-wyrde,
ne to wac wiga   ne to wan-hydig,
ne to forht ne to fægen   ne to feoh-gifre
ne næfre gielpes to georn   ær he geare cunne.
Beorn sceal gebidan,   þonne he beot spriceð,
oþþæt collen-ferð   cunne gearwe
hwider hreþra gehygd   hweorfan wille.
    "Ongietan sceal gleaw hæle   hu gæstlic bið,
þonne eall þisse worulde wela   weste stondeð,
swa nu missenlice   geond þisne middan-geard
winde biwaune   weallas stondaþ,
hrime bihrorene,   hryðge þa ederas.
Weorniað þa win-salo,   waldend licgað
dreame bidrorene,   duguþ eal gecrong
wlonc bi wealle.   Sume wig fornom,
ferede in forð-wege.   Sumne fugel oþbær
ofer heanne holm;   sumne se hara wulf
deaðe gedælde;   sumne dreorig-hleor
in eorð-scræfe   eorl gehydde.

for the one who must very frequently send
his weary heart over the binding of the waves.
   "Therefore I cannot imagine for all the world
why my heart should not grow dark
when I wholly consider the life of nobles,   60
how they suddenly left the floor,
proud young retainers. Thus this middle earth
perishes and falls each and every day;
therefore a man cannot become wise before he has
a share of winters in the worldly kingdom. The wise man   65
     must be patient,
must not be too hot-hearted nor too hasty in speech
nor too weak a warrior nor too foolhardy
nor too fearful nor too happy nor too greedy for wealth
nor ever too eager to boast before he clearly knows.
A man must wait when he would boast   70
until bold-spirited he may clearly know
where the thought of his heart will turn.
   "The wise man must understand how ghastly it will be
when all the riches of this world will stand waste
as now variously throughout this middle earth   75
walls stand blown by the wind,
covered by frost, the buildings exposed to storms.
The wine halls decay, the lords lie
bereft of joy, the whole company has perished,
proud by the wall. War took some,   80
they departed on the way forth. The bird bore one off
over the high sea; the gray wolf shared one
with death; a sad-faced man hid
one in the grave.

85   "Yþde swa þisne eard-geard   ælda scyppend
oþþæt, burg-wara   breahtma lease,
eald enta geweorc   idlu stodon.
    Se þonne þisne weal-steal   wise geþohte
ond þis deorce lif   deope geondþenceð,

90 frod in ferðe,   feor oft gemon
wæl-sleahta worn,   ond þas word acwið:
    "'Hwær cwom mearg? Hwær cwom mago?   Hwær
                                   cwom maþþum-gyfa?
Hwær cwom symbla gesetu?   Hwær sindon sele-
                                     dreamas?
Eala beorht bune!   Eala byrn-wiga!

95 Eala þeodnes þrym!   Hu seo þrag gewat,
genap under niht-helm,   swa heo no wære!
Stondeð nu on laste   leofre duguþe
weal wundrum heah,   wyrmlicum fah.
Eorlas fornoman   asca þryþe,

100 wæpen wæl-gifru,   wyrd seo mære,
ond þas stan-hleoþu   stormas cnyssað,
hrið hreosende   hrusan bindeð,
wintres woma,   þonne won cymeð,
nipeð niht-scua,   norþan onsendeð

105 hreo hægl-fare   hæleþum on andan.
Eall is earfoðlic   eorþan rice,
onwendeð wyrda gesceaft   weoruld under heofonum.
Her bið feoh læne,   her bið freond læne,
her bið mon læne,   her bið mæg læne,

110 eal þis eorþan gesteal   idel weorþeð!'"

"The creator of men thus devastated this dwelling place   85
until, devoid of the noise of the inhabitants,
the old works of giants stood empty.
The one who with wise thought, then, deeply ponders
this foundation and this dark life,
the one experienced in heart often remembers from long   90
    ago
the great number of slaughters and speaks these words:
  "'Where has the horse gone? Where the warrior? Where
    the treasure?
Where the seats of feasts? Where are the hall joys?
Oh, the bright cup! Oh, the mailed warrior!
Oh, the prince's glory! How that time departed,   95
grew dark under the night helmet as if it hadn't been!
In the track of the beloved company now stands
a wall wondrously high, decorated with serpents.
The hosts of spears carried away the earls,
weapons greedy for slaughter, fate the mighty,   100
and storms batter the rocky slopes,
the falling snow storm binds the ground,
the tumult of winter when the darkness comes,
the night shadow grows black, from the north it sends
a stormy shower of hail in malice against human beings.   105
All is difficult in the earthly kingdom,
the ordered course of fate changes the world under the
    heavens.
Here money is fleeting, here friend is fleeting,
here man is fleeting, here kinsman is fleeting,
all the foundation of this earth becomes empty!'"   110

Swa cwæð snottor on mode,   gesæt him sundor æt rune.
Til biþ se þe his treowe gehealdeþ;   ne sceal næfre his torn
                                                              to rycene
beorn of his breostum acyþan   nemþe he ær þa bote
                                                              cunne
eorl mid elne gefremman.   Wel bið þam þe him are seceð,
115 frofre to Fæder on heofonum   þær us eal seo fæstnung
                                                              stondeð.

Thus spoke the one wise in mind, sat apart in meditation.
Good is the one who keeps the faith; a man should never
     too hastily make known
the affliction of the heart unless he knows beforehand how
     to work
the remedy with courage. Well is it for the one who seeks
     favor,
consolation from the Father in the heavens where for us all   115
     stability stands.

The Gifts of Mortals

Fela bið on foldan   forð-gesynra
geongra geofona,   þa þa gæst-berend
wegað in gewitte,   swa her weoruda God,
meotud meahtum swið,   monnum dæleð,
5   syleð sundor-giefe,   sendeð wide
agne spede,   þara æghwylc mot
dryht-wuniendra   dæl onfon.
Ne bið ænig þæs   earfoð-sælig
mon on moldan,   ne þæs med-spedig,
10   lytel-hydig,   ne þæs læt-hydig,
þæt hine se ar-gifa   ealles biscyrge
modes cræfta   oþþe mægen-dæda,
wis on gewitte   oþþe on word-cwidum,
þy læs ormod sy   ealra þinga,
15   þara þe he geworhte   in woruld-life,
geofona gehwylcre.   Næfre God demeð
þæt ænig eft þæs   earm geweorðe.
Nænig eft þæs swiþe   þurh snyttru-cræft
in þeode þrym   þisses lifes
20   forð gestigeð,   þæt him folca weard
þurh his halige giefe   hider onsende
wise geþohtas   ond woruld-cræftas,
under anes meaht   ealle forlæte,
þy læs he for wlence   wuldor-geofona ful,

The Gifts of Mortals

Many new gifts are visible
on earth, those that soul bearers
carry in their minds, according as the God of hosts,
the measurer strong in might, deals them out to human
    beings,
gives special gifts, sends them widely   5
by his own power, a portion of which each
of those living among the people may receive.
There is no person so unhappy
on earth, nor so unprosperous,
so lacking in courage, nor so slow thinking,   10
that the giver of benefits should deprive him of all
skills of mind or mighty deeds,
wisdom in understanding or in language,
lest he become despairing of all things,
of each gift, that he made in   15
this worldly life. God never decrees
that any should become so wretched.
No one through wisdom-craft
should rise up in the glory of the people
during this life so mightily that the guardian of the folk   20
through his holy gift should send here
wise thoughts and worldly skills,
should allow all those to be in one person's power,
lest he, full of glorious gifts in pride,

25   mon mode swið   of gemete hweorfe
    ond þonne forhycge   hean-spedigran;
    ac he gedæleð   se þe ah domes geweald,
    missenlice   geond þisne middan-geard
    leoda leoþo-cræftas   lond-buendum.
30   Sumum her ofer eorþan   æhta onlihð,
    woruld-gestreona.   Sum bið won-spedig,
    heard-sælig hæle,   biþ hwæþre gleaw
    modes cræfta.   Sum mægen-strengo
    furþor onfehð.   Sum freolic bið
35   wlitig on wæstmum.   Sum biþ woð-bora,
    giedda giffæst.   Sum biþ gearu-wyrdig.
    Sum bið on huntoþe   hreð-eadigra
    deora dræfend.   Sum dyre bið
    woruld-ricum men.   Sum bið wiges heard,
40   beado-cræftig beorn,   þær bord stunað.
    Sum in mæðle mæg   mod-snottera
    folc-rædenne   forð gehycgan,
    þær witena biþ   worn ætsomne.
    Sum mæg wrætlice   weorc ahyggan
45   heah-timbra gehwæs;   hond bið gelæred,
    wis ond gewealden,   swa bið wyrhtan ryht,
    sele asettan,   con he sidne ræced
    fæste gefegan   wiþ fær-dryrum.
    Sum mid hondum mæg   hearpan gretan;
50   ah he gleo-beames   gearo-brygda list.
    Sum bið rynig,   sum ryht-scytte,
    sum leoða gleaw,   sum on londe snel,
    feþe-spedig.   Sum on fealone wæg
    stefnan steoreð;   stream-rade con,
55   weorudes wisa,   ofer widne holm,

a person strong in mind, should turn from moderation   25
and then despise those of few gifts;
but he who holds the power of judgment apportions
variously throughout this middle earth
the skills of people to land dwellers.
To one here on earth he grants possessions,   30
worldly treasures. One lacks prosperity,
an unfortunate man; he, however, is wise
in the skills of the mind. One receives
superior strength. One is stately,
beautiful in form. One is an orator,   35
talented in songs. One is fluent of speech.
One in hunting is a tracker of
glorious animals. One is dear to men
of worldly power. One is hard in war,
a battle-crafty man, where shields clash.   40
One in the assembly of wise ones can
resolve upon a decree of the people
where many sages are gathered together.
One can wondrously devise the work
of each lofty building; his hand is trained,   45
wise and controlled, as is right for the worker,
to set up a hall, he knows how to join firmly
the spacious hall against sudden fall.
One can play the harp with his hands;
he possesses the art of deft playing of the instrument.   50
One is good in counsel, one a straight shooter,
one skilled in songs, one speedy on land,
fleet of foot. One on the fallow wave
steers the prow; the leader of the troop
knows the sea path over the wide water,   55

þonne sæ-rofe   snelle mægne
arum bregdað   yð-borde neah.
Sum bið syndig,   sum searo-cræftig
goldes ond gimma,   þonne him gumena weard
60   hateð him to mærþum   maþþum renian.
Sum mæg wæpen-þræce,   wige to nytte,
mod-cræftig smið   monige gefremman,
þonne he gewyrceð   to wera hilde
helm oþþe hup-seax   oððe heaþu-byrnan,
65   scirne mece   oððe scyldes rond,
fæste gefeged   wið flyge gares.
Sum bið ar-fæst   ond ælmes-georn,
þeawum geþyde.   Sum bið þegn gehweorf
on meodu-healle.   Sum bið meares gleaw,
70   wicg-cræfta wis.   Sum gewealden-mod
þafað in geþylde   þæt he þonne sceal.
Sum domas con   þær dryht-guman
ræd eahtiað.   Sum bið hræd-tæfle.
Sum bið gewittig   æt win-þege,
75   beor-hyrde god.   Sum bið bylda til
ham to hebbanne.   Sum bið here-toga,
fyrd-wisa from.   Sum biþ folc-wita.
Sum biþ æt þearfe   þrist-hydigra
þegn mid his þeodne.   Sum geþyld hafað,
80   fæst-gongel ferð.   Sum bið fugel-bona,
hafeces cræftig.   Sum bið to horse hwæt.
Sum bið swið-snel,   hafað searolic gomen,
gleo-dæda gife   for gum-þegnum,
leoht ond leoþu-wac.   Sum bið leof-wende,
85   hafað mod ond word   monnum geþwære.
Sum her geornlice   gæstes þearfe

when the ones hardy at sea with quick strength
pull with oars close to the side of the ship.
One is skilled in swimming, one expert
with gold and silver, when the guardian of men
commands him to arrange treasures with splendor.   60
One, the clever smith, can fashion
many weapons, useful in battle,
when for combat of men he makes
helmet or short sword or battle shirts,
shining blade or boss of shield,   65
joined fast against the flight of the spear.
One is pious and eager to give alms,
virtuous in his habits. One is a retainer
active in the mead hall. One is horse savvy,
wise in steed craft. One strong-hearted one   70
endures patiently what he must.
One knows laws where warriors
take counsel. One is quick at tables.
One is witty at the wine banquet,
a good beer lord. One is a good builder   75
at raising a home. One is a commander,
a wise chieftain. One is a public councilor.
One to his lord is a bold retainer
in time of need. One has patience,
a steady heart. One is a fowler,   80
skilled with a hawk. One is quick on a horse.
One is very agile, light and limber of limb,
has a special pastime, the gift
of mirthful deeds before people. One is agreeable,
has temperament and words pleasant to people.   85
One eagerly engages inwardly here

mode bewindeþ   ond him metudes est
ofer eorð-welan   ealne geceoseð.
Sum bið deor-mod   deofles gewinnes,
90   bið a wið firenum   in gefeoht gearo.
Sum cræft hafað   circ-nytta fela,
mæg on lof-songum   lifes waldend
hlude hergan;   hafað healice
beorhte stefne.   Sum bið boca gleaw,
95   larum leoþu-fæst.   Sum biþ list-hendig
to awritanne   word-geryno.
      Nis nu ofer eorþan   ænig monna
mode þæs cræftig,   ne þæs mægen-eacen,
þæt hi æfre anum   ealle weorþen
100   gegearwade,   þy læs him gilp sceððe,
oþþe fore þære mærþe   mod astige,
gif he hafaþ ana   ofer ealle men
wlite ond wisdom   ond weorca blæd;
ac he missenlice   monna cynne
105   gielpes styreð   ond his giefe bryttað,
sumum on cystum,   sumum on cræftum,
sumum on wlite,   sumum on wige;
sumum he syleð monna   milde heortan,
þeaw-fæstne geþoht;   sum bið þeodne hold.
110   Swa weorðlice   wide tosaweð
Dryhten his duguþe.   A þæs dom age,
leoht-bære lof,   se us þis lif giefeð
ond his milde mod   monnum cyþeð.

the needs of the soul and chooses for himself the favor
of the measurer over all earthly wealth.
One is brave minded in strife with the devil,
is always ready in the fight against sins.   90
One has skill in many church services,
can in songs of praise loudly extol
the ruler of life; that one has an exalted,
bright voice. One is wise in books,
able in learning. One is handy   95
at writing profound sayings.
    There is no one now over the earth
so skillful in mind, nor so mighty,
that all the gifts should ever be
vested in one person alone, lest pride should injure him,   100
or the heart should rise up because of that fame
if he alone above all people
had beauty and wisdom and glory of works;
but he variously reproves humankind
for boasting and grants his gifts,   105
to one in virtues, to one in skills,
to one in beauty, to one in battle;
to one he gives a mild heart,
a moral thought; one is loyal to his lord.
Thus the Lord appropriately scatters   110
his gifts widely. May he always have glory for this,
luminous praise, he who gives us life
and shows his gentle mind to humankind.

Precepts

Ðus frod fæder   freo-bearn lærde,
mod-snottor mon,   maga cystum eald,
wordum wis-fæstum   þæt he wel þunge:
"Do a þætte duge,   deag þin gewyrhtu;
5   God þe biþ symle   goda gehwylces
frea ond fultum,   feond þam oþrum
wyrsan gewyrhta.   Wene þec þy betran,
efn elne þis   a þenden þu lifge.
Fæder ond modor   freo þu mid heortan,
10   maga gehwylcne,   gif him sy meotud on lufan.
Wes þu þinum yldrum   arfæst symle,
fæger-wyrde,   ond þe in ferðe læt
þine lareowas   leofe in mode,
þa þec geornast   to gode trymmen."
15   Fæder eft his sunu   frod gegrette
oþre siþe: "Heald elne þis!
Ne freme firene,   ne næfre freonde þinum,
mæge man ne geþafa,   þy læs þec meotud oncunne,
þæt þu sy wommes gewita.   He þe mid wite gieldeð,
20   swylce þam oþrum   mid ead-welan."
Ðriddan syþe   þonc-snottor guma
breost-gehygdum   his bearn lærde:

Precepts

Thus the wise father, the man prudent in mind,
experienced in the virtues of the kinsmen, taught the child
    of gentle birth
with learned words so that the child might prosper well:
"Always do what's virtuous, your works will avail;
God will always be a lord and support for you   5
in each good thing, an enemy to others
in worse deeds. Accustom yourself to the better,
practice this boldly always while you live.
Love your father and mother with your heart,
each kinsman, if the measurer is in their love.   10
Always be respectful to your elders,
fair speaking, and in your heart let
your teachers be dear in mind,
those who most eagerly exhort you to the good."
    The wise father greeted his son   15
a second time: "Hold this boldly.
Do not commit crimes, don't ever condone sin in your
    friend
or in your kinsman lest the measurer should reproach
you as an accomplice in evil. He will repay you with
    punishment,
as he will repay others with prosperity."   20
    A third time the man wise
in his breast-thoughts instructed his child:

"Ne gewuna wyrsa   widan feore
ængum eahta,   ac þu þe anne genim
25   to gesprecan symle   spella ond lara
ræd-hycgende.   Sy ymb rice swa hit mæge."
        Feorþan siðe   fæder eft lærde
mod-leofne magan,   þæt he gemunde þis:
"Ne aswic sundor-wine,   ac a symle geheald
30   ryhtum gerisnum.   Ræfn elne þis,
þæt þu næfre fæcne weorðe   freonde þinum."
        Fiftan siþe   fæder eft ongon
breost-geþoncum   his bearn læran:
"Druncen beorg þe   ond dollic word,
35   man on mode   ond in muþe lyge,
yrre ond æfeste   ond idese lufan.
Forðon sceal æwisc-mod   oft siþian,
se þe gewiteð   in wifes lufan,
fremdre meowlan.   Þær bið a firena wen,
40   laðlicre scome,   long nið wið God,
geotende gielp.   Wes þu a giedda wis,
wær wið willan,   worda hyrde."
        Siextan siþe   swæs eft ongon
þurh bliðne geþoht   his bearn læran:
45   "Ongiet georne   hwæt sy god oþþe yfel,
ond toscead simle   scearpe mode
in sefan þinum   ond þe a þæt selle geceos.
A þe bið gedæled;   gif þe deah hyge,
wunað wisdom in,   ond þu wast geare
50   ondgit yfles,   heald þe elne wið,
feorma þu symle   in þinum ferðe god."

"Do not ever associate with a worse person
for any reason, but you should always take the one
wise of stories and learning as a councilor.   25
Let his status be what it may."
     For a fourth time the father again taught
the precious kinsman so that he should remember this:
"Don't desert your bosom friend, but always hold
rightly to what is fitting. Boldly do this,   30
that you should never be deceitful to your friend."
     For the fifth time the father again began
with the thoughts of his heart to teach his child:
"Fortify yourself against drunkenness and foolish words,
sin in the heart and lies in the mouth,   35
anger and avarice and the love of women.
Therefore he must often depart ashamed,
he who falls in love with a woman,
with an unfamiliar maiden. There will always be an
          expectation of sins,
hateful shame, long enmity against God,   40
flowing arrogance. Be ever wise in songs,
wary of desires, a guardian of your words."
     For the sixth time, the dear one began again
with a gentle thought to teach his son:
"Understand eagerly what is good or evil,   45
always distinguish them in your heart
with a sharp intellect and always choose the better for
          yourself.
It will always be separated out for you; if thought avails you,
if wisdom dwells in it, and if you clearly have
an understanding of evil, hold yourself boldly against it,   50
always cherish good in your heart."

Seofeþan siþe   his sunu lærde
fæder, frod guma,   sægde fela geongum:
"Seldan snottor guma   sorgleas blissað,
55   swylce dol seldon   drymeð sorgful
ymb his forð-gesceaft   nefne he fæhþe wite.
Wær-wyrde sceal   wisfæst hæle
breostum hycgan,   nales breahtme hlud."
     Eahtoþan siþe   eald fæder ongon
60   his mago monian   mildum wordum:
"Leorna lare   lær-gedefe,
wene þec in wisdom,   weoruda scyppend
hafa þe to hyhte,   haligra gemynd,
ond a soð to syge,   þonne þu secge hwæt."
65   Nigeþan siþe   nægde se gomola,
eald uðwita   sægde eaforan worn:
"Nis nu fela folca   þætte fyrn-gewritu
healdan wille,   ac him hyge brosnað,
ellen colað,   idlað þeodscype;
70   ne habbað wiht for þæt,   þeah hi wom don
ofer meotudes bibod.   Monig sceal ongieldan
sawel-susles.   Ac læt þinne sefan healdan
forð fyrn-gewritu   ond Frean domas,
þa þe her on mægðe gehwære   men forlætaþ
75   swiþor asigan   þonne him sy sylfum ryht."
     Teoþan siþe   torn-sorgna ful
eald eft ongon   eaforan læran:
"Snyttra bruceþ   þe fore sawle lufan
warnað him wommas   worda ond dæda
80   on sefan symle   ond soþ fremeð;

For the seventh time the father, the wise man,
taught his son, said many things to the young one:
"A wise man seldom rejoices without sorrow,
just as the fool seldom sings aloud sorrowfully   55
about his future unless he knows feud.
A sensible man, cautious in speech, must
ponder in heart, never be loud with noise."
    For the eighth time the old father began
to admonish his kinsman with mild words: 60
"Ponder teachings fittingly learned,
train yourself in wisdom, have for yourself the creator
of hosts and the memory of the saints as your hope,
and always truth as your victory, when you say something."
    For the ninth time the aged one spoke,   65
the old sage said much to his offspring:
"There are not now many people who want
to keep the ancient writings, but their thought crumbles,
courage cools, the community grows idle;
although they commit evil, against the creator's command,   70
they get nothing for it. Many must pay
with soul torment. But let your heart hold
the ancient writings and the judgments of the Lord,
those which people in every country allow
to decline much more than would be right for them."   75
    For the tenth time full of cares
the old one again began to teach his offspring;
"He uses wisdom well who for the love of his soul
guards himself against sins of words and of deeds
always in his heart and promotes the truth;   80

biŏ him geofona gehwylc   Gode geyced;
meahtum spedig   þonne he mon flyhð.
Yrre ne læt þe   æfre gewealdan,
heah in hreþre,   heoro-worda grund
85 wylme bismitan,   ac him warnað þæt
on geheortum hyge.   Hæle sceal wis-fæst
ond gemetlice,   modes snottor,
gleaw in gehygdum,   georn wisdomes,
swa he wið ælda mæg   eades hleotan.
90 Ne beo þu no to tælende,   ne to tweo-spræce,
ne þe on mode læt   men to fracoþe,
ac beo leofwende;   leoht on gehygdum
ber breost-cofan.   Swa þu, min bearn, gemyne
frode fæder lare   ond þec a wið firenum geheald."

each of his gifts will be increased by God;
he will be prosperous in strength when he flees sin.
Do not let anger ever control you,
high in your heart, the abyss of hostile speech, defile
you with fervor, but the wise man guards himself against   85
that in courageous thought. A man must be sensible
and moderate, wise of mind,
prudent in thoughts, eager for wisdom,
so he can obtain happiness among people.
Do not be too reproving, nor too two tongued,   90
nor allow yourself in your mind to be too vile to others,
but be kind; light in thoughts,
maintain your inner self. Thus, my son, remember
the wise teaching of your father and always hold yourself
        against sins."

The Seafarer

Mæg ic be me sylfum   soð-gied wrecan,
siþas secgan,   hu ic geswinc-dagum
earfoð-hwile   oft þrowade,
bitre breost-ceare   gebiden hæbbe,
5   gecunnad in ceole   cear-selda fela,
atol yþa gewealc,   þær mec oft bigeat
nearo nihtwaco   æt nacan stefnan,
þonne he be clifum cnossað   calde geþrungen.
Fruron mine fet,   forste gebunden,
10   caldum clommum,   þær þa ceare seofedun
hat ymb heortan;   hungor innan slat
mere-werges mod.   Þæt se mon ne wat
þe him on foldan   fægrost limpeð,
hu ic earm-cearig   is-cealdne sæ
15   winter wunade   wræccan lastum,
wine-mægum bidroren,
bihongen hrim-gicelum;   hægl scurum fleag.
Þær ic ne gehyrde   butan hlimman sæ,
is-caldne wæg,   hwilum ylfete song
20   dyde ic me to gomene,   ganetes hleoþor
ond huilpan sweg   fore hleahtor wera,
mæw singende   fore medo-drince.
Stormas þær stan-clifu beotan   þær him stearn oncwæð
isig-feþera;   ful oft þæt earn bigeal,

The Seafarer

I can recite a true song about myself,
relate my experiences, how in days of toil I
have often suffered times of hardship,
endured bitter breast care,
known in the ship many an abode of care,   5
the terrible tossing of the waves, where the anxious
night-watch often held me at the ship's prow,
when, oppressed by cold, the ship tosses along the cliffs.
My feet were frozen, bound by frost,
by cold fetters, where those cares sighed   10
hot around my heart; hunger from within tore
the spirit of the sea-weary one. The man on land for whom
things happen most pleasantly does not know
how I, careworn, occupied the
ice-cold sea in winter on the paths of exile,   15
deprived of friendly kinsmen,
hung round with icicles; hail flew in showers.
There I heard nothing except the roaring sea,
the ice-cold wave, at times taking the song of the wild swan
as my entertainment, the cry of the gannet   20
and the sound of the curlew instead of the laughter of men,
the singing seagull instead of mead.
Storms beat the rocky cliffs where the icy-feathered tern
answered them; very often, the dewy-feathered eagle
    screeched

25   urig-feþra;   nænig hleo-mæga
       fea-sceaftig ferð   frefran meahte.
         Forþon him gelyfeð lyt,   se þe ah lifes wyn
       gebiden in burgum,   bealo-siþa hwon,
       wlonc ond win-gal,   hu ic werig oft
30   in brim-lade   bidan sceolde.
       Nap niht-scua;   norþan sniwde;
       hrim hrusan bond;   hægl feol on eorþan,
       corna caldast.   Forþon cnyssað nu
       heortan geþohtas   þæt ic hean streamas,
35   sealt-yþa gelac   sylf cunnige;
       monað modes lust   mæla gehwylce
       ferð to feran,   þæt ic feor heonan
       el-þeodigra   eard gesece.
       Forþon nis þæs mod-wlonc   mon ofer eorþan,
40   ne his gifena þæs god,   ne in geoguþe to þæs hwæt,
       ne in his dædum to þæs deor,   ne him his dryhten to þæs
                                   hold
       þæt he a his sæ-fore   sorge næbbe,
       to hwon hine dryhten   gedon wille.
       Ne biþ him to hearpan hyge   ne to hring-þege,
45   ne to wife wyn   ne to worulde hyht,
       ne ymbe owiht elles,   nefne ymb yða gewealc,
       ac a hafað longunge   se þe on lagu fundað.
       Bearwas blostmum nimað,   byrig fægriað,
       wongas wlitigað,   woruld onetteð;
50   ealle þa gemoniað   modes fusne
       sefan to siþe,   þam þe swa þenceð
       on flod-wegas   feor gewitan.

in reply; not any protecting kinsmen   25
could console the wretched heart.
   And so the one who has experienced the joy of life while
      remaining
in the cities, a few bitter experiences, proud and flushed
with wine, little believes how I, weary, often
had to stay on the seaway.   30
The night shadow grew dark; it snowed from the north;
frost bound the ground; hail, the coldest of grains,
fell on the earth. And so the thoughts of my heart
now urge that I should explore
the high seas, the rolling of the salty waves myself;   35
the desire of my mind admonishes my heart
to travel each time to seek
the land of strangers far from here.
And yet there is no one so proud minded on earth
nor so fortunate in gifts, nor so vigorous in youth,   40
nor so brave in deeds, nor so devoted to his lord
that he does not always have anxiety on the sea voyage
as to what purpose his lord might have in store.
His thought is not for the harp nor for ring giving,
nor for joy with a woman nor for bliss in the world,   45
nor for anything else except the rolling of the waves,
but the one who sets out to sea always has longing.
The groves begin blossoming, the cities grow fair,
the plains become beautiful, the world hastens on;
all these things admonish the one eager of spirit, urge   50
the mind on the journey, for the one who thinks thus
to depart far away on the ocean paths.

Swylce geac monað   geomran reorde,
singeð sumeres weard,   sorge beodeð
bitter in breost-hord.   Þæt se beorn ne wat,
seft-eadig secg,   hwæt þa sume dreogað
þe þa wræc-lastas   widost lecgað.
    Forþon nu min hyge hweorfeð   ofer hreþer-locan,
min mod-sefa   mid mere-flode
ofer hwæles eþel   hweorfeð wide,
eorþan sceatas,   cymeð eft to me
gifre ond grædig;   gielleð anfloga,
hweteð on hwæl-weg   hreþer unwearnum
ofer holma gelagu.   Forþon me hatran sind
Dryhtnes dreamas   þonne þis deade lif,
læne on londe.   Ic gelyfe no
þæt him eorð-welan   ece stondað.
Simle þreora sum   þinga gehwylce,
ær his tid gegang,   to tweon weorþeð:
adl oþþe yldo   oþþe ecg-hete
fægum from-weardum   feorh oðþringeð.
Forþon þæt bið eorla gehwam   æfter-cweþendra
lof lifgendra   last-worda betst,
þæt he gewyrce,   ær he on weg scyle,
fremum on foldan   wið feonda niþ,
deorum dædum   deofle togeanes,
þæt hine ælda bearn   æfter hergen,
ond his lof siþþan   lifge mid englum
awa to ealdre,   ecan lifes blæd,
dream mid dugeþum.   Dagas sind gewitene,
ealle onmedlan   eorþan rices;

The cuckoo likewise urges with a sad voice,
the guardian of summer sings, announces sorrow,
bitter in the breast. The man does not know,   55
the warrior blessed with comfort, what those particular
ones endure who lay the tracks of exile most widely.
   And so my thought goes beyond my breast,
my heart with the sea flood
goes widely over the domain of the whale,   60
over the expanse of the earth, comes to me again
ravenous and greedy; the lone flyer cries out,
incites the heart irresistibly on the whale way,
over the expanse of the seas. And so for me hotter
are the joys of the Lord than this dead life,   65
fleeting on land. I do not believe
that earthly treasures last forever.
Always, without fail, one of three things
will be cause for uncertainty before the appointed time:
disease or old age or deadly violence   70
will force the soul out of the one fated to die and about to
     depart.
And so for each man the best words left behind him
will be the praise of those speaking after him, of the living,
that, before he had to depart, he performed good deeds
on earth against the malice of enemies,   75
brave deeds against the devil,
so that the children of humans may praise them afterward,
and their praise may live among the angels
forever and ever, the glory of eternal life,
joy among the troops. The days have departed,   80
all splendor of the kingdom of earth;

nearon nu cyningas   ne caseras
ne gold-giefan   swylce iu wæron,
þonne hi mæst mid him   mærþa gefremedon
85   ond on dryht-licestum   dome lifdon.
Gedroren is þeos duguð eal,   dreamas sind gewitene,
wuniað þa wacran   ond þas woruld healdaþ,
brucað þurh bisgo.   Blæd is gehnæged.
Eorþan indryhto   ealdað ond searað,
90   swa nu monna gehwylc   geond middan-geard.
Yldo him on fareð,   onsyn blacað,
gomel-feax gnornað,   wat his iu-wine,
æþelinga bearn,   eorþan forgiefene.
Ne mæg him þonne se flæsc-homa   þonne him þæt
                                        feorg losað
95   ne swete forswelgan   ne sar gefelan,
ne hond onhreran   ne mid hyge þencan.
Þeah þe græf wille   golde stregan
broþor his geborenum,   byrgan be deadum
maþmum mislicum   þæt hine mid wille,
100 ne mæg þære sawle   þe biþ synna ful
gold to geoce   for Godes egsan,
þonne he hit ær hydeð   þenden he her leofað.
  Micel biþ se meotudes egsa   forþon hi seo molde
                                        oncyrreð;
se gestaþelade   stiþe grundas,
105 eorþan sceatas   ond up-rodor.
  Dol biþ se þe him his Dryhten ne ondrædeþ;   cymeð him
                                        se deað unþinged.

there are not now kings nor caesars
nor gold givers as there once were,
when among themselves they performed the greatest
of glorious deeds and lived in magnificent fame.   85
All that company has perished, the joys have departed,
the weaker ones remain and control this world,
gain the use of it by toil. Glory is brought low.
The very noble ones of the earth grow old and wither,
as now does each person throughout the middle earth.   90
Old age comes on him, his face grows pale,
the hoary-haired one mourns, know his friends from
        former days,
the children of nobles, having given up the earth.
When he loses his life that fleshly covering cannot
swallow sweetness or feel pain   95
or move hands or think with the mind.
Although a brother may want to strew the grave with gold
for his born brother, bury him among the dead
with various treasures that he wants with him,
gold cannot, when he hides it here beforehand while he   100
lives, be of help before the terror of God
for the soul that is full of sins.
    Great will be the terror of the creator from which the
        earth will turn aside;
he established the strong foundations,
the expanses of the earth, and heaven above. Foolish is the   105
one who does not dread his Lord; death comes on him
        unexpected.

Eadig bið se þe eaþ-mod leofaþ;   cymeð him seo ar of
                          heofonum,
meotod him þæt mod gestaþelað   forþon he in his meahte
                          gelyfeð.
Stieran mon sceal strongum mode   ond þæt on staþelum
                          healdan,
110   ond gewis werum,   wisum clæne;
scyle monna gehwylc   mid gemete healdan
wiþ leofne lufan   ond wið laþne bealo,
þeah þe he hine wille fyres   fulne habban
oþþe on bæle   forbærnedne
115   his geworhtne wine.   Wyrd biþ swiþre,
meotud meahtigra   þonne ænges monnes gehygd.
Uton we hycgan   hwær we ham agen,
ond þonne geþencan   hu we þider cumen,
ond we þonne eac tilien   þæt we to moten
120   in þa ecan   eadignesse
þær is lif gelong   in lufan Dryhtnes,
hyht in heofonum.   Þæs sy þam halgan þonc,
þæt he usic geweorþade,   wuldres ealdor,
ece Dryhten,   in ealle tid.
Amen.

Blessed is the one who lives humbly; mercy comes to him
    from the heavens,
the creator establishes in them that spirit because they
    believe in his might.
Everyone must exert self-control with a strong spirit and
    keep it in place
and steadfast in its pledges, pure in its ways;   110
everyone should hold in moderation
love of friend and spite for foe
even if the foe may want him steeped in fire
or the fast friend consumed
on a funeral pyre. Fate is stronger,   115
the creator mightier than the thought of any man.
Let us think where we have our home
and then consider how we may get there,
and we then should also strive that we may proceed there
in the eternal bliss where life is inseparable   120
from the love of the Lord, hope in the heavens.
Thanks be to the holy one for this
that he, the prince of glory,
the eternal Lord, has honored us through all time.
Amen.

Vainglory

Hwæt, me frod wita   on fyrn-dagum
sægde, snottor ar,   sundor-wundra fela.
Word-hord onwreah   witgan larum
beorn boca gleaw,   bodan ær-cwide,
5   þæt ic soðlice   siþþan meahte
ongitan bi þam gealdre   Godes agen bearn,
wil-gest on wicum,   ond þone wacran swa some
scyldum bescyredne   on gescead witan.
Þæt mæg æghwylc mon   eaþe geþencan,
10   se þe hine ne læteð   on þas lænan tid
amyrran his gemyndum   modes gælsan
ond on his dæg-rime   druncen to rice,
þonne monige beoð   mæþel-hegendra,
wlonce wig-smiþas   win-burgum in,
15   sittaþ æt symble,   soð-gied wrecað,
wordum wrixlað,   witan fundiaþ
hwylc æsc-stede   inne in ræcede
mid werum wunige   þonne win hweteð
beornes breost-sefan.   Breahtem stigeð,
20   cirm on corþre,   cwide scralletaþ
missenlice.   Swa beoþ mod-sefan
dalum gedæled;   sindon dryht-guman
ungelice.   Sum on ofer-hygdo

Vainglory

Yes, a wise sage in days gone by,
a prudent messenger, told me many special wonders.
The man skilled in books through the teachings of the
     prophet
unfolded his word hoard, the former speech of the herald,
so that I could then truthfully   5
by means of that teaching perceive God's own son,
welcome guest in the habitations, and could distinguish
the weaker one as well, deprived through sins.
Anyone can easily imagine that,
anyone who does not allow appetite of mind   10
to obstruct thoughts during this transitory time
and in this lifetime does not allow drunkenness to reign
when many deliberating ones,
proud war smiths, are in the wine cities,
sitting at the feast, uttering true reports,   15
exchanging words, aspiring to know
which battlefield memory stays with men
inside the hall when wine incites
the warrior's heart. The revelry rises,
uproar among the troop, speeches sound loudly,   20
variously. Thus hearts are
divided; warriors are
not alike. One in arrogance

þrymme þringeð,   þrinteð him in innan
25 ungemedemad mod;   sindan to monige þæt.
Bið þæt æf-þonca   eal gefylled
feondes flige-pilum,   facen-searwum;
breodað he ond bælceð,   boð his sylfes
swiþor micle   þonne se sella mon,
30 þenceð þæt his wise   welhwam þince
eal unforcuþ.   Biþ þæs oþer swice,
þonne he þæs facnes   fintan sceawað.
Wrenceþ he ond blenceþ,   worn geþenceþ
hinder-hoca,   hyge-gar leteð,
35 scurum sceoteþ.   He þa scylde ne wat
fæhþe gefremede,   feoþ his betran
eorl fore æfstum,   læteð inwit-flan
brecan þone burg-weal,   þe him bebead meotud
þæt he þæt wig-steal   wergan sceolde;
40 siteþ symbelwlonc,   searwum læteð
wine gewæged   word ut faran,
þræfte þringan   þrymme gebyrmed,
æfæstum onæled,   ofer-hygda ful,
niþum nearo-wrencum.   Nu þu cunnan meaht,
45 gif þu þyslicne   þegn gemittest
wunian in wicum,   wite þe be þissum
feawum forð-spellum   þæt þæt biþ feondes bearn
flæsce bifongen;   hafað fræte lif,
grund-fusne gæst   gode orfeormne,
50 wuldor-cyninge.   Þæt se witga song,
gearo-wyrdig guma,   ond þæt gyd awræc:
"Se þe hine sylfne   in þa sliþnan tid
þurh ofer-hygda   up ahlæneð,
ahefeð heah-modne,   se sceal hean wesan
55 æfter neo-siþum   niþer gebiged,

presses on violently, his spirit swelling up inside him
unmeasured; there are too many like that.   25
He is all filled with the enemy's flying arrows
of insults, with treacheries;
he cries out and shouts, boasts about himself
much more than the better man does,
thinks that his way seems completely   30
reputable to everyone. There will be another end of that
when he sees the result of this treachery.
He twists and deceives, considers many
tricks, lets go the wily thought,
shoots in showers. He does not know the offense   35
he has made with his hostility, hates his better
leader with malice, allows the treacherous shaft
to break the city wall, the rampart
that the measurer commanded that he should defend;
he sits elated with feasting, deceived by wine,   40
treacherously lets his words flow out,
to press with contentiousness, swelled up with violence,
ignited with malice, strife, evil tricks,
full of pride. Now you can know,
if you meet a retainer like this   45
dwelling in the villages, know by these
few declarations that that is the child of the enemy
enclosed in flesh; he has a perverse life,
a spirit hastening to hell destitute of good,
of the glorious king. The prophet sang of that,   50
the man ready of speech, and made this song:
"Whoever sets himself up
in this cruel time through pride,
lifts himself up high-minded, shall be made low
after the death journey, humiliated below   55

41

wunian witum fæst,   wyrmum beþrungen.
Þæt wæs geara iu   in Godes rice
þætte mid englum   ofer-hygd astag,
wid-mære gewin.   Wroht ahofan,
heardne here-siþ,   heofon widledan,
forsawan hyra sellan,   þa hi to swice þohton
ond þrym-cyning   þeoden-stoles
ricne beryfan,   swa hit ryht ne wæs,
ond þonne gesettan   on hyra sylfra dom
wuldres wyn-lond.   Þæt him wige forstod
Fæder frum-sceafta;   wearð him seo feohte to grim.
    Ðonne bið þam oþrum   ungelice
se þe her on eorþan   eað-mod leofað,
ond wiþ gesibbra gehwone   simle healdeð
freode on folce   ond his feond lufað,
þeah þe he him abylgnesse   oft gefremede
willum in þisse worulde.   Se mot wuldres dream
in haligra hyht   heonan astigan
on engla eard.   Ne biþ þam oþrum swa,
se þe on ofer-medum   eargum dædum
leofaþ in leahtrum,   ne beoð þa lean gelic
mid wuldor-cyning."   Wite þe be þissum,
gif þu eað-modne   eorl gemete,
þegn on þeode,   þam bið simle
gæst gegæderad,   Godes agen bearn,
wilsum in worlde,   gif me se witega ne leag.
Forþon we sculon a hycgende   hælo rædes
gemunan in mode   mæla gehwylcum
þone selestan   sigora waldend.
Amen.

60
65
70
75
80

to dwell fast in tortures, encircled by worms.
That was long ago in years in the kingdom of God
that among the angels pride rose up,
well-known strife. They hatched a crime,
a hard battle expedition, to defile heaven,   60
to renounce their better, when they intended treachery
and thought to deprive the powerful king of glory
of the princely throne, as was not right,
and then occupy the joy-land of glory according to
their own judgment. The Father of creation prevented   65
that through war; the fight was too fierce for them.
    Then it will be different for the other one
who here on earth humble-minded lives
and with each kinsman always holds
peace among the folk and loves his enemy,   70
although he often did him harm
willfully in this world. Toward the joy of glory
in the hope of the saints he may rise from here
into the land of angels. It will not be so for the other,
who in pride with slothful deeds   75
lives in vices, nor will the rewards be the same
from the glory king." Know by these things,
if you should meet a humble-minded man,
a retainer among the people, to that one will always be
joined the spirit, God's own son,   80
delightful in the world, if the prophet doesn't deceive me.
Therefore, ever mindful of the design of salvation,
we must keep in mind at all times
the best ruler of victories.
Amen.

Widsith

Widsið maðolade,   word-hord onleac,
se þe monna mæst   mægþa ofer eorþan,
folca geondferde;   oft he on flette geþah
mynelicne maþþum.   Him from Myrgingum
5   æþele onwocon.   He mid Ealhhilde,
fælre freoþu-webban,   forman siþe
Hreð-cyninges   ham gesohte
eastan of Ongle,   Eormanrices,
wraþes wær-logan.   Ongon þa worn sprecan:
10   "Fela ic monna gefrægn   mægþum wealdan!
Sceal þeodna gehwylc   þeawum lifgan,
eorl æfter oþrum   eðle rædan,
se þe his þeoden-stol   geþeon wile.
Þara wæs Hwala   hwile selast,
15   ond Alexandreas   ealra ricost
monna cynnes,   ond he mæst geþah
þara þe ic ofer foldan   gefrægen hæbbe.
Ætla weold Hunum,   Eormanric Gotum,
Becca Baningum,   Burgendum Gifica.
20   Casere weold Creacum   ond Celic Finnum,
Hagena Holmrygum   ond Heoden Glommum.
Witta weold Swæfum,   Wada Hælsingum,
Meaca Myrgingum,   Mearchealf Hundingum.

Widsith

Widsith spoke, unlocked his word hoard,
he who passed through most nations
and peoples across the earth; he often received desirable
treasure in the hall. His noble origins arose
from the Myrgings. With Ealhild, the   5
gracious peace weaver, he sought for the
first time from the east of Anglen the home of the king
of the Goths, of Eormanric, the cruel troth breaker.
He then began to speak many things:
"I have heard of many men ruling nations.   10
Each prince must live by customs,
one earl after the other ruling the homeland,
he who wants his throne to prosper.
Of those, Hwala was the best for a while
and Alexander the Great the most powerful of all mankind,   15
and he prospered most of those
I have heard of across the earth.
Attila ruled the Huns, Eormanric the Goths,
Becca the Banings, Gifica the Burgundians.
Caesar ruled the Greeks and Celic the Finns,   20
Hagena the Rugas and Heoden the Glommas.
Witta ruled the Swabians, Wada the Hælsings,
Meaca the Myrgings, Mearchealf the Hundings.

Þeodric weold Froncum,   Þyle Rondingum,
25   Breoca Brondingum,   Billing Wernum.
Oswine weold Eowum   ond Ytum Gefwulf,
Fin Folcwalding   Fresna cynne.
Sigehere lengest   Sæ-Denum weold,
Hnæf Hocingum,   Helm Wulfingum,
30   Wald Woingum,   Wod Þyringum,
Sæferð Sycgum,   Sweom Ongendþeow,
Sceafthere Ymbrum,   Sceafa Longbeardum,
Hun Hætwerum   ond Holen Wrosnum.
Hringweald wæs haten   Herefarena cyning.
35   Offa weold Ongle,   Alewih Denum;
se wæs þara manna   mod-gast ealra.
No hwæþre he ofer Offan   eorlscype fremede,
ac Offa geslog   ærest monna,
cniht-wesende,   cyne-rica mæst.
40   Nænig efen-eald him   eorlscipe maran
on orette.   Ane sweorde
merce gemærde   wið Myrgingum
bi Fifeldore;   heoldon forð siþþan
Engle ond Swæfe,   swa hit Offa geslog.
45   Hroþwulf ond Hroðgar   heoldon lengest
sibbe ætsomne   suhtor-fædran,
siþþan hy forwræcon   wicinga cynn
ond Ingeldes   ord forbigdan,
forheowan æt Heorote   Heaðobeardna þrym.
50   Swa ic geondferde fela   fremdra londa
geond ginne grund.   Godes ond yfles
þær ic cunnade   cnosle bidæled,
freo-mægum feor   folgade wide.

Theodoric ruled the Franks, Thyle the Rondings,
Breoca the Brondings, Billing the Wernas.   25
Oswine ruled the Eowan and Gefwulf the Jutes,
Fin the son of Folcwalda the race of the Frisians.
Sigehere ruled the Sea-Danes longest,
Hnæf the Hocings, Helm the Wulfings,
Wald the Woings, Wod the Thuringians,   30
Sæferth the Secgan, Ongendtheow the Swedes,
Sceafthere the Ymbras, Sceafa the Lombards,
Hun the Hætweres, and Holen the Wrosnas.
Hringweald was called king of the Herefaran.
Offa ruled the Angles, Alewih the Danes;   35
he was the boldest of all those men.
He did not, however, achieve heroic deeds beyond Offa's,
but Offa, first among men, while a boy,
won the greatest of kingdoms.
No one his age showed greater heroism   40
in battle. With his lone sword
he fixed the boundary against the Myrgings
at Fifeldore; afterward the Angles and
Swabians held it as Offa had won it.
Hrothwulf and Hrothgar, uncle and nephew,   45
kept the peace together longest
since they had driven away the race of the Vikings
and humiliated the vanguard of Ingeld,
cut to pieces the Heathobard host at Heorot.
So I traveled through many a foreign land   50
throughout the wide world. Good and evil
I experienced there bereft of kin,
far from free kinsmen I served widely.

Forþon ic mæg singan   ond secgan spell,
55 mænan fore mengo   in meodu-healle
hu me cyne-gode   cystum dohten.
Ic wæs mid Hunum   ond mid Hreðgotum,
mid Sweom ond mid Geatum   ond mid Suþ-Denum.
Mid Wenlum ic wæs ond mid Wærnum   ond mid
                                        wicingum.
60 Mid Gefþum ic wæs ond mid Winedum   ond mid
                                        Gefflegum.
Mid Englum ic wæs ond mid Swæfum   ond mid
                                        Ænenum.
Mid Seaxum ic wæs ond mid Sycgum   ond mid
                                        Sweordwerum.
Mid Hronum ic wæs ond mid Deanum   ond mid
                                        Heaþoreamum.
Mid Þyringum ic wæs   ond mid Þrowendum,
65 ond mid Burgendum,   þær ic beag geþah;
me þær Guðhere forgeaf   glædlicne maþþum
songes to leane.   Næs þæt sæne cyning!
Mid Froncum ic wæs ond mid Frysum   ond mid
                                        Frumtingum.
Mid Rugum ic wæs ond mid Glommum   ond mid
                                        Rumwalum.
70 Swylce ic wæs on Eatule   mid Ælfwine,
se hæfde mon-cynnes,   mine gefræge,
leohteste hond   lofes to wyrcenne,
heortan unhneaweste   hringa gedales,
beorhtra beaga,   bearn Eadwines.
75 Mid Sercingum ic wæs   ond mid Seringum;
mid Creacum ic wæs ond mid Finnum   ond mid Casere,

Therefore I can sing and tell a tale,
declare before the company in the mead hall   55
how the nobles were kind to me with choice gifts.
I was with the Huns and with the Goths,
with the Swedes and with the Geats and with the South-
    Danes.
With the Wenlas I was and with the Wernas and with the
    Vikings.
With the Gibids I was and with the Wends and with the   60
    Gefflegas.
With the Angles I was and with the Swabians and with the
    Ænenas.
With the Saxons I was and the Secgas and with the
    Swordsmen.
With the Hronas I was and with the Danes and with the
    Heathoremes.
With the Thuringians I was and with the Throwendas,
and with the Burgundians, where I received a ring;   65
Guthhere gave me the bright treasure there
as a reward for a song. That was not a negligent king!
With the Franks I was and with the Frisians and with the
    Frumtings.
With the Rugas I was and with the Glommas and with the
    Romans.
Likewise I was in Italy with Ælfwine,   70
who had, I've heard, the quickest hand
among mankind in gaining praise,
a most unmiserly heart in giving out rings,
bright bracelets, the son of Eadwine.
With the Saracens I was and with the Serings   75
with the Greeks I was and with the Finns and with Caesar,

se þe win-burga   geweald ahte,
wiolena ond wilna,   ond Wala rices.
Mid Scottum ic wæs ond mid Peohtum   ond mid
                                    Scridefinnum;
80   mid Lidwicingum ic wæs ond mid Leonum   ond mid
          Longbeardum,
      mid hæðnum ond mid hæleþum   ond mid Hundingum.
      Mid Israhelum ic wæs   ond mid Exsyringum,
      mid Ebreum ond mid Indeum   ond mid Egyptum.
      Mid Moidum ic wæs ond mid Persum   ond mid
                                    Myrgingum,
85   ond Mofdingum   ond ongend Myrgingum,
      ond mid Amothingum.   Mid East-Þyringum ic wæs
      ond mid Eolum ond mid Istum   ond Idumingum.
      Ond ic wæs mid Eormanrice   ealle þrage,
      þær me Gotena cyning   gode dohte;
90   se me beag forgeaf,   burg-warena fruma,
      on þam siex hund wæs   smætes goldes,
      gescyred sceatta   scilling-rime;
      þone ic Eadgilse   on æht sealde,
      minum hleo-dryhtne,   þa ic to ham bicwom,
95   leofum to leane,   þæs þe he me lond forgeaf,
      mines fæder eþel,   frea Myrginga.
      Ond me þa Ealhhild   oþerne forgeaf,
      dryht-cwen duguþe,   dohtor Eadwines.
      Hyre lof lengde   geond londa fela,
100   þonne ic be songe   secgan sceolde

he who had control of joyful cities, of riches
and of desirable things and of the kingdom of the Romans.
With the Irish I was and with the Picts and with the Scride-
    Finns;
with the Lidwicings I was and with the Leonas and with the   80
    Lombards,
with heathens and with warriors and with the Hundings.
With the Israelites I was and with the Assyrians,
with the Hebrews and with the Indians and with the
    Egyptians.
With the Medes I was and with the Persians and with the
    Myrgings
and the Mofdings and against the Myrgings   85
and with the Amothings. With the East Thuringians I was
and with the Eolas and with the Istas and the Idumings.
And I was with Eormanric continually,
where the king of the Goths was good and kind to me;
he gave me a ring, the leader of the city dwellers,   90
in which was six hundred coins of pure gold,
counted in shillings;
I gave that into Eadgil's possession,
to my protecting lord, when I came home,
as a reward to the beloved one because he, the lord   95
of the Myrgings, gave me land, the homeland of my father.
And then Ealhild, noble queen to the troop,
daughter of Eadwine, gave me another.
Her praise extended through many lands,
when I had to relate through song   100

hwær ic under swegle   selast wisse
gold-hrodene cwen   giefe bryttian.
Ðonne wit Scilling   sciran reorde
for uncrum sige-dryhtne   song ahofan
105   —hlude bi hearpan   hleoþor swinsade—
þonne monige men,   modum wlonce,
wordum sprecan,   þa þe wel cuþan,
þæt hi næfre song   sellan ne hyrdon.
Ðonan ic ealne geondhwearf   eþel Gotena;
110   sohte ic a gesiþa   þa selestan;
þæt wæs inn-weorud   Earmanrices.
Heðcan sohte ic ond Beadecan   ond Herelingas,
Emercan sohte ic ond Fridlan   ond Eastgotan,
frodne ond godne   fæder Unwenes.
115   Seccan sohte ic ond Beccan,   Seafolan ond Þeodric,
Heaþoric ond Sifecan,   Hliþe ond Incgenþeow.
Eadwine sohte ic ond Elsan,   Ægelmund ond Hungar,
ond þa wloncan gedryht   Wiþmyrginga.
Wulfhere sohte ic ond Wyrmhere;   ful oft þær wig ne
                                             alæg,
120   þonne Hræda here   heardum sweordum
ymb Wistla-wudu   wergan sceoldon
ealdne eþel-stol   Ætlan leodum.
Rædhere sohte ic ond Rondhere,   Rumstan ond
                                          Gislhere,
Wiþergield ond Freoþeric,   Wudgan ond Haman;
125   ne wæran þæt gesiþa   þa sæmestan
þeah þe ic hy anihst   nemnan sceolde.
Ful oft of þam heape   hwinende fleag
giellende gar   on grome þeode;

where I knew the best gold-adorned
queen beneath the sky was distributing gifts.
When Scilling and I in a clear voice
raised a song for our victorious lord
—loud to the harp it sounded melodiously—   105
then many people, proud in mind,
spoke in words, those who really knew,
that they never heard a better song.
From there I traveled through all the lands of the Goths;
always I sought the best of companions;   110
that was Eormanric's household.
Hethca I sought and Beadeca and Harlungs,
Emerca I sought and Fridla and Ostrogotha,
the wise and good father of Unwen.
Secca I sought and Becca, Seafola and Theodoric,   115
Heathoric and Sifeca, Hlithe and Incengtheow.
Eadwine I sought and Elsa, Ægelmund and Hungar,
and the proud troop of the Withmyrgings.
Wulfhere I sought and Wyrmhere; very often war did not
      cease there
when the army of the Goths with hard swords   120
at the Vistula wood had to defend
the ancient hereditary seat against Attila's people.
Rædhere I sought and Rondhere, Rumstan and Gislhere,
Withergield and Frederick, Wudga and Hama;
those companions were not the worst ones   125
although I must name them last.
Very often the yelling spear flew whistling
from that troop into the hostile people;

wræccan þær weoldan   wundnan golde
130   werum ond wifum,   Wudga ond Hama.
Swa ic þæt symle onfond   on þære feringe,
þæt se biþ leofast   lond-buendum
se þe him God syleð   gumena rice
to gehealdenne   þenden he her leofað."
135   Swa scriþende   gesceapum hweorfað
gleo-men gumena   geond grunda fela,
þearfe secgað,   þonc-word sprecaþ,
simle suð oþþe norð   sumne gemetað
gydda gleawne,   geofum unhneawne,
140   se þe fore duguþe wile   dom aræran,
eorlscipe æfnan,   oþþæt eal scæceð,
leoht ond lif somod;   lof se gewyrceð,
hafað under heofonum   heah-fæstne dom.

the exiles Wudga and Hama held sway there
with twisted gold over men and women.   130
Thus I always found in my traveling
that he will be most dear to land dwellers
whom God gives power over the kingdom of
men while he lives here."
Thus moving through creation the minstrels   135
of men roam through many countries,
say what they need, speak words of thanks,
south or north always meeting someone
wise in tales, generous in gifts,
he who before the company wants to spread glory,   140
perform manly deeds until light and life
depart all together; he earns praise,
has immutable glory under the heavens.

The Fortunes of Mortals

Ful oft þæt gegongeð   mid Godes meahtum
þætte wer ond wif   in woruld cennað
bearn mid gebyrdum   ond mid bleom gyrwað,
tennaþ ond tætaþ   oþþæt seo tid cymeð,
5   gegæð gear-rimum,   þæt þa geongan leomu,
lif-fæstan leoþu,   geloden weorþað.
Fergað swa ond feþað   fæder ond modor,
giefað ond gierwaþ.   God ana wat
hwæt him weaxendum   winter bringað.
10   Sumum þæt gegongeð   on geoguð-feore
þæt se ende-stæf   earfeð-mæcgum
wealic weorþeð.   Sceal hine wulf etan,
har hæð-stapa;   hin-siþ þonne
modor bimurneð.   Ne bið swylc monnes geweald.
15 Sumne sceal hungor ahiþan;   sumne sceal hreoh fordrifan,
sumne sceal gar agetan;   sumne guð abreotan.
Sum sceal leomena leas   lifes neotan,
folmum ætfeohtan;   sum on feðe lef,
seono-bennum seoc,   sar cwanian,
20   murnan meotud-gesceaft   mode gebysgad.
Sum sceal on holte   of hean beame
fiþerleas feallan: bið on flihte seþeah,
laceð on lyfte,   oþþæt lengre ne bið

The Fortunes of Mortals

Very often it happens through God's might
that a man and a woman bring children
into the world through birth and adorn them with colors,
coax them and cheer them until the time comes,
happens through a number of years, that the young limbs,   5
the members endowed with life, become grown.
Thus father and mother carry them along and walk with
them, give to them and dress them. God alone knows
what winters will bring them as they are growing up.
For some sufferers it happens that the end   10
woefully occurs during youth.
The wolf, the hoary heath stalker,
will devour him; his mother will then mourn
his departure. Such is not under human control.
Hunger will destroy one; rough weather will drive one off;   15
a spear will pour one's blood out; battle will destroy one.
One must live his life lightless,
grope about with his hands; one, lame of foot,
sick with sinew wounds, troubled in mind,
will lament his pain, mourn the decree of fate.   20
One will fall from a high tree in the forest,
featherless: that one is flying anyway,
playing in the air, until no longer

westem wudu-beames.   Þonne he on wyrt-ruman
25   sigeð sworcen-ferð,   sawle bireafod,
fealleþ on foldan;   feorð biþ on siþe.
Sum sceal on feþe   on feor-wegas
nyde gongan   ond his nest beran,
tredan urig-last   el-þeodigra,
30   frecne foldan;   ah he feormendra
lyt lifgendra,   lað biþ æghwær
fore his wonsceaftum   wineleas hæle.
Sum sceal on geapum   galgan ridan,
seomian æt swylte,   oþþæt sawl-hord,
35   ban-cofa blodig,   abrocen weorþeð.
Þær him hrefn nimeþ   heafod-syne,
sliteð salwig-pad   sawelleasne;
noþer he þy facne mæg   folmum biwergan,
laþum lyft-sceaþan;   biþ his lif scæcen,
40   ond he feleleas,   feores or-wena,
blac on beame   bideð wyrde,
bewegen wæl-miste.   Bið him werig noma.
Sumne on bæle sceal   brond aswencan,
fretan frecne lig   fægne monnan;
45   þær him lif-gedal   lungre weorðeð,
read reþe gled;   reoteð meowle,
seo hyre bearn gesihð   brondas þeccan.
Sumum meces ecg   on meodu-bence
yrrum ealo-wosan   ealdor oþþringeð,
50   were win-sadum;   bið ær his worda to hræd.
Sum sceal on beore   þurh byreles hond
meodu-gal mæcga;   þonne he gemet ne con
gemearcian his muþe   mode sine,

a fruit hanging from the tree. Then to the foot of it,
dark minded, bereft of soul, he plummets,   25
falls to the earth; the spirit journeys on.
One will go on distant paths on foot
by necessity and bear his provisions,
tread the wet ground of foreign nations,
the dangerous earth; with few living   30
entertainers, the friendless one is hated
everywhere because of miseries.
One must ride the broad gallows,
sway in death, until the soul holder,
the bloody bone casket, becomes broken.   35
There the raven plucks out the eyes,
the dark-plumaged one tears the soulless one;
neither can he defend against that evil with his hands,
against the hateful airborne robber; his life is gone,
and insensible, hopeless of life,   40
pale on the tree, he awaits fate,
covered with slaughter mist. His name is cursed.
Fire shall afflict one on the funeral pyre,
the fearful flame will consume the doomed one;
there separation from life happens quickly,   45
the cruel ember reddens with blood; the woman weeps,
she sees the flames swallow up her child.
From one, an ale tippler in his wrath,
a man sated with wine, the edge of the sword on the mead
bench takes his life; he was too quick with his words before. 50
One through beer from the cupbearer's hand will
become a mead-mad man; then he will know no measure,
will not give boundary to his mouth with his mind,

ac sceal ful earmlice   ealdre linnan,
55   dreogan dryhten-bealo   dreamum biscyred,
ond hine to sylf-cwale   secgas nemnað,
mænað mid muþe   meodu-gales gedrinc.
Sum sceal on geoguþe   mid Godes meahtum
his earfoð-sið   ealne forspildan,
60   ond on yldo eft   eadig weorþan,
wunian wyn-dagum   ond welan þicgan,
maþmas ond meodu-ful   mæg-burge on,
þæs þe ænig fira mæge   forð gehealdan.
Swa missenlice   meahtig Dryhten
65   geond eorþan sceat   eallum dæleð,
scyreþ ond scrifeð   ond gesceapo healdeð:
sumum ead-welan;   sumum earfeþa dæl,
sumum geogoþe glæd;   sumum guþe blæd,
gewealdenne wig-plegan;   sumum wyrp oþþe scyte,
70   torhtlicne tiir;   sumum tæfle cræft,
bleo-bordes gebregd.   Sume boceras
weorþað wis-fæste.   Sumum wundor-giefe
þurh gold-smiþe   gearwad weorþað;
ful oft he gehyrdeð   ond gehyrsteð wel,
75   bryten-cyninges beorn,   ond he him brad syleð
lond to leane.   He hit on lust þigeð.
Sum sceal on heape   hæleþum cweman,
blissian æt beore   benc-sittendum;
þær biþ drincendra   dream se micla.
80   Sum sceal mid hearpan   æt his hlafordes
fotum sittan,   feoh þicgan,
ond a snellice   snere wræstan,

but he must very wretchedly yield up his life,
endure great misfortune bereft of joys,   55
and people will say he killed himself, will decry
the drinking of the mead-mad man with their mouths.
One during youth through God's might will
waste the whole time of hardship,
and in old age again become blessed,   60
dwell in joyous days and partake of prosperity,
treasures and the mead cup among his family,
in as much as anyone can hold on to such things.
Thus the mighty Lord throughout the expanse
of the earth deals out variously to all,   65
determines, allots, and controls fortunes:
to one, wealth; to one, a share of miseries;
to one, gladness in youth; to one, glory in war,
controlled battle play; to one, throwing or shooting,
radiant fame; to one, skill at tables,   70
quick movement on the colored board. Some
become wise scholars. To one wondrous gifts
in goldsmithing are granted;
very often he will harden and ornament well,
the man of the powerful king, and he will give him broad   75
land in reward. He will gladly accept it.
One in the troop will please the people,
gladden the bench sitters through beer;
there will be great joy among the drinkers.
One will sit with his harp at his lord's   80
feet, receive payment,
and always quickly twang the harp string,

lætan scralletan   sceacol, se þe hleapeð,
nægl neomegende;   biþ him neod micel.
85 Sum sceal wildne fugel   wloncne atemian,
heafoc on honda,   oþþæt seo heoro-swealwe
wynsum weorþeð;   deþ he wyrplas on,
fedeþ swa on feterum   fiþrum dealne,
lepeþ lyft-swiftne   lytlum gieflum,
90 oþþæt se wælisca   wædum ond dædum
his æt-giefan   eað-mod weorþeð
ond to hago-stealdes   honda gelæred.
Swa wrætlice   weoroda nergend
geond middan-geard   monna cræftas
95 sceop ond scyrede   ond gesceapo ferede
æghwylcum on eorþan   eormen-cynnes.
Forþon him nu ealles þonc   æghwa secge,
þæsþe he fore his miltsum   monnum scrifeð.

let the plectrum sound loudly, the one that leaps,
the sweet sounding pick; it will be a great delight for him.
One must train the wild, proud bird,   85
the hawk, to his hand, until the falcon
becomes pleasant; he puts jesses on it,
feeds in its fetters the one exulting in feathers,
gives the one swift in the air little morsels,
until the servile one in dress and deeds   90
becomes obedient to his feeder
and guided to the hand of its provider.
Thus wondrously the savior of hosts
throughout middle earth created and allotted
skills of people and conveyed the fortunes   95
to each of humankind on earth.
Therefore let everyone thank him now for all
that he, through his mercy, ordains for human beings.

Maxims I

Frige mec frodum wordum.   Ne læt þinne ferð onhælne,
degol þæt þu deopost cunne.   Nelle ic þe min dyrne
                    gesecgan
gif þu me þinne hyge-cræft hylest   ond þine heortan
                    geþohtas.
Gleawe men sceolon gieddum wrixlan.   God sceal mon
                    ærest hergan
5   fægre, Fæder userne,   forþon þe he us æt frymþe geteode
lif ond lænne willan;   he usic wile þara leana gemonian.
    Meotud sceal in wuldre,   mon sceal on eorþan
    geong ealdian.   God us ece biþ;
    ne wendað hine wyrda   ne hine wiht dreceþ
10   adl ne yldo   ælmihtigne;
    ne gomelað he in gæste,   ac he is gen swa he wæs,
    þeoden geþyldig.   He us geþonc syleð,
    missenlicu mod,   monge reorde.
    Feorh-cynna fela   fæþ-meþ wide
15   eg-lond monig.   Eardas rume
    meotud arærde   for mon-cynne,
    ælmihtig God,   efen-fela bega
    þeoda ond þeawa.   Þing sceal gehegan
    frod wiþ frodne;   biþ hyra ferð gelic,

Maxims I

Ask me with wise words. Don't let your heart, what you
    know
most profoundly, be hidden, concealed. I won't tell you my
    secret
if you hide from me the power of your mind and the
    thoughts of your heart.
The wise must exchange sayings. One must first fairly
    praise God,
our Father, because in the beginning he granted us   5
life and fleeting desire; he will remind us of those rewards.
The measurer must be in glory, man must be on earth,
the young grow old. God will be eternal for us;
fates do not change him nor does disease
nor age trouble him, the almighty, at all;   10
he does not age in spirit, but he is yet as he was,
a patient prince. He gives us thoughts,
diverse minds, many voices.
Many an island far and wide
embraces many living kinds. The creator, almighty God,   15
has established spacious regions for humankind,
as many peoples as customs.
The wise must hold a meeting
with the wise; their hearts are alike,

65

20   hi a sace semaþ,   sibbe gelærað,
      þa ær won-sælge   awegen habbað.
      Ræd sceal mid snyttro,   ryht mid wisum,
      til sceal mid tilum.   Tu beoð gemæccan;
      sceal wif ond wer   in woruld cennan
25   bearn mid gebyrdum.   Beam sceal on eorðan
      leafum liþan,   leomu gnornian.
      Fus sceal feran,   fæge sweltan
      ond dogra gehwam   ymb gedal sacan
      middan-geardes.   Meotud ana wat
30   hwær se cwealm cymeþ,   þe heonan of cyþþe gewiteþ.
      Umbor yceð,   þa ær-adl nimeð;
      þy weorþeð on foldan swa fela   fira cynnes.
      Ne sy þæs magu-timbres   gemet ofer eorþan,
      gif hi ne wanige   se þas woruld teode.
35   Dol biþ se þe his Dryhten nat,   to þæs oft cymeð deað
                            unþinged.
      Snotre men sawlum beorgað,   healdað hyra soð mid ryhte.
      Eadig bið se þe in his eþle geþihð,   earm se him his frynd
                            geswicað.
      Nefre sceal se him his nest aspringeð;   nyde sceal þrage
                            gebunden.
      Bliþe sceal bealoleas heorte.   Blind sceal his eagna þolian,
40   oftigen biþ him torhtre gesihþe.   Ne magon hi tunglu
                            bewitian,

they always settle conflicts, teach peace,   20
which the unhappy have previously destroyed.
Counsel must come with wisdom, right with the wise,
the good must come with the good. Two are mates;
a woman and man must bring forth in the world
a child through birth. A tree on earth must   25
be bereft of its leaves, must mourn its branches.
The one ready to depart must go, the doomed must die
and every day fight against the separation
from middle earth. The creator alone knows
where the death comes that departs out of the native land.   30
He adds infants, early disease takes them;
that is why so many of the human race came to be in the
        world.
There would not be a limit to the number of children on
        earth
if he who made this world did not decrease it.
    Foolish is the one who does not know his Lord, because   35
        death often comes unexpected.
Intelligent people guard their souls, rightly hold onto their
        truth.
Blessed is the one who thrives in the homeland, miserable
        the one whom friends desert.
Never shall he be blessed whose food fails him; he will be
        bound for a time by necessity.
The innocent heart will be blessed. The blind must lose
        their eyes;
clear sight is taken from them; they cannot observe the   40
        stars,

swegl-torht sunnan ne monan.   Þæt him biþ sar in his
                                                                        mode,
onge þonne he hit ana wat   ne weneð þæt him þæs
                                                                ed-hwyrft cyme.
Waldend him þæt wite teode,   se him mæg wyrpe syllan,
hælo of heofod-gimme,   gif he wat heortan clæne.
45 Lef mon læces behofað.   Læran sceal mon geongne
                                                                    monnan,
trymman ond tyhtan þæt he teala cunne,   oþþæt hine mon
                                                                    atemedne hæbbe,
sylle him wist ond wædo,   oþþæt hine mon on gewitte
                                                                    alæde.
Ne sceal hine mon cild-geongne forcweþan   ær he hine
                                                                    acyþan mote;
þy sceal on þeode geþeon   þæt he wese þrist-hycgende.
50 Styran sceal mon strongum mode.   Storm oft holm
                                                                gebringeþ,
geofen in grimmum sælum;   onginnað grome fundian
fealwe on feorran to londe,   hwæþer he fæste stonde.
Weallas him wiþre healdað,   him biþ wind gemæne.
     Swa biþ sæ smilte,   þonne hy sund ne weceð,
55 swa beoþ þeoda geþwære   þonne hy geþingad habbað;
gesittað him on gesundum þingum,   ond þonne mid
                                                                gesiþum healdaþ
cene men gecynde rice.   Cyning biþ anwealdes georn;
lað se þe londes monað,   leof se þe mare beodeð.
     Þrym sceal mid wlenco,   þriste mid cenum,
60   sceolun bu recene   beadwe fremman.

68

the heavenly bright sun or moon. For him that is painful in
    his mind,
oppressive when he alone knows it and does not expect that
    a change will come.
The ruler set that punishment for him, he who may give a
    cure,
health for the jewel in the head, if he knows his heart is
    pure.
A feeble person needs a physician. A young person must be   45
taught to know things well until you have tamed him,
give him food and clothes until you have led him to under-
    standing.
You must not revile him while he is youthful before he can
    prove himself;
in that way he will prosper among the people so that he be-
    comes brave minded.
One must steer with a strong mind. Storm often brings the   50
sea, the ocean, into severe conditions; angry, fallow waves
    from afar begin
rushing to land, testing whether or not it will stand firm.
Walls hold out against them, wind is common to both.
  As the sea is calm when it does not awaken its waters,
so people are peaceful when they have come to agreement;   55
they sit in prosperity, and then brave men with their
    companions
control the lawful kingdom. A king is eager for power;
hateful is the one who demands land, beloved the one who
    offers more.
Glory goes with pride, the bold with the brave,
both must do battle at once.   60

Eorl sceal on eos boge,   eorod sceal getrume ridan,
fæste feþa stondan.   Fæmne æt hyre bordan geriseð;
wid-gongel wif word gespringeð,   oft hy mon wommum
                            bilihð,
hæleð hy hospe mænað,   oft hyre hleor abreoþeð.
65   Sceomiande man sceal in sceade hweorfan;   scir in leohte
                          geriseð.
Hond sceal heofod inwyrcan,   hord in streonum bidan,
gif-stol gegierwed stondan   hwonne hine guman gedælen.
Gifre biþ se þam golde onfehð;   guma þæs on heah-setle
                          geneah;
lean sceal, gif we leogan nellað,   þam þe us þas lisse
                          geteode.

B

70   Forst sceal freosan,   fyr wudu meltan,
eorþe growan,   is brycgian,
wæter helm wegan,   wundrum lucan
eorþan ciþas.   An sceal inbindan
forstes fetre   fela-meahtig God;
75   winter sceal geweorpan;   weder eft cuman,
sumor swegle hat,   sund unstille.
Deop deada wæg   dyrne bið lengest;
holen sceal inæled,   yrfe gedæled
deades monnes.   Dom biþ selast.
80   Cyning sceal mid ceape   cwene gebicgan,

The earl must ride the warhorse's arched back, the
     mounted troop must ride as a host,
foot soldiers must stand fast. It is proper for a maid to be at
     her embroidery;
a wandering woman spreads words, often she is blamed for
     wrongs,
men speak of her with reproach, her cheek often withers.
A shamed person must move in the shadow; it is proper for   65
     bright things to be in the light.
The head must work the hand, the hoard wait in its trea-
     sures,
the gift-throne stand ready when men share it out.
Greedy is the one who receives the gold; the man on the
     high seat does not lack;
there must be compensation, if we do not want to lie, to the
     one who granted us these favors.

B

Frost must freeze, fire melt wood,   70
earth grow, ice form a bridge,
water wear a helmet, wondrously lock away
earth's seeds. One alone, most mighty God,
shall unbind the frost's fetters;
winter must pass; good weather will come again,   75
summer hot from the sun, the ocean restless.
The deep path of the dead will be secret longest;
holly must be burned, the inheritance from a dead
person divided. Fame is best.
A king must buy a queen with goods,   80

bunum ond beagum;   bu sceolon ærest
geofum god wesan.   Guð sceal in eorle,
wig geweaxan,   ond wif geþeon
leof mid hyre leodum,   leoht-mod wesan,
85   rune healdan,   rum-heort beon
mearum ond maþmum,   meodo-rædenne
for gesið-mægen   symle æghwær
eodor æþelinga   ærest gegretan,
forman fulle   to frean hond
90   ricene geræcan,   ond him ræd witan
bold-agendum   bæm ætsomne.
    Scip sceal genægled,   scyld gebunden,
leoht linden bord;   leof wil-cuma
Frysan wife   þonne flota stondeð;
95   biþ his ceol cumen   ond hyre ceorl to ham,
agen æt-geofa,   ond heo hine in laðaþ,
wæsceð his warig hrægl   ond him syleþ wæde niwe,
liþ him on londe   þæs his lufu bædeð.
Wif sceal wiþ wer wære gehealdan,   oft hi mon wommum
                        belihð;
100   fela bið fæst-hydigra,   fela bið fyrwet-geornra,
freoð hy fremde monnan   þonne se oþer feor gewiteþ.
Lida biþ longe on siþe;   a mon sceal seþeah leofes wenan,
gebidan þæs he gebædan ne mæg.   Hwonne him eft
                        gebyre weorðe,
ham cymeð, gif he hal leofað,   nefne him holm gestyreð,
105   mere hafað mundum   mægð-egsan wyn.
    Ceap-eadig mon   cyning-wic þonne

with goblets and rings; both must first
be good at giving gifts. Battle, war must grow
in a man, and a woman must thrive,
dear among her people, be lighthearted,
hold secrets, be open hearted   85
with horses and with treasures; always, everywhere
in dealing out mead before the band of warriors
she must greet first the chief of the nobles,
instantly offer the first cup
to her lord's hand, and know what is good sense for them   90
both as holders together of the homestead.
   A ship must be nailed, a shield, the light
linden wood board, bound; dear is the welcome one
to the Frisian wife when the boat is moored;
the vessel has come and her husband is home,   95
her own provider, and she leads him in,
washes his dirty clothes and gives him new garments,
lies with him on land as his love requires.
A woman must be true to her man, often she is blamed for
     wrongs;
many are constant, many are curious,   100
they love strangers when the other one goes far away.
A sailor is long on the journey; even so, one should expect
     the loved one,
 wait for that which he cannot urge along. When he has the
     chance again,
he comes home, if he lives uninjured, unless the sea
     restrains him,
the ocean has the maiden's own joy, in its hands.   105
The rich merchant will then buy a kingly dwelling

leodon cypeþ   þonne liþan cymeð;
wuda ond wætres nyttað   þonne him biþ wic alyfed,
mete bygeþ, gif he maran þearf   ærþon he to meþe weorþe.
110 Seoc se biþ þe to seldan ieteð;   þeah hine mon on sunnan
                                                        læde,
ne mæg he be þy wedre wesan,   þeah hit sy wearm on
                                                        sumera,
ofercumen biþ he, ær he acwele,   gif he nat hwa hine
                                                        cwicne fede.
Mægen mon sceal mid mete fedan,   morþor under eorþan
                                                        befeolan,
hinder under hrusan,   þe hit forhelan þenceð;
115 ne biþ þæt gedefe deaþ   þonne hit gedyrned weorþeð.
    Hean sceal gehnigan,   hadl gesigan,
    ryht rogian.   Ræd biþ nyttost,
    yfel unnyttost;   þæt unlæd nimeð.
    God bið genge   ond wiþ God lenge.
120 Hyge sceal gehealden,   hond gewealden,
    seo sceal in eagan,   snyttro in breostum,
    þær bið þæs monnes   mod-geþoncas.
Muþa gehwylc mete þearf,   mæl sceolon tidum gongan.
    Gold geriseþ   on guman sweorde,
125 sellic sige-sceorp,   sinc on cwene,
    god scop gumum,   gar-niþ werum,
    wig towiþre   wic-freoþa healdan.
    Scyld sceal cempan,   sceaft reafere,
    sceal bryde beag,   bec leornere,
130 husl halgum men,   hæþnum synne.

for his people when he comes sailing home;
he enjoys wood and water when a dwelling is granted him,
buys food if he needs more before he becomes too tired.
Sick will be the one who eats too seldom; although   110
      someone should lead him into the sun,
he cannot exist on the weather, although it be warm in the
      summer,
he will be overcome before he dies if he does not know
      someone to keep him alive with nourishment.
One must nourish strength with food, conceal murder
      under the earth,
far down under the ground, whoever wants to hide it;
that is no fitting death when it is secret.   115
   The humble person must bow, the prone one fall,
the straight flourish. Counsel is most useful,
evil most useless; the wicked one chooses that.
Good will prevail and belongs with God.
Thought must be directed, the hand controlled,   120
the pupil must be in the eye, wisdom in the breast,
where the understanding of human beings is.
Each mouth needs food, meals must come on time.
It is fitting that gold is on a man's sword,
a rare ornament of victory, that treasure is on a queen,   125
that there is a good poet for people, that men take up
spears to preserve a dwelling's protection in time of war.
A shield must be with the warrior, a shaft with the raider,
a ring must be with the bride, books with the student,
the eucharist with holy men, sins with the heathens.   130

Woden worhte weos,   wuldor alwalda,
rume roderas;   þæt is rice God,
sylf soð-cyning,   sawla nergend,
se us eal forgeaf   þæt we on lifgaþ,
135   ond eft æt þam ende   eallum wealdeð
monna cynne.   Þæt is meotud sylfa.

C

Ræd sceal mon secgan,   rune writan,
leoþ gesingan,   lofes gearnian,
dom areccan,   dæges onettan.
140   Til mon tiles   ond tomes meares,
cuþes ond gecostes   ond calc-rondes;
nænig fira   to fela gestryneð.
Wel mon sceal wine healdan   on wega gehwylcum;
oft mon fereð feor bi tune,   þær him wat freond
                                      unwiotodne.
145   Wineleas, won-sælig mon   genimeð him wulfas to geferan,
fela-fæcne deor.   Ful oft hine se gefera sliteð;
gryre sceal for greggum,   græf deadum men;
hungre heofeð,   nales þæt heafe bewindeð,
ne huru wæl wepeð   wulf se græga,
150   morþor-cwealm mæcga,   ac hit a mare wille.
Wræd sceal wunden;   wracu heardum men.
Boga sceal stræle,   sceal bam gelic
mon to gemæccan.   Maþþum oþres weorð,

Woden made idols, the almighty made heaven,
the spacious skies; that is powerful God,
the true king himself, the savior of souls,
who gave us all everything on which we live
and again at the end will entirely rule   135
the human race. That is the creator himself.

C

One should talk sense, write down mysteries,
sing songs, earn praise
pronounce judgment, hasten while it is day.
A good man keeps in mind a good and tame horse,   140
known and tried and round hoofed;
no man gets too much.
One must be true to a friend on each path;
one often travels far around a homestead, where he knows
        he has no certain friend.
Friendless, the unhappy man takes wolves as companions,   145
very treacherous animals. Very often that companion tears
        him;
there must be terror on account of the gray one, a grave for
        the dead man;
the gray wolf laments its hunger, not at all circles the grave
        with a dirge,
indeed does not mourn over the slaughter,
the murder of men, but it always wants more.   150
    A wound must have a bandage; a cruel man, revenge.
A bow must have an arrow, both alike must
have a man as a companion. One treasure is worth another,

gold mon sceal gifan.   Mæg God syllan
155   eadgum æhte   ond eft niman.
Sele sceal stondan,   sylf ealdian.
Licgende beam   læsest groweð.
Treo sceolon brædan   ond treow weaxan,
sio geond bilwitra   breost ariseð.
160   Wærleas mon ond won-hydig,
ætren-mod ond ungetreow,
þæs ne gymeð God.
Fela sceop meotud þæs þe fyrn gewearð,   het siþþan swa
forð wesan.
Wæra gehwylcum wislicu   word gerisað,
165   gleo-men gied   ond guman snyttro.
Swa monige beoþ men ofer eorþan,   swa beoþ mod-
geþoncas;
ælc him hafað sundor-sefan.
Longað þonne þy læs   þe him con leoþa worn,
oþþe mid hondum con   hearpan gretan,
170   hafaþ him his gliwes giefe,   þe him God sealde.
Earm biþ se þe sceal ana lifgan,
wineleas wunian,   hafaþ him wyrd geteod;
betre him wære þæt he broþor ahte,   begen hi anes
monnes,
eorles eaforan wæran   gif hi sceoldan eofor onginnan
175   oþþe begen beran;   biþ þæt sliþ-hende deor.
A scyle þa rincas   gerædan lædan
ond him ætsomne swefan;
næfre hy mon tomælde,
ær hy deað todæle.

one must give gold. God can give wealth
to the fortunate and take it back again.   155
A hall must stand, grow old by itself.
The tree lying down grows least.
Trees must broaden and faith be fruitful,
it rises in the hearts of the innocent.
Of the faithless and careless one,   160
venomous and untrue,
God will not take heed.
The creator shaped much of that which happened long ago,
commanded that it should be so from then on.
For every one, wise words are fitting,
song for the minstrel and prudence for the man.   165
There are as many people on earth as there are thoughts;
each person has a separate understanding.
The one who knows many songs
or knows how to greet the harp with hands longs less,
and has the gift of music inside, which God gave.   170
Miserable is the one who has to live alone,
fate has ordained that he should exist friendless;
it would be better for him to have a brother, for both of
        them to be from one man,
sons of a nobleman if they must attack a boar
or beset a bear; that is a fell-pawed beast.   175
Warriors must always have weapons with them
and sleep side by side;
let no one ever hinder them with words
before death separates them.

180 Hy twegen sceolon tæfle ymbsittan   þenden him hyra
                                    torn toglide,
    forgietan þara geocran gesceafta,   habban him gomen on
                                         borde;
    idle hond æmetlan geneah tæfles monnes   þonne teoselum
                                     weorpeð.
    Seldan in sidum ceole,   nefne he under segle yrne . . .
    werig scealc wiþ winde roweþ;   ful oft mon wearnum tihð
185 eargne þæt he elne forleose;   drugað his ar on borde.
        Lot sceal mid lyswe,   list mid gedefum;
        þy weorþeð se stan forstolen.
        Oft hy wordum toweorpað,
        ær hy bacum tobreden;
190   geara is hwær aræd.
    Wearð fæhþo fyra cynne   siþþan furþum swealg
    eorðe Abeles blode.   Næs þæt an-dæge nið;
    of þam wroht-dropan   wide gesprungon
    micel mon ældum,   monegum þeodum
195 bealo-blonden niþ.   Slog his broðor swæsne
    Cain, þone cwealm serede;   cuþ wæs wide siþþan,
    þæt ece nið ældum scod,   swa aþol-warum.
        Drugon wæpna gewin   wide geond eorþan,
        ahogodan ond ahyrdon   heoro sliþendne.
200   Gearo sceal guð-bord,   gar on sceafte,
        ecg on sweorde   ond ord spere,
        hyge heardum men.   Helm sceal cenum,
        ond a þæs heanan hyge   hord unginnost.

Two will sit at the game board while their troubles slip away,   180
forgetting sad events, having pleasure at the table;
an empty hand is enough for an idle gambler when he
        throws the dice.
Seldom in a broad ship, unless it's moving under sail . . .
a weary man rows against the wind; very often the sluggish
        man attracts reproaches
that he lacks courage; his oar dries up on board.   185
Guile must accompany the evil man, skill the virtuous one;
in that way, the stone gets stolen.
Often they cast words
before they turn their backs;
the ready man is prepared everywhere.   190
A state of feud came to the human race after
the earth swallowed Abel's blood. That strife was not
        restricted to one day;
from that criminal bloodshed sprang
great evil widely among men, pernicious strife
among many peoples. Cain, whom death spared,   195
slew his dear brother; it was widely known since
that eternal strife was oppressive to men as to dwellers in a
        plague.
They endured the clash of weapons widely throughout the
earth, thinking about and hardening wounding swords.
 The battle shield must be ready, the spear on the shaft,   200
the edge on the sword, and the point on the spear,
spirit on the hard man. To the bold, a helmet,
and always to the one of lowly spirit the most meager
        hoard.

The Order of the World

Wilt þu, fus hæle,   fremdne monnan,
wisne woð-boran   wordum gretan,
fricgan fela-geongne   ymb forð-gesceaft,
biddan þe gesecge   sidra gesceafta
5   cræftas cyndelice   cwic-hrerende,
þa þe dogra gehwam   þurh dom Godes
bringe wundra fela   wera cneorissum.
Is þara anra gehwam   orgeate tacen,
þam þurh wisdom   woruld ealle con
10   behabban on hreþre,   hycgende mon,
þæt geara iu,   gliwes cræfte,
mid gieddingum   guman oft wrecan,
rincas ræd-fæste;   cuþon ryht sprecan,
þæt a fricgende   fira cynnes
15   ond secgende   searo-runa gespon
a gemyndge mæst   monna wiston.
Forþon scyle ascian,   se þe on elne leofað,
deop-hydig mon,   dygelra gesceafta,
bewritan in gewitte   word-hordes cræft,
20   fæstnian ferð-sefan,   þencan forð teala;
ne sceal þæs aþreotan   þegn modigne
þæt he wislice   woruld fulgonge.

    Leorna þas lare.   Ic þe lungre sceal
meotudes mægen-sped   maran gesecgan,

The Order of the World

Resolve, eager one, to greet the stranger,
the wise singer, with words,
ask the much-traveled one about the created world,
bid that he should tell you about the living and moving
natural powers of the spacious creations,   5
which every day through the judgment of God
bring many wonders to the human race.
Each one of those wonders is a well-known sign
to the one who through wisdom knows how to comprehend
the whole world in his heart, the person thinking about   10
what formerly in days gone by, men, resolute warriors,
by the power of music often recited
in songs; they knew how to speak rightly
always questioning and saying,
always mindful, what the best of mankind   15
knew of the web of mysteries.
Therefore, whoever will live in courage,
the deeply meditating one, must ask the secret creations,
inscribe in mind the craft of the word hoard,
make firm the heart, think properly;   20
a noble-minded attendant must not grow tired
of engaging wholly and wisely in the world.
    Learn this lesson. I must quickly
tell you of the creator's abundance of strength greater

25   þonne þu hyge-cræftig   in hreþre mæge
      mode gegripan.   Is sin meaht forswiþ.
      Nis þæt monnes gemet   mold-hrerendra,
      þæt he mæge in hreþre   his heah geweorc
      furþor aspyrgan   þonne him frea sylle
30   to ongietanne   Godes agen bibod;
      ac we sculon þoncian   þeodne mærum
      awa to ealdre,   þæs þe us se eca cyning
      on gæste wlite   forgiefan wille
      þæt we eaðe magon   up-cund rice
35   forð gestigan,   gif us on ferðe geneah
      ond we willað healdan   heofon-cyninges bibod.
      Gehyr nu þis here-spel   ond þinne hyge gefæstna.
          Hwæt, on frymþe gescop   Fæder ælmihtig,
      heah hordes weard,   heofon ond eorðan,
40   sæs sidne grund,   sweotule gesceafte,
      þa nu in þam þream   þurh þeodnes hond
      heaþ ond hebbaþ   þone halgan blæd.
      Forþon eal swa teofanade,   se þe teala cuþe,
      æghwylc wiþ oþrum;   sceoldon eal beran
45   stiþe stefn-byrd,   swa him se steora bibead
      missenlice gemetu   þurh þa miclan gecynd.
      Swa hi to worulde   wlite forþ berað
      dryhtnes duguþe   ond his dæda þrym,
      lixende lof   in þa longan tid,
50   fremmaþ fæstlice   frean ece word
      in þam frum-stole   þe him frea sette,
      hluttor heofones weard,   healdað georne
      mere gemære;   meaht forð tihð

than you, sagacious at heart, can   25
grasp with your mind. His might is very great.
It is not within the compass of people moving on earth
that they may further investigate his exalted works
in their hearts than the Lord should give them
for understanding God's own commandment;   30
but we must thank the famous prince
for ever and ever so that the eternal king
will give us a beautiful spirit
so that we may easily ascend from here
into the kingdom above if our heart is not lacking   35
and we want to keep the command of the heavenly king.
Hear now this glorious discourse and make fast your mind.
  Behold, the Father almighty, the high guardian of the
treasure hoard, created in the beginning heaven and earth,
the broad bottom of the sea, the distinct creatures   40
that now in those three regions through the prince's hand
exalt and raise up holy praise.
Therefore he who rightly knows joined all,
each to the other; all had to bear
firm direction, as the ordainer enjoined on them,   45
their various degrees through that mighty act of generation.
So they, the tried warriors of the Lord,
carry forth his beauty and the glory of his deeds to the
world, his splendid praise during that long period,
firmly perform the Lord's eternal word   50
in the original seat that the Lord, the shining guardian
of heaven, established, eagerly hold
the illustrious course; his might draws forth

heofon-condelle   ond holmas mid,
55   laþað ond lædeþ   lifes agend
in his anes fæþm   ealle gesceafta.
Swa him wide-ferh   wuldor stondeþ,
ealra demena   þam gedefestan,
þe us þis lif gescop,   ond þis leohte beorht
60   cymeð morgna gehwam   ofer mist-hleoþu
wadan ofer wægas   wundrum gegierwed,
ond mid ær-dæge   eastan snoweð
wlitig ond wynsum   wera cneorissum;
lifgendra gehwam   leoht forð biereð
65   bronda beorhtost,   ond his brucan mot
æghwylc on eorþan,   þe him eagna gesihð
sigora soð-cyning   syllan wolde.
Gewiteð þonne mid þy wuldre   on west-rodor
forð-mære tungol   faran on heape,
70   oþþæt on æfenne   ut gar-secges
grundas pæþeð;   glom oþer cigð;
niht æfter cymeð,   healdeð nyd-bibod
halgan Dryhtnes.   Heofon-torht swegl
scir gescyndeð   in gesceaft Godes
75   under foldan fæþm,   farende tungol.
Forþon nænig fira   þæs frod leofað
þæt his mæge æ-springe   þurh his ægne sped witan,
hu geond grund færeð   gold-torht sunne
in þæt wonne genip   under wætra geþring,
80   oþþe hwa þæs leohtes   lond-buende
brucan mote,   siþþan heo ofer brim hweorfeð.
     Forþon swa teofenede,   se þe teala cuþe,
dæg wiþ nihte,   deop wið hean,

the heavenly candles and the seas,
the owner of life invites and leads   55
in the oneness of his embrace all of creation.
Thus forever the glory stands
of the kindest of all judges,
who created this life for us, and this brightness of light,
wondrously adorned, comes every morning   60
over the misty slopes passing over the waves,
and at daybreak comes from the east
beautiful and pleasant for the generations of men;
for each of the living, the brightest of torches
carries forth light, and everyone on earth   65
to whom the true king of victories wanted to give
eyesight may enjoy it.
Then with that glory the very great star
departs to go in company into the western sky
until in the evening it treads the ocean's depths   70
as its path; another darkness calls;
the night comes afterward, obeying the command
of the holy Lord. The heavenly bright sun,
the traveling star, resplendent hastens
in God's creation under the bosom of the earth.   75
Therefore no human being lives who is so wise
that he, by his own faculties, may know its waning,
how the gold-bright sun fares through the lowest part
into that dark mist under the tumult of waters,
or who dwelling in the land may enjoy   80
that light after it moves beyond the shore.
    Therefore, he who rightly has the power thus joined
day with night, deep with lofty,

lyft wið lagu-stream,   lond wiþ wæge,

85   flod wið flode,   fisc wið yþum.

Ne waciað þas geweorc,   ac he hi wel healdeð;
stondað stiðlice   bestryþed fæste
miclum meaht-locum   in þam mægen-þrymme
mid þam sy ahefed   heofon ond eorþe.

90   Beoð þonne eadge   þa þær in wuniað,
hyhtlic is þæt heorð-werud.   Þæt is herga mæst,
eadigra unrim,   engla þreatas.

Hy geseoð symle   hyra sylfra cyning,
eagum on wlitað,   habbað æghwæs genoh.

95   Nis him wihte won,   þam þe wuldres cyning
geseoþ in swegle;   him is symbel ond dream
ece unhwylen   eadgum to frofre.

Forþon scyle mon gehycgan   þæt he meotude hyre;
æghwylc ælda bearna   forlæte idle lustas,

100   læne lifes wynne;   fundige him to lissa blisse;
forlæte hete-niþa   gehwone sigan
mid synna fyrnum;   fere him to þam sellan rice.

air with river, land with sea,
flood with flood, fish with wave.   85
These works do not weaken, but he holds them well;
they stand firmly, erected fast
with great bonds in that majestic power
with which heaven and earth may be upheld.
Those who live there are blessed,   90
joyous is that household. That is the greatest of armies,
countless blessed ones, hosts of angels.
They always see their king himself,
gaze on him with their eyes, have enough of each good.
They want for nothing, those who see the king of glory   95
in heaven; for the blessed is feast and joy
eternal, everlasting, as a comfort.
Therefore, everyone must resolve that he obey the creator;
let each human child relinquish idle desires,
the transitory joy of life; let each aspire to the bliss of grace; 100
let each allow violent hatreds to subside;
let each journey to that better kingdom.

The Rhyming Poem

Me lifes onlah   se þis leoht onwrah,
ond þæt torhte geteoh,   tillice onwrah.
Glæd wæs ic gliwum,   glenged hiwum,
blissa bleoum,   blostma hiwum.
5   Secgas mec segon   —symbel ne alegon—
feoh-giefe gefegon;   frætwed wægon
wicg ofer wongum   wennan gongum,
lisse mid longum   leoma gehongum.
Þa wæs wæstmum aweaht,   world onspreht,
10   under roderum areaht,   ræd-mægne oferþeaht.
Giestas gengdon,   gerscype mengdon,
lisse lengdon,   lustum glengdon.
Scrifen scrad glad   þurh gescad in brad,
wæs on lagu-streame lad,   þær me leoþu ne biglad.
15   Hæfde ic heanne had,   ne wæs me in healle gad,
þæt þær rof weord rad.   Oft þær rinc gebad,
þæt he in sele sæge   sinc-gewæge,
þegnum geþyhte.   Þenden wæs ic in mægen,
horsce mec heredon,   hilde generedon,
20   fægre feredon,   feondon biweredon.

The Rhyming Poem

He who revealed this light gave me life
and brought forth that brightness, graciously revealed it.
Joyously was I glad, in hues was I clad,
in colors of delights, in the blossoms' hues.
Men saw me—feasts did not fail—   5
they joined in the gift of life; ornamented horses
carried me over the plains in joyous courses,
gently past trees with long branches.
Then the world was awakened in fruitfulness, it was
        enlivened, spread out
under the firmament, covered with productive force of life.   10
The guests came, mingled with noisy talk,
pleasantly lingered, were joyfully adorned.
The appointed ship sailed through the passage onto the
        broad course,
was on the ocean path where the vessel did not fail me.
I had high rank; for me, nothing was lacking in the hall   15
where the proud troop moved about. A warrior often
        waited there
in the hall so that he might see the weight of treasure,
useful to retainers. While I was strong,
the brave praised me, protected me in battle,
fairly upheld me, defended me from enemies.   20

Swa mec hyht-giefu heold,   hyge-dryht befeold,
staþol-æhtum steold,   stepe-gongum weold
swylce eorþe ol,   ahte ic ealdor-stol,
galdor-wordum gol.   Gomen sibbe ne ofoll,
25 ac wæs gefest gear,   gellende sner,
wuniendo wær   wil-bec bescær.
Scealcas wæron scearpe,   scyl wæs hearpe,
hlude hlynede,   hleoþor dynede,
swegl-rad swinsade,   swiþe ne minsade.
30 Burg-sele beofode,   beorht hlifade,
ellen eacnade,   ead beacnade,
freaum frodade,   fromum godade,
mod mægnade,   mine fægnade,
treow telgade,   tir welgade,
35 blæd blissade,
gold gearwade,   gim hwearfade,
sinc searwade,   sib nearwade.
From ic wæs in frætwum,   freolic in geatwum;
wæs min dream dryhtlic,   drohtað hyhtlic.
40 Foldan ic freoþode,   folcum ic leoþode,
lif wæs min longe,   leodum in gemonge,
tirum getonge,   teala gehonge.
Nu min hreþer is hreoh,   heow-siþum sceoh,
nyd-bysgum neah;   gewiteð nihtes in fleah
45 se ær in dæge wæs dyre.   Scriþeð nu deop in feore
brond-hord geblowen,   breostum in forgrowen,
flyhtum toflowen.   Flah is geblowen
miclum in gemynde;   modes gecynde

Thus the hope-gift held me, the household retainers
surrounded me, I held the high seat, ruled their goings
as the earth gave nourishment, I possessed the high throne,
sang the words of charms. The joy of peace did not
    decrease,
but the year was constant in gifts, resounding harp string,   25
continuing pledge, cut off the river of affliction.
Men were sharp; clear was the harp,
loudly it sounded, the song resounded,
the music melodious, diminished not for us.
The hall cowered, brightly towered,   30
courage teemed, happiness beamed,
for the lords was wisdom, for the strong was good,
the heart grew great, the memories rejoiced,
faith branched forth, glory abounded,
renown exulted,   35
gold was ready, the gem turned,
treasure cheated, kinship narrowed.
   Strong was I in my armaments, noble in my array;
my pleasure had been lordly, my way of life hopeful.
With the earth I made peace, my folk I appeased,   40
my life was long among my people,
in contact with glory, well disposed.
   Now my heart is troubled, timid from departing hues,
to trouble now more near; that leaves in flight at night
what before in day was dear. A burning thought   45
now moves deep into my life, has grown into my chest,
has flown far and wide apart. Hostility has blossomed
much in mind; bottomless, unrestrained sorrow

greteð ungrynde   grorn efenpynde;
50   bealo-fus byrneð,   bittre toyrneð.
Werig winneð,   widsið onginneð,
sar ne sinniþ,   sorgum cinnið,
blæd his blinnið,   blisse linnið,
listum linneð,   lustum ne tinneð.
55   Dreamas swa her gedreosað,   dryhtscype gehreosað,
lif her men forleosað,   leahtras oft geceosað;
treow-þrag is to trag,   seo untrume genag,
steapum eatole misþah,   ond eal stund genag.
    Swa nu world wendeþ,   wyrde sendeþ,
60   ond hetes henteð,   hæleþe scyndeð.
Wen-cyn gewiteð,   wæl-gar sliteð,
flah-mah fliteþ,   flan mon hwiteð,
borg-sorg biteð,   bald ald þwiteþ,
wræc-fæc wriþað,   wraþ að smiteþ,
65   sin-gryn sidað,   searo-fearo glideþ,
grom-torn græfeþ,   græf hæft hafað,
searo-hwit solaþ,   sumur-hat colað,
fold-wela fealleð,   feondscipe wealleð,
eorð-mægen ealdaþ,   ellen colað.
70   Me þæt wyrd gewæf,   ond gehwyrft forgeaf,
þæt ic grofe græf,   ond þæt grimme græf
flean flæsce ne mæg,   þonne flan-hred dæg
nyd-grapum nimeþ,   þonne seo neaht becymeð
seo me eðles ofonn   ond mec her eardes onconn.

attacks the nature of the mind;
prone to sin, it burns, bitterly surges.   50
The weary one labors, the wide journey begins,
pain does not abate, gapes with sorrows,
his renown ceases, he desists from joy,
he parts from skills, goes not at will.
Pleasures decline here, lordship falls,   55
people lose their lives here, often choose vices;
the time of faithfulness is very bad; it has sunk down ill,
has mountainously, terribly degenerated, sinking all the
      time.
  So the world turns, sends fate
and pursues hate, incites people.   60
The joyous kin departs, the slaughter-spear tears,
the hostilely determined one fights, wickedness polishes
      the arrow,
sorrow that comes from borrowing gnaws, the bold cuts off
      the old,
a time of exile fetters, wrath fouls the oath,
continual grief spreads wide, cunning glides,   65
fierce anger mines deep, the grave imprisons,
brilliant whiteness gets defiled, summer heat cools,
the land's wealth falls, enmity wells up,
the power of earth grows old, courage grows cold.
Fate wove for me and the cycle of time apportioned   70
that I dug a grave, and that grim grave
flesh cannot flee when the arrow-swift day
with inevitable grips will seize, when the night will come
that will deprive me of native land and attack me here in my
      homeland.

75 Þonne lic-homa ligeð,   lima wyrm friteþ,
    ac him wenne gewigeð   ond þa wist geþygeð,
    oþþæt beoþ þa ban an,
    ond æt nyhstan nan   nefne se neda tan
    balawun her gehloten.   Ne biþ se hlisa adroren.
80 Ær þæt eadig geþenceð;   he hine þe oftor swenceð,
    byrgeð him þa bitran synne,   hogaþ to þære betran wynne,
    gemon morþa lisse,   þær sindon miltsa blisse
    hyhtlice in heofona rice.   Uton nu halgum gelice
    scyldum biscyrede   scyndan generede,
85 wommum biwerede,   wuldre generede,
    þær mon-cyn mot   for meotude rot
    soðne God geseon,   ond aa in sibbe gefean.

Then the body will lie, the worm will gnaw the limbs,   75
and it will experience joy and take the feast,
until all alone there will be naught but bone,
and at the last none except the inescapable lot
appointed for men. That fame will not fall away.
The blessed one thinks about that beforehand; he more   80
    often undertakes penance,
protects himself from grievous sin, ponders better joys,
remembers the joy of rewards, where the bliss of mercies is
hopeful in the kingdom of heaven. Let us hurry like the
saints cut off from sins, saved,
defended from faults, gloriously saved,   85
where mankind, glad before the measurer, will be allowed
to see the true God and always rejoice in peace.

Deor

Welund him be wurman   wræces cunnade,
an-hydig eorl   earfoþa dreag,
hæfde him to gesiþþe   sorge ond longaþ,
winter-cealde wræce;   wean oft onfond,
5   siþþan hine Niðhad on   nede legde,
swoncre seono-bende   on syllan monn.
     Þæs ofereode;   þisses swa mæg.

Beadohilde ne wæs   hyre broþra deaþ
on sefan swa sar   swa hyre sylfre þing,
10   þæt heo gearolice   ongieten hæfde
þæt heo eacen wæs;   æfre ne meahte
þriste geþencan,   hu ymb þæt sceolde.
     Þæs ofereode;   þisses swa mæg.

We þæt Mæðhilde   monge gefrugnon:
15   wurdon grundlease   Geates frige
þæt hi seo sorg-lufu   slæp ealle binom.
     Þæs ofereode;   þisses swa mæg.

Ðeodric ahte   þritig wintra
Mæringa burg;   þæt wæs monegum cuþ.
20   Þæs ofereode;   þisses swa mæg.

We geascodan   Eormanrices
wylfenne geþoht;   ahte wide folc
Gotena rices;   þæt wæs grim cyning.

Deor

Welund experienced exile among his damascened work,
the resolute warrior endured hardships,
had sorrow and longing for companions,
winter-cold exile; he often found woe,
after Nithhad laid constraints upon him,   5
supple sinew-bonds on the better man.
    That passed away; so can this.

Beadohild was not as pained in heart about
the death of her brothers as she was about her own state,
that she had clearly perceived   10
that she was with child; she could never
think unflinchingly about how that must turn out.
    That passed away; so can this.

We have heard about the moans of Mæthhild:
Geat's passions were bottomless   15
so that sorrowful love took all sleep from her.
    That passed away; so can this.

Theodric possessed for thirty winters
the fortress of the Goths; that was known to many.
    That passed away; so can this.   20

We have learned of Eormanric's
wolfish thought; he controlled widely the people
of the kingdom of the Goths; that was a cruel king.

Sæt secg monig   sorgum gebunden,
25 wean on wenum,   wyscte geneahhe
þæt þæs cyne-rices   ofercumen wære.
   Þæs ofereode;   þisses swa mæg.

Siteð sorg-cearig,   sælum bidæled,
on sefan sweorceð,   sylfum þinceð
30 þæt sy endeleas   earfoða dæl.
Mæg þonne geþencan,   þæt geond þas woruld
witig Dryhten   wendeþ geneahhe:
eorle monegum   are gesceawað,
wislicne blæd,   sumum weana dæl.

35 Þæt ic bi me sylfum   secgan wille,
þæt ic hwile wæs   Heodeninga scop,
dryhtne dyre.   Me wæs Deor noma.
Ahte ic fela wintra   folgað tilne,
holdne hlaford,   oþ-þæt Heorrenda nu,
40 leoð-cræftig monn   lond-ryht geþah
þæt me eorla hleo   ær gesealde.
   Þæs ofereode;   þisses swa mæg.

Many a warrior sat bound with sorrows,
in expectation of woe, wished frequently   25
that that kingdom should be overcome.
    That passed away; so can this.

The sorrowful one sits, bereft of joys,
darkening in spirit, it seems to him
that his portion of hardships is endless.   30
He may then think that throughout this world
the wise Lord makes frequent changes:
to many a person he grants honor,
true glory, to some a portion of woe.

I want to relate this about myself,   35
that for a while I was the poet of the Heodeningas,
dear to my lord. My name was Deor.
For many winters I possessed a good service,
a gracious lord, until Heorrenda now,
the man skilled in song craft, received the land-right   40
that the protector of men before gave to me.
    That passed away; so can this.

Wulf and Eadwacer

Leodum is minum   swylce him mon lac gife;
willað hy hine aþecgan,   gif he on þreat cymeð.
    Ungelic is us.
Wulf is on iege,   ic on oþerre.
5   Fæst is þæt eg-lond,   fenne biworpen.
Sindon wæl-reowe   weras þær on ige;
willað hy hine aþecgan,   gif he on þreat cymeð.
    Ungelice is us.
Wulfes ic mines wid-lastum   wenum dogode;
10   þonne hit wæs renig weder   ond ic reotugu sæt,
þonne mec se beadu-cafa   bogum bilegde,
wæs me wyn to þon,   wæs me hwæþre eac lað.
Wulf, min wulf,   wena me þine
seoce gedydon,   þine seld-cymas,
15   murnende mod,   nales mete-liste.
Gehyrest þu, Eadwacer?   Uncerne earmne hwelp
bireð wulf to wuda.
    Þæt mon eaþe tosliteð   þætte næfre gesomnad wæs,
uncer giedd geador.

Wulf and Eadwacer

For my people, it is as if someone gave them a gift of sacri-
    fice;
they want to kill him if he comes into their company.
  It's different for us.
Wolf is on one island, I on another.
Secure is that land, surrounded by a fen.   5
Cruel men are there on that island;
they want to kill him if he comes into their company.
  It's different for us.
I dogged my Wolf with far-wandering expectations;
when it was rainy weather and I sat mournful,   10
when the one active in battle embraced me,
it was a joy to me; it was also hateful to me.
Wolf, my wolf, my longings for you
have made me sick, your rare visits,
a mourning mind, not at all want of food.   15
Do you hear, Eadwacer, vigilant one? Wolf will bear our
wretched whelp off to the forest.
One may easily tear apart what was never joined,
our song together.

The Wife's Lament

Ic þis giedd wrece   bi me ful geomorre,
minre sylfre sið.   Ic þæt secgan mæg,
hwæt ic yrmþa gebad,   siþþan ic up aweox,
niwes oþþe ealdes,   no ma þonne nu.

5   A ic wite wonn   minra wræc-siþa.
      Ærest min hlaford gewat   heonan of leodum
ofer yþa gelac;   hæfde ic uht-ceare
hwær min leod-fruma   londes wære.
Ða ic me feran gewat   folgað secan,

10   wineleas wrecca,   for minre wea-þearfe.
Ongunnon þæt þæs monnes   magas hycgan
þurh dyrne geþoht   þæt hy todælden unc
þæt wit gewidost   in woruld-rice
lifdon laðlicost,   ond mec longade.

15   Het mec hlaford min   her hired niman;
ahte ic leofra lyt   on þissum lond-stede,
holdra freonda.   Forþon is min hyge geomor.
      Ða ic me ful gemæcne   monnan funde
—heard-sæligne,   hyge-geomorne,

20   mod-miþendne,   morþor-hycgendne—
bliþe gebæro   ful oft wit beotedan
þæt unc ne gedælde   nemne deað ana
owiht elles;   eft is þæt onhworfen;
is nu seo neawest   swa hit no wære,

The Wife's Lament

I recite this poem about myself, very sad,
about my own experience. I can relate
what miseries I've endured recently and long ago
since I grew up, never more than now.
I have always suffered the torment of my exile journeys.   5
   First my husband departed from his people
over the tossing of the waves; I had anxiety before dawn
about where my lord might be in the land.
Then, to seek place in a retinue, I, a friendless exile,
set out traveling because of my grievous need.   10
The kinsmen of that man began to consider
through secret thought that they might separate us
so that we two, as far apart as possible in the worldly
      kingdom,
would live most horribly, and it made me suffer longing.
My husband commanded me to take up my household here;   15
I had in this plot of ground few loved ones,
gracious friends. Therefore my mind is sad.
   When I found a man very similar to me
—luckless, humorless,
secretive, intending violence—   20
with joyful demeanor, we two very often boasted
that nothing but death would separate us at all;
afterward, that changed;
our closeness, our friendship is now as if it

25 freondscipe uncer.   Sceal ic feor ge neah
mines fela-leofan   fæhðu dreogan.
   Heht mec mon wunian   on wuda-bearwe,
under ac-treo   in þam eorð-scræfe.
Eald is þes eorð-sele;   eal ic eom oflongad.
30 Sindon dena dimme,   duna up-hea,
bitre burg-tunas,   brerum beweaxne,
wic wynna leas.   Ful oft mec her wraþe begeat
from-siþ frean.   Frynd sind on eorþan,
leofe lifgende,   leger weardiað,
35 þonne ic on uhtan   ana gonge
under ac-treo   geond þas eorð-scrafu.
Þær ic sittan mot   sumor-langne dæg,
þær ic wepan mæg   mine wræc-siþas,
earfoþa fela;   forþon ic æfre ne mæg
40 þære mod-ceare   minre gerestan,
ne ealles þæs longaþes   þe mec on þissum life begeat.
   A scyle geong mon   wesan geomor-mod,
heard heortan geþoht,   swylce habban sceal
bliþe gebæro,   eac þon breost-ceare,
45 sin-sorgna gedreag.   Sy æt him sylfum gelong
eal his worulde wyn,   sy ful wide fah
feorres folc-londes,   þæt min freond siteð
under stan-hliþe   storme behrimed,
wine werig-mod,   wætre beflowen
50 on dreor-sele.   Dreogeð se min wine
micle mod-ceare;   he gemon to oft
wynlicran wic.   Wa bið þam þe sceal
of langoþe   leofes abidan.

hadn't been. Far and near I must   25
endure the hostility of my beloved.
    I was ordered to live in a grove,
under an oak tree in the earth cave.
This earth hall is old; I am completely possessed with
longing. The valleys are dark, the hills steep,   30
the earthworks bitter, covered with briars,
a settlement deprived of joys. Very often my husband's
departure cruelly held me here. Lovers are on earth,
beloved living ones, occupying their beds,
while I walk alone at dawn   35
under the oak tree through this earth cave.
There I may sit the summer-long day,
where I can lament my exile journeys,
my many hardships; therefore I cannot ever
gain rest from my grief   40
nor from all the longing that has held me in this life.
    A young person must always be sad in mind,
the thought of the heart hard, and will also have
a joyful demeanor, heart anxiety in addition,
a multitude of perpetual sorrows. May all joy in the world   45
be dependent on the self alone, may the person be outlawed
    very far away
to a distant country so that my friend will sit
under a rocky slope covered with frost by a storm,
a weary-minded friend, conveyed by water
to desolate lodgings. My friend will suffer   50
great grief, will often remember
a more joyful dwelling. Woe is for the one who must
await a beloved one with longing.

Resignation (B): An Exile's Lament

... hwæþre ic me ealles þæs   ellen wylle
habban ond hlyhhan   ond me hyhtan to,
frætwian mec on forð-weg   ond fundian
sylf to þam siþe   þe ic asettan sceal,
5   gæst gearwian,   ond me þæt eal for Gode þolian
bliþe mode;   nu ic gebunden eom
fæste in minum ferþe.   Huru me Frea witeð
sume þara synna   þe ic me sylf ne conn
ongietan gleawlice.   Gode ic hæbbe
10   abolgen, brego mon-cynnes;   forþon ic þus bittre wearð
gewitnad for þisse worulde,   swa min gewyrhto wæron
micle fore monnum,   þæt ic martirdom
deopne adreoge.   Ne eom ic dema gleaw,
wis fore weorude;   forþon ic þas word spræce
15   fus on ferþe,   swa me on frymðe gelomp
yrmþu ofer eorþan,   þæt ic a þolade
geara gehwylce   (Gode ealles þonc!)
mod-earfoþa   ma þonne on oþrum,
fyrhto in folce;   forþon ic afysed eom
20   earm of minum eþle.   Ne mæg þæs an-hoga,
leod-wynna leas,   leng drohtian,
wineleas wræcca,   (is him wrað meotud),
gnornað on his geoguþe,

Resignation (B): An Exile's Lament

. . . even so, I want to have courage
and laugh and hope for myself because of all that,
adorn myself for the onward course and aspire
to that journey that I must take,
prepare my soul, and endure all that for God   5
with a blithe spirit; now I am firmly
bound in my heart. Indeed, the Lord will reproach me for
some of the sins that I do not know how
to perceive wisely in myself. I have enraged
God, the ruler of mankind; therefore, I have become   10
bitterly afflicted here in this world, since my transgressions
were great before human beings so that I am enduring
extreme martyrdom. I am not discerning in judgments,
wise before the multitude; therefore I have spoken these
words eager in my heart, since for me from the beginning   15
misery happened on earth so that I always suffered
each year (thanks be to God for all that!)
more griefs of mind, fear among the people,
than was in others; therefore wretched, I have been driven
from my homeland. The solitary one, the friendless exile,   20
deprived of home joys, cannot live much longer
with that (the creator is angry with him),
grieves in his youth,

ond him ælce mæle   men fullestað,
25   ycað his yrmþu,   ond he þæt eal þolað,
sar-cwide secga,   ond him bið a sefa geomor,
mod morgen-seoc.   Ic bi me tylgust
secge þis sar-spel   ond ymb siþ spræce,
longunge fus,   ond on lagu þence,
30   nat min . . .
hwy ic gebycge   bat on sæwe,
fleot on faroðe;   nah ic fela goldes
ne huru þæs freondes,   þe me gefylste
to þam sið-fate,   nu ic me sylf ne mæg
35   fore minum won-æhtum   willan adreogan.
Wudu mot him weaxan,   wyrde bidan,
tanum lædan;   ic for tæle ne mæg
ænigne mon-cynnes   mode gelufian
eorl on eþle.   Eala Dryhten min,
40   meahtig mund-bora!   Þæt ic eom mode seoc,
bittre abolgen,   is seo bot æt þe
gelong æfter life.   Ic on leohte ne mæg
butan earfoþum   ænge þinga
fea-sceaft hæle   foldan gewunian;
45   þonne ic me to fremþum   freode hæfde,
cyðþu gecweme   me wæs a cearu symle
lufena to leane,   swa ic alifde nu.
Giet biþ þæt selast   þonne mon him sylf ne mæg
wyrd onwendan   þæt he þonne wel þolige.

and on every occasion people help him
and thereby increase his misery, and he endures all that,   25
people's hurtful speech, and his heart is always sad,
his mind sick in the morning. I most firmly
tell this woeful tale about myself and speak about a journey
eager with longing, and think about the sea;
my mind does not know . . .   30
with what I may buy passage on a boat on the sea,
a ship on the edge of the flood; I do not have much gold
nor indeed many friends who might help me
in that journey, now that I myself cannot
accomplish my wish because of my poverty.   35
A tree may grow, await its fate,
sprout its branches; because of disgrace, I cannot
love in my heart any man
in my homeland. Oh, my Lord,
mighty protector! Because I am sick at heart,   40
bitterly offended, the remedy after life
is dependent on you. I, a forlorn man, cannot
inhabit in any way the earth
without hardships in the light;
when I maintained the peace, agreeable kinship,   45
with strangers, their care was always for me
a reward for love, as I have now admitted.
Still it is always best when one cannot
avoid fate that he should then endure it well.

Pharaoh

"Saga me hwæt þær weorudes   wære ealles
on Farones fyrde   þa hy folc Godes
þurh feondscipe   fylgan ongunnon."
    "Nat ic hit be wihte,   butan ic wene þus:
þæt þær screoda wære   gescyred rime
siex hundred godra   searo-hæbbendra;
þæt eal fornam   yþa fær-gripe
wraþe wyrde   in woruld-rice."

Pharaoh

"Tell me what part of all the host in Pharaoh's army
was there when they through enmity
began pursuing the people of God."
    "I don't know at all, but I expect thus:
that six hundred chariots full of good warriors   5
were counted there in number;
the sudden grip of waves took all that
by a cruel fate in the worldly kingdom."

The Husband's Message

Nu ic onsundran þe   secgan wille
. . . treo-cyn   ic tudre aweox;
in mec æld . . .   sceal
ellor landes settan . . .   Ic,
5   sealte streamas   . . . sse.
Ful oft ic on bates . . .   gesohte
þær mec mon-dryhten   min . . .
ofer heah hafu;   eom nu her cumen
on ceol-þele,   ond nu cunnan scealt
10   hu þu ymb mod-lufan   mines frean
on hyge hycge.   Ic gehatan dear
þæt þu þær tirfæste   treowe findest.

Hwæt, þec þonne biddan het   se þisne beam agrof
þæt þu sinc-hroden   sylf gemunde
15   on gewit-locan   word-beotunga,
þe git on ær-dagum   oft gespræcon,
þenden git moston   on meodu-burgum
eard weardigan,   an lond bugan,
freondscype fremman.   Hine fæhþo adraf
20   of sige-þeode;   heht nu sylfa þe
lustum læran,   þæt þu lagu drefde,
siþþan þu gehyrde   on hliþes oran
galan geomorne   geac on bearwe.

The Husband's Message

Now I want to tell you privately
. . . a species of tree I grew up from childhood;
in me men . . . must
elsewhere in the land set . . .
salt streams . . .   5
Very often on a boat's . . . sought
where my master . . . me
over the high seas; I have now come here
on a ship, and now you must know
how you might think in your mind   10
about my lord's love. I dare promise
that you will find glorious fidelity there.

Yes, he who engraved this tree ordered me to ask you
that you, treasure-adorned, should yourself remember
in your mind the promises   15
that you two in earlier days often spoke,
while you could occupy a dwelling
in the mead cities, abide in the same land,
improve your friendship. A feud drove him
from the victorious people; now he himself has ordered me   20
to tell you gladly that you should stir up the sea
after you have heard on the cliff's edge
the sad cuckoo sing in the wood.

Ne læt þu þec siþþan   siþes getwæfan,
25 lade gelettan   lifgendne monn.

Ongin mere secan,   mæwes eþel,
onsite sæ-nacan,   þæt þu suð heonan
ofer mere-lade   monnan findest,
þær se þeoden is   þin on wenum.
30 Ne mæg him worulde   willa gelimpan
mara on gemyndum,   þæs þe he me sægde,
þonne inc geunne   alwaldend God
. . . ætsomne   siþþan motan
secgum ond gesiþum   s . . .
35 næglede beagas;   he genoh hafað
fædan goldes . . .
. . . d el-þeode   eþel healde,
fægre foldan
. . . ra hæleþa,   þeah þe her min wine . . .
40 nyde gebæded,   nacan ut aþrong,
ond on yþa gelagu   . . . sceolde
faran on flot-weg,   forð-siþes georn,
mengan mere-streamas.   Nu se mon hafað
wean oferwunnen;   nis him wilna gad,
45 ne meara ne maðma   ne meodo-dreama,
ænges ofer eorþan   eorl-gestreona,
þeodnes dohtor,   gif he þin beneah.
Ofer eald gebeot   incer twega,
gehyre ic ætsomne   ᚻ ᚱ geador
50 ᛏ � ᛒ ᚷ ᛗ aþe benemnan,
þæt he þa wære   ond þa wine-treowe
be him lifgendum   læstan wolde,
þe git on ær-dagum   oft gespræconn.

116

Afterward, do not let any living man
divert you from the journey, hinder your course.   25

Start seeking the sea, the homeland of the seagull,
board the ship so that to the south
you will find the man over the ocean track,
where your lord is waiting in expectation of you.
There is no greater desire in the world in his mind,   30
from what he told me,
than that all-ruling God should grant you two
. . . together may afterward
to warriors and companions . . .
studded rings; he has enough   35
of burnished gold
. . . in a foreign country he holds his home,
a fair land . . .
. . . of heroes, although here my friend . . .
compelled by need, pushed out the boat,   40
and on the expanses of waves . . . had
to travel on the sea, eager for the journey,
to stir up the ocean currents. Now the man has
overcome woe; there is no lack of delights for him,
not horses, not treasures, not the joys of mead,   45
not any of noble stores of wealth on earth,
prince's daughter, if he may possess you.
Contrary to the old vow of both of you,
I hear *S R* together
EA W and *M* declare an oath,   50
that, while he lived, he would carry out
the pledge and the oath of fidelity
that you two often agreed upon in days past.

The Ruin

Wrætlic is þes weal-stan,   wyrde gebræcon;
burg-stede burston,   brosnað enta geweorc.
Hrofas sind gehrorene,   hreorge torras,
hring-geat berofen,   hrim on lime,
5   scearde scur-beorge   scorene, gedrorene,
ældo undereotone.   Eorð-grap hafað
waldend wyrhtan   —forweorone, geleorene—
heard-gripe hrusan,   oþ hund cnea
wer-þeoda gewitan.   Oft þæs wag gebad
10   ræg-har ond read-fah   rice æfter oþrum,
ofstonden under stormum;   steap geap gedreas.
Worað giet se weall-steall   wæpnum geheapen;
fel on foldan   forð-gesceaft bærst
grimme gegrunden,   grund eall forswealg
15   . . . scan   heo . . .
. . . g or-þonc   ærsceaft . . .
. . . g   lam-rindum gebeag;
mod monade   myne swiftne gebrægd
hwæt-red in hringas,   hyge-rof gebond
20   weall-walan wirum   wundrum togædre.

The Ruin

Wondrous is this wall stone; disastrous events have
    shattered it;
the fortified cities have broken apart, the work of giants
    decays.
Roofs have fallen, towers are ruinous,
the ring gate is destroyed, frost is on the mortar,
the gaping protectors against storms are rent, have   5
    collapsed,
undermined by age. The earth's grasp,
the hard grip of the ground, has hold of the master builders
—perished, gone—until a hundred generations
of people have departed. Often this building wall,
gray with lichen and stained red, endured one kingdom   10
    after another,
remained standing under storms; high, curved, it caved in.
The wall place still molders, hewn by weapons;
it fell to the earth, its future burst
fiercely ground down, the ground swallowed all
. . . it shone . . .   15
. . . the monument of skill, the ancient work . . .
. . . bent by crusts of mud;
a mind stimulated that thought-swift plan,
ingenious in rings, the bold-minded one wondrously
bound the foundations together with wires.   20

Beorht wæron burg-ræced,   burn-sele monige,
heah horn-gestreon,   here-sweg micel,
meodo-heall monig   monn-dreama full,
oþþæt þæt onwende   wyrd seo swiþe.
25 Crungon walo wide,   cwoman wol-dagas,
swylt eall fornom   secg-rofra wera;
wurdon hyra wig-steal   westen staþolas,
brosnade burg-steall.   Betend crungon
hergas to hrusan.   Forþon þas hofu dreorgiað,
30 ond þæs teafor-geapa   tigelum sceadeð
hrost-beages hrof.   Hryre wong gecrong
gebrocen to beorgum,   þær iu beorn monig
glæd-mod ond gold-beorht   gleoma gefrætwed,
wlonc ond win-gal   wig-hyrstum scan;
35 seah on sinc, on sylfor,   on searo-gimmas,
on ead, on æht,   on eorcan-stan,
on þas beorhtan burg   bradan rices.
Stan-hofu stodan,   stream hate wearp
widan wylme;   weal eall befeng
40 beorhtan bosme,   þær þa baþu wæron,
hat on hreþre.   Þæt wæs hyðelic.
Leton þonne geotan . . .
ofer harne stan   hate streamas
un . . .
45 . . . oþþæt hring-mere.   Hate . . .
. . .   þær þa baþu wæron.
Þonne is . . .
. . . re.   Þæt is cynelic þing,
hu se . . .   burg . . .

Bright were the city buildings, many bathing halls,
an abundance of high gables, much martial noise,
many mead halls full of human joys,
until fate the mighty changed that.
Slaughtered men widely fell dead, days of pestilence came,   25
death took away all of the valiant men;
their bastions became waste places,
the city decayed. The rebuilders, the armies,
fell dead on the ground. Therefore these buildings grow
desolate, and the red curved roof above the vault   30
sheds its tiles. The ruin fell to the plain
broken into mounds of stone where long ago many a man
happy and gold bright, proud and flushed with wine,
adorned with splendor, shone in his war gear;
he gazed on treasure, on silver, on jewels,   35
on wealth, on property, on precious stones,
on this bright city of the spacious kingdom.
The stone buildings stood, the stream gushed with heat
in a broad surge; a wall embraced everything
in its bright bosom where the baths were,   40
hot to the core. That was advantageous.
Then they let pour . . .
over the gray stone hot streams
. . .
. . . until the circular pool. Hot . . .   45
. . . where the baths were.
Then is . . .
. . . That is a noble thing,
how the . . . city . . .

POEMS FROM
THE ANGLO-SAXON
MINOR POEMS

Durham

Is ðeos burch breome   geond Breoten-rice,
steppa gestaðolad,   stanas ymbutan
wundrum gewæxen.   Weor ymbeornad,
ea yðum stronge,   and ðer inne wunað
     feola fisca kyn   on floda gemonge.
And ðær gewexen is   wuda-fæstern micel;
wuniad in ðem wycum   wilda deor monige,
in deope dalum   deora ungerim.
Is in ðere byri eac   bearnum gecyðed
     ðe ar-festa   eadig Cudberch
and ðes clene   cyninges heafud,
Osuualdes, Engle leo,   and Aidan biscop,
Eadberch and Eadfrið,   æðele geferes.
Is ðer inne midd heom   Æðelwold biscop
     and breoma bocera Beda,   and Boisil abbot,
ðe clene Cudberte   on gecheðe
lerde lustum,   and he his lara wel genom.
Eardiæð æt ðem eadige   in in ðem minstre
unarimeda   reliquia,
     ðær monia wundrum gewurðað,   ðes ðe writ seggeð;
midd ðene Drihnes wer   domes bideð.

Durham

This city is famous throughout the kingdom of the Britons,
steeply established, stones round about it
wondrously grown. The Wear surrounds it,
the river strong with waves, and there within
the mixture of flowing waters dwell many kinds of fish.   5
And a great fastness of wood has grown there;
in that habitation many wild animals dwell,
in the deep valleys countless animals.
There is also known to men in that city
the pious, blessed Cuthbert   10
and the head of the pure king,
of Oswald, protector of the English, and bishop Aidan,
Eadbert and Eadfrith, noble companions.
There with them is bishop Æthelwold
and the famous scholar Bede, and abbot Boisil,   15
who gladly taught the pure Cuthbert
in his youth, and he received his teaching well.
With the blessed one in that minster dwell
countless relics
where many things wondrously occur, as the written   20
     account says;
with the man of God, they await judgment.

The Rune Poem

ᚠ [feoh] byþ frofur   fira gehwylcum.
    Sceal ðeah manna gehwylc   miclun hyt dælan
    gif he wile for Drihtne   domes hleotan.
ᚢ [ur] byþ an-mod   and ofer-hyrned,
5   ela-frecne deor,   feohteþ mid hornum,
    mære mor-stapa;   þæt is modig wuht.
ᚦ [þorn] byþ ðearle scearp;   ðegna gehwylcum
    anfeng ys yfyl,   ungemetun reþe
    manna gehwylcun   ðe him mid resteð.
10 ᚩ [os] byþ ord-fruma   ælcre spræce,
    wisdomes wraþu   and witena frofur,
    and eorla gehwam   eadnys and tohiht.
ᚱ [rad] byþ on recyde   rinca gehwylcum
    sefte, and swiþ-hwæt   ðam ðe sitteþ on ufan
15   meare mægen-heardum   ofer mil-paþas.
ᚳ [cen] byþ cwicera gehwam   cuþ on fyre,
    blac and beorhtlic;   byrneþ oftust
    ðær hi æþelingas   inne restaþ.
ᚷ [gyfu] gumena byþ   gleng and herenys,
20   wraþu and wyrþscype,   and wræcna gehwam
    ar and ætwist   ðe byþ oþra leas.
ᚹ [wyn]ne bruceþ   ðe can weana lyt,
    sares and sorge,   and him sylfa hæfþ
    blæd and blysse   and eac byrga geniht.

The Rune Poem

Wealth is a comfort for everyone.
 But everyone must dispense it abundantly
 if he wants to obtain favorable judgment from the Lord.
The *aurochs* is resolute and great-horned,
 a very fierce animal, fights with its horns,   5
 a famous traverser of the moors; that is a bold creature.
The *thorn* is very sharp; it is evil
 for every man clutching it, immeasurably cruel
 to anyone who rests with it.
The *mouth* is the origin of each language,   10
 the support of wisdom and consolation of the wise,
 and for each and every one, happiness and hope.
Riding is easy for each warrior in the hall,
 and very hard for the one who sits
 on the very strong mare on the milestoned paths.   15
The *torch* to each living being is known by its fire,
 shining and bright; it burns most often
 where the nobles rest inside.
The *liberality* of men is an adornment and praise,
 a help and a glory, and the grace and sustenance   20
 for every wretch who is bereft of others.
They experience *joy* who know few woes,
 pain, and sorrow, and who have dignity and happiness
 and also an abundance of fortified settlements for
  themselves.

25 � H [hægl] byþ hwitust corna;   hwyrft hit of heofones lyfte,
   wealcaþ hit windes scura,   weorþeþ hit to wætere syððan.
   ᚾ [nyd] byþ nearu on breostan,   weorþeþ hi ðeah oft niþa
                                                        bearnum
   to helpe and to hæle gehwæþre,   gif hi his hlystaþ æror.
   ᛁ [is] byþ ofer-ceald,   ungemetum slidor,
30   glisnaþ glæs-hluttur,   gimmum gelicust,
      flor forste geworuht,   fæger ansyne.
      ᛄ [ger] byþ gumena hiht   ðon God læteþ,
      halig heofones cyning,   hrusan syllan
      beorhte bleda   beornum and ðearfum.
35   ᛇ [eoh] byþ utan   unsmeþe treow,
      heard, hrusan fæst,   hyrde fyres,
      wyrt-rumun underwreþyd,   wynan on eþle.
      ᛈ [peorð] byþ symble   plega and hlehter
      wlancum . . .   ðar wigan sittaþ
40   on beor-sele   bliþe ætsomne.
      ᛉ [eolhx]-secg eard hæfþ   oftust on fenne,
      wexeð on wature,   wundaþ grimme,
      blode breneð   beorna gehwylcne
      ðe him ænigne   onfeng gedeð.
45   ᛋ [sigel] se-mannum   symble biþ on hihte,
      ðonn hi hine feriaþ   ofer fisces beþ,
      oþ hi brim-hengest   bringeþ to lande.
      ᛏ [Tir] biþ tacna sum,   healdeð trywa wel
      wiþ æþelingas,   a biþ on færylde,
50   ofer nihta genipu   næfre swiceþ.
      ᛒ [beorc] byþ bleda leas   bereþ efne swa ðeah
      tanas butan tudder,   biþ on telgum wlitig,

Hail is the whitest of grains; it whirls from the air of heaven,   25
    showers of wind toss it, it turns to water afterward.
Need is confining for the heart although often it turns into a
    help and a salvation for the children of men if they listen
      to it beforehand.
Ice is very cold, immeasurably slippery,
    it glistens bright as glass, most like gems,   30
    a floor made by frost, fair in countenance.
Summer is the hope of men when God,
    holy king of heaven, lets the earth give forth
    bright fruits for both the rich and the poor.
The *yew* is a tree unsmooth on the outside,   35
    hard, fixed in the earth, a guardian of fire,
    supported by its roots, a joy in the native land.
Peorth is always play and laughter
    for the proud . . . where warriors sit
    in the beer hall happily together.   40
Eohl-sedge most often has its place in a fen,
    grows in the water, wounds fiercely,
    reddens with blood everyone
    who lays hold of it.
The *sun* is always a hope for seafarers   45
    when they convey the sea steed over the fish's bath
    until it brings them to land.
Tir is a certain sign, keeps faith well
    with nobles, is always in motion
    above the night-clouds, never fails.   50
The *birch* is free of fruit yet bears
    shoots without seed, is beautiful in its branches,

heah on helme   hrysted fægere,
geloden leafum,   lyfte getenge.
55   ᛗ [eh] byþ for eorlum   æþelinga wyn,
hors hofum wlanc,   ðær him hæleþas ymb,
welege on wicgum,   wrixlaþ spræce,
and biþ unstyllum   æfre frofur.

ᛗ [mann] byþ on myrgþe   his magan leof;
60   sceal þeah anra gehwylc   oðrum swican,
for ðam Dryhten wyle   dome sine
þæt earme flæsc   eorþan betæcan.

ᛚ [lagu] byþ leodum   langsum geþuht,
gif hi sculun neþun   on nacan tealtum,
65   and hi sæ-yþa   swyþe bregaþ,
and se brim-hengest   bridles ne gymeð.

ᛝ [Ing] wæs ærest   mid East-Denum
gesewen secgun,   oþ he siððan eft
ofer wæg gewat,   wæn æfter ran;
70   ðus heardingas   ðone hæle nemdun.

ᛟ [eþel] byþ oferleof   æghwylcum men,
gif he mot ðær rihtes   and gerysena on
brucan on bolde   bleadum oftast.

ᛞ [dæg] byþ Drihtnes sond,   deore mannum,
75   mære metodes leoht,   myrgþ and tohiht
eadgum and earmum,   eallum brice.

ᚨ [ac] byþ on eorþan   elda bearnum
flæsces fodor;   fereþ gelome
ofer ganotes bæþ;   gar-secg fandaþ
80   hwæþer ac hæbbe   æþele treowe.

ᚫ [æsc] biþ ofer-heah,   eldum dyre,
stiþ on staþule,   stede rihte hylt
ðeah him feohtan on   firas monige.

high in its crown, fairly adorned,
   growing with leaves, reaches into the air.
The *warhorse* is the joy of princes before nobles,   55
   the steed proud in its hooves, where heroes,
   rich men on horseback, exchange words about it,
   and is always a comfort to the restless.
A *human being* in delight is dear to his kin;
   nevertheless each one has to depart from the others   60
   because the Lord wants, by his decree,
   to cover the wretched flesh with earth.
Water seems endless to people
   if they have to venture out on the tilting ship,
   and the ocean waves greatly terrify them,   65
   and the sea steed does not heed the bridle.
Ing was first seen by people
   among the East Danes, until he afterward
   departed over the waves again, his chariot running after;
   thus warriors named that hero.   70
The *native land* is very dear to everyone,
   if there in their home they may enjoy
   what is right and proper most often in prosperity.
Day is a sending of the Lord, dear to humankind,
   the glorious light of the creator, a pleasure and a hope   75
   for the blessed and the wretched, useful to all.
The *oak* is the nourishment of pork
   for the sons of men; it often fares
   over the gannet's bath; the ocean tests
   whether the oak has noble faith.   80
The *ash* is very tall, dear to humankind,
   strong at its base, rightly holds its place
   although many men fight against it.

ᚣ [yr] byþ æþelinga   and eorla gehwæs
85   wyn and wyrþ-mynd,   byþ on wicge fæger,
      fæstlic on færelde,   fyrd-geatewa sum.
   ᛡ [iar] byþ ea-fix,   and ðeah a bruceþ
      fodres on foldan,   hafaþ fægerne eard,
      wætre beworpen,   ðær he wynnum leofaþ.
90   ᛠ [ear] byþ egle   eorla gehwylcun
      ðonn fæstlice   flæsc onginneþ
      hraw colian,   hrusan ceosan
      blac to gebeddan;   bleda gedreosaþ,
      wynna gewitaþ,   wera geswicaþ.

The *bow* is a joy and honor
   for every noble and warrior, is fair on a horse,   85
   reliable on a journey, a kind of battle gear.
The *eel* is a river fish, yet it always enjoys
   its food on land, has a fair dwelling,
   surrounded by water, where it lives with joy.
Earth is horrible for everyone   90
   when inexorably the flesh, the corpse,
   begins to cool, the pallid one to choose
   soil as a bedfellow; fruits fail,
   joys depart, pledges cease.

Solomon and Saturn

I

Saturnus cwæð:
"Hwæt. Ic ig-landa   eallra hæbbe
boca onbyrged   þurh gebregd-stafas,
lar-cræftas onlocen   Libia and Greca,
swylce eac istoriam   Indea rices.

5 Me þa treahteras   tala wisedon
on þam micelan bec   . . .
     m.ces heardum.
Swylce ic næfre on eallum þam fyrn-gewrytum   findan
                                                  ne mihte
soðe samnode.   Ic sohte þa git

10 hwylc wære modes   oððe mægen-þrymmes,
elnes oððe æhte   oððe eorlscipes
se gepalm-twigoda   Pater Noster.
Sille ic þe ealle,   sunu Dauides,
þeoden Israela,   ðritig punda

15 smætes goldes   and mine suna twelfe,
gif þu mec gebringest   þæt ic si gebryrded
ðurh þæs cantices cwyde   Cristes linan,
gesemesð mec mid soðe,   and ic mec gesund fare,
wende mec on willan   on wæteres hrigc

20 ofer Cofer-flod   Caldeas secan."

134

Solomon and Saturn

I

Saturn said:
"Yes. I have eaten the books of all
islands through learned arts,
unlocked the knowledge of the Libyans and Greeks
as well as the history of the kingdom of the Indians.
The commentators guided me through the accounts   5
in the great book . . .
    with the hard . . . of a sword.
Such things I could never find truly gathered in all
the ancient writings. I still sought then
what sort of mind or majesty,   10
of virtue or wealth or nobility,
is the palm-twigged Pater Noster.
I will give you all, son of David,
prince of Israel, thirty pounds
of refined gold and my twelve sons,   15
if you bring me to the point where I may be overawed
through the word of the canticle of Christ's line of letters,
satisfy me with the truth, and I will leave safe and sound,
take myself willingly on the water's ridge
over the river Chobar to seek the Chaldeans."   20

Salomon cwæð:
"Unlæde bið on eorþan,   unnit lifes,
wesðe wisdomes,   weallað swa nieten,
feld-gongende   feoh butan gewitte,
se þurh ðone cantic ne can   Crist geherian.

25 Worað he windes full,   worpað hine deofol
on dom-dæge,   draca egeslice,
bismorlice,   of blacere liðran
irenum aplum;   ealle beoð aweaxen
of edwittes   iða heafdum.

30 Þonne him bið leofre   ðonne eall ðeos leohte gesceaft,
gegoten fram ðam grunde   goldes and seolfres,
feðer-sceatum full   fyrn-gestreona,
gif he æfre ðæs organes   owiht cuðe.
Fracoð he bið ðonne and fremde   Frean ælmihtigum;

35 englum ungesibb,   ana hwearfað."

Saturnus cwæð:
"Ac hwa mæg eaðost   ealra gesceafta
ða haligan duru   heofona rices
torhte ontynan   on getæl-rime?"

Salomon cwæð:
"Ðæt gepalm-twigede   Pater Noster

40 heofonas ontyneð,   halige geblissað,
metod gemiltsað,   morðor gefylleð,
adwæsceð deofles fyr,   Dryhtnes onæleð.
Swylce ðu miht mid ðy beorhtan gebede   blod onhætan,
ðæs deofles dros,   þæt him dropan stigað,

45 swate geswiðed,   seofan intingum,
egesfullicran   ðonne seo ærene gripu,
ðonne heo for twelf fyra   tydernessum
ofer gleda gripe   gifrust wealleð.

136

Solomon said:
"Unhappy will the one be on earth, useless in life,
empty of wisdom, will wander like an animal,
like cattle traversing the field without sense,
who cannot praise Christ through the canticle.
He wanders full of wind, and the devil, the dragon   25
will cast him down on judgment day terribly,
ignominiously, with iron apples
from a black sling; all are grown
from the heads of waves of disgrace.
Then it will be dearer to him than all this bright creation,   30
poured from the foundation of gold and silver,
the four corners full of ancient treasures,
if he had known anything of the song, the Pater Noster.
He will then be vile and estranged from the almighty Lord,
hostile to angels, he will turn away alone."   35
    Saturn said:
"But who of all creatures most easily and
splendidly can open the holy doors in order
of the kingdom of heaven?"
    Solomon said:
"The palm-twigged Pater Noster
opens the heavens, blesses the holy,   40
makes the measurer merciful, fells murder,
puts out the devil's fire, starts the Lord's.
Likewise with bright prayer you may heat the blood,
the devil's dross, so that the drops rise in him,
forced by the blood, by the matter of the heart,   45
more terribly than the brass cauldron
when it most greedily boils above the grip of flames
because of the twelve weaknesses of human beings.

Forðon hafað se cantic   ofer ealle Cristes bec
50 wid-mærost word;   he gewritu læreð,
stefnum steoreð,   and him stede healdeð
heofona rices;   here-geatewa wigeð."

    Saturnus cwæð:
"Ac hulic is se organ   in-gemyndum
to begonganne   ðam ðe his gast wile
55 meltan wið morðre,   mergan of sorge,
asceadan of scyldum?   Huru him scippend geaf
wuldorlicne wlite.   Mec ðæs on worolde full oft
fyrwit frineð;   fus gewiteð,
mod gemengeð.   Nænig manna wat,
60 hæleða under hefenum,   hu min hige dreoseð,
bysig æfter bocum;   hwilum me bryne stigeð,
hige heortan neah   hædre wealleð."

    Salomon cwæð:
"Gylden is se Godes cwide,   gimmum astæned,
hafað sylfren leaf;   sundor mæg æghwylc
65 ðurh gastes gife   god-spel secgan.
He bið seofan snytro   and saule hunig
and modes meolc,   mærþa gesælgost.
He mæg ða saule   of sien-nihte
gefeccan under foldan,   næfre hie se feond to ðæs niðer
70 feterum gefæstnað;   ðeah he hie mid fiftigum
clusum beclemme,   he ðone cræft briceð
and ða or-ðancas   ealle tosliteð.
Hungor he ahieðeð,   helle gestrudeð,
wylm toweorpeð,   wuldor getimbreð.
75 He is modigra   middan-gearde,
staðole strengra   ðonne ealra stana gripe.

Therefore over all of Christ's books, the canticle, the Pater
    Noster,
has the most widely famous words; it teaches scripture,   50
steers through voices, and holds for them a place
in the kingdom of heaven; it carries war gear."
    Saturn said:
"But how is the song, the Pater Noster, to be revered
in memory by the one who wishes to refine
his spirit from the dross of crime, to purify it from sorrow,   55
to separate it from faults? Indeed the creator gave it
a wondrous appearance. Very often curiosity prompts me
to ask about it in the world; it rises rapidly,
stirs up the heart. No human knows,
no hero under the heavens, how my mind becomes weak,   60
busy in pursuit of books; at times, a burning rises up in me,
the mind seethes anxiously near to the heart."
    Solomon said:
"Golden is the speech of God, adorned with jewels,
it has silver leaves; each one through the grace
of the Spirit can separately relate the gospel.   65
It is the wisdom of the heart and the soul's honey
and the mind's milk, the most blessed of glories.
It can fetch the soul from perpetual night
under the earth, no matter how far down
the enemy fastens it with fetters; though he   70
bind it with fifty locks, it will break the power
and completely rip apart the skillful work.
It destroys hunger, ravages hell,
breaks the surge, builds glory.
It is bolder than the foundation of   75
middle earth, stronger than the grip of all stones.

Lamena he is læce,   leoht wincendra,
swilce he is deafra duru,   dumbra tunge,
scyldigra scyld,   scyppendes seld,
80   flodes ferigend,   folces nerigend,
yða yrfe-weard,   earmra fisca
and wyrma welm,   wildeora holt,
on westenne weard,   weorð-mynta geard.
And se ðe wile geornlice   ðone Godes cwide
85   singan soðlice,   and hine siemle wile
lufian butan leahtrum,   he mæg ðone laðan gæst,
feohtende feond,   fleonde gebrengan,
gif ðu him ærest on ufan   ierne gebrengest
prologa prima,   ðam is ᚳ ᚹ nama.
90   Hafað guð-mæcga   gierde lange,
gyldene gade,   and a ðone grymman feond
swið-mod sweopað,   and him on swaðe fylgeð
ᚠ ᚪ ofer-mægene   and hine eac ofslihð.
ᛏ ᛏ hine teswað   and hine on ða tungan sticað,
95   wræsteð him ðæt woddor   and him ða wongan brieceð.
ᛗ ᛖ hiene yflað,   swa he a wile
ealra feonda gehwane   fæste gestondan.
Ðonne hiene on unðanc ᚱ ᚱ   ieorrenga geseceð,
boc-stafa brego,   bregdeð sona
100   feond be ðam feaxe,   læteð flint brecan
scines sconcan;   he ne besceawað no
his leomona lið,   ne bið him læce god.
Wendeð he hiene ðonne under wolcnum,   wig-steall
                                         seceð,

It is the healer of the lame, the light of the blind,
just as it is the door of the deaf, the tongue of the dumb,
the shield of the guilty, the hall of the creator,
the bearer of the flood, the savior of the people,   80
the hereditary guardian of the waves, of the miserable
     fishes,
and the surging of serpents, the forest of wild animals,
the guardian in the wasteland, the enclosure of dignities.
And whoever will eagerly sing the speech of God
truthfully and will always love   85
it without sins can cause the hated guest,
the fighting enemy, to flee,
if you first bring on him from above the angry one,
prologa prima, the prime first letter, which is named *P.*
The warrior has a long rod,   90
a golden goad, and always the brave one
swipes at the fierce enemy, and with overpowering might
A follows in its track and also strikes it.
T harms it and stabs it in the tongue,
wrings its neck and breaks its jaws.   95
E hurts it since it will always
stand firm against every enemy.
Then to its displeasure, *R,* the lord of letters,
will angrily seek it, immediately pull
the enemy by the hair, let the flint break   100
the shin of the evil spirit; he will not pay attention
to the joints of the limbs, and a physician will not do it any
    good.
It will then wend its way under the clouds, seek an
    entrenchment,

heolstre behelmed.   Huru him bið æt heartan wa,
105   ðonne he hangiende   helle wisceð,
ðæs ængestan   eðel-rices.
Ðonne hine forcinnað   ða cirican getuinnas,
N ond ᚩ O samod   æghwæðer brengeð
sweopan of siðe;   sargiað hwile
110   fremdne flæsc-homan,   feorh ne bemurnað.
Ðonne ᚻ S cymeð,   engla geræswa,
wuldores stæf,   wraðne gegripeð
feond be ðam fotum,   læteð foreweard hleor
on strangne stan,   stregdað toðas
115   geond helle heap.   Hydeð hine æghwylc
æfter sceades sciman;   sceaða bið gebisigod,
Satanes ðegn   swiðe gestilled.
Swilce hiene ᛏ Q and ᚾ V   cwealme gehnægað,
frome folc-togan,   farað him togegnes,
120   habbað leoht speru,   lange sceaftas,
swið-mode sweopan,   swenga ne wyrnað,
deorra dynta;   him bið ðæt deofol lað.
Ðonne hine I and ᚱ L   and se yrra ᚲ C
guðe begyrdað   (geap stæf wigeð
125   biterne brogan),   bigað sona
helle hæftling,   ðæt he on hinder gæð.
Ðonne hiene ᚢ F and ᛗ M   utan ymbðringað,
scyldigne sceaðan,   habbað scearp speru,
atole earh-fare,   æled lætað
130   on ðæs feondes feax   flana stregdan,
biterne brogan;   banan heardlice
grimme ongieldað   ðæs hie oft gilp brecað.

covered with darkness. Indeed, there will be woe in its
    heart,
when, hanging, it will wish for hell, 105
for the most confining homeland.
Then the twins of the church, *N* and *O* together,
will repudiate it, each will bring a
whip from the journey; for a while they will inflict pain
on the alien body, not care about its life. 110
Then *S* will come, leader of angels,
the letter of glory, will seize the hostile
enemy by the feet, will have its forward cheek
fall on strong stone, will strew teeth
throughout the throng of hell. Each one will hide himself 115
in the shadow's gloom; the criminal will be busy,
the retainer of Satan very stilled.
Ǫ and *V* will likewise vanquish it with pain,
bold leaders will move toward it,
will have spears of light, long shafts, 120
resolute whips, they will not be sparing of blows,
of formidable strokes; that devil will be loathsome to them.
Then *I* and *L* and wrathful *C*
will surround it with war (the rounded letter carries
bitter terror), will immediately bend 125
hell's captive so that it falls back.
Then *F* and *M* will throng around the guilty criminal
from the outside, will have sharp spears,
a horrible flight of arrows, will let
the flame of arrows, a bitter terror, 130
spread into the enemy's hair; they will severely,
grimly pay the slayer because they often failed to perform a
    boast.

Ðonne hine æt niehstan   nearwe stilleð
ᛋ G se geapa,   ðone God sendeð
135   freondum on fultum,   færeð æfter ᛗ D
fif-mægnum full.   Fyr bið se ðridda
stæf stræte neah;   stille bideð.
H onetteð,   engel hine scierpeð,
Cristes cempan,   on cwicum wædum
140   Godes spyrigendes   geonges hrægles.
Ðonne hine on lyfte   lif-getwinnan
under tungla getrumum   tuigena ordum,
sweopum seolfrynum,   swiðe weallað,
oððæt him ban blicað,   bledað ædran;
145   gar-torn geotað   gifrum deofle.
Mæg simle se Godes cwide   gumena gehwylcum
ealra feonda gehwane   fleondne gebrengan
ðurh mannes muð,   manfulra heap
sweartne geswencan,   næfre hie ðæs syllice
150   bleoum bregdað.   Æfter ban-cofan
feðer-homan onfoð.   Hwilum flotan gripað.
Hwilum hie gewendað   in wyrmes lic
stronges and sticoles;   stingeð nieten,
feld-gongende   feoh gestrudeð.
155   Hwilum he on wætere   wicg gehnægeð,
hornum geheaweð,   oððæt him heortan blod,
famig flodes bæð,   foldan geseceð.
Hwilum he gefeterað   fæges mannes,
handa gehefegað,   ðonne he æt hilde sceall
160   wið lað werud   lifes tiligan;
awriteð he on his wæpne   wæll-nota heap
bealwe boc-stafas,   bill forscrifeð,
meces mærðo.   Forðon nænig man scile

Next then *G,* the rounded,
whom God sends as a support to friends,
will forcibly still it, *D* will follow after   135
full with five virtues. Fire is the third
letter near the street; calm, it waits.
H will hurry, an angel, the warrior of Christ,
will clothe it in the living garments
of a follower of God's fresh attire.   140
Then the life-twins will fiercely
surge it into the air under a host of stars
with the points of twigs, with silver whips,
until its bones show, its veins bleed;
they will pour forth the rage of battle onto the greedy devil.   145
The speech of God through a person's mouth
for everyone can cause all enemies,
the host of evil ones, to flee,
can assail the black ones, notwithstanding their strangely
changing colors. They will take on plumage   150
on their bodies. Sometimes they will seize a sailor.
Sometimes they will turn into the likeness of a
strong and scaly serpent; it stings the wild animal,
ravages the cattle walking in the field.
Sometimes in the water it vanquishes the horse,   155
hews it with horns, until its heart's blood
seeks the foamy bath of the river and the ground.
Sometimes it binds the man fated to die,
makes heavy his hands, when he in battle must
fight for his life against a hostile company;   160
it inscribes on his weapon a host of baleful inscriptions,
deadly letters, blunts his sword,
the glory of a blade. Therefore no one

oft orðances   ut abredan
165   wæpnes ecgge,   ðeah ðe him se wlite cweme,
ac symle he sceal singan,   ðonne he his sweord geteo,
Pater Noster,   and ðæt palm-treow
biddan mid blisse,   ðæt him bu gife
feorh and folme,   ðonne his feond cyme."
170   ". . . swice,   ær he soð wite,
ðæt ða sienfullan   saula sticien
mid hettendum   helle tomiddes.
Hateð ðonne heah-cining   helle betynan,
fyres fulle,   and ða feondas mid."
175   Hæfde ða se snotra   sunu Dauides
forcumen and forcyðed   Caldea eorl.
Hwæðre was on sælum   se ðe of siðe cwom
feorran gefered;   næfre ær his ferhð ahlog.

II

Hwæt. Ic flitan gefrægn   on fyrn-dagum
180   mod-gleawe men,   middan-geardes ræswan,
gewesan ymbe hira wisdom;   wyrs deð se ðe liehð
oððe ðæs soðes ansæceð.   Saloman was bremra,
ðeah ðe Saturnus   sumra hæfde,
bald breost-toga,   boca cæga,
185   leornenga locan.   Land eall geondhwearf,
Indea mere,   east Corsias,
Persea rice,   Palestinion,
Niniuen ceastre   and norð Predan,
Meda maððum-selas,   Marculfes eard,
190   Saulus rice,   swa he suð ligeð

without forethought must draw out
the edge of the weapon even though its appearance is   165
    pleasing,
but he always must sing, when he draws his sword,
the Pater Noster and pray to that palm tree
with joy that it might give him both
life and limb when his enemy comes."
". . . should weaken before he knows the truth,   170
that the sinful souls should remain fixed
with enemies in the middle of hell.
The high king then will command hell to be closed,
full of fire, and the enemies along with it."
The wise son of David had then   175
overcome and reproached the man of the Chaldeans.
He was happy, however, he who had come on the journey,
had traveled from afar; never before had his heart laughed.

II

Yes. I have heard of wise men quarreling
in days of old, leaders of middle earth   180
disputing about their wisdom; the one who lies
or denies the truth does worse. Solomon was more famous,
although Saturn, the brave leader of minds,
had the keys of certain books,
of the enclosure of learning. He went through all the lands,   185
the border of India, the east Cossias,
the Persian kingdom, Palestine,
the city of Nineveh and the north Parthians,
the Medes's treasure halls, the land of Marculf,
Saul's kingdom, as it lies in the south   190

ymbe Geallboe   and ymb Geador norð,
Filistina flet,   fæsten Creca,
wudu Egipta,   wæter Mathea,
cludas Coreffes,   Caldea rice,
195   Creca cræftas,   cynn Arabia,
lare Libia,   lond Syria,
Pitðinia,   Buðanasan,
Pamhpilia,   Pores gemære,
Macedonia,   Mesopotamie,
200   Cappadocia,   Cristes eðel:
Hieryhco, Galilea,   Hierusalem ...
       "...   oððe ic swigie,
nyttes hycgge,   ðeah ic no sprece.
Wat ic ðonne, gif ðu gewitest   on Wendel-sæ
205   ofer Cofor-flod   cyððe secean,
ðæt ðu wille gilpan   ðæt ðu hæbbe gumena bearn
forcumen and forcyðð ed.   Wat ic ðæt wæron Caldeas
guðe ðæs gielpne   and ðæs gold-wlonce,
mærða ðæs modige,   ðær to ðam moning gelomp
210   suð ymbe Sanere feld.   Sæge me from ðam lande
ðær nænig fyra ne mæg   fotum gestæppan."
       Saturnus cuæð:
"Se mæra was haten   sæ-liðende
weallende Wulf,   wer-ðeodum cuð
Filistina,   freond Nebrondes.
215   He on ðam felda ofslog   fif ond twentig
dracena on dæg-red,   and hine ða deað offeoll;
forðan ða foldan ne mæg   fira ænig,
ðone merc-stede,   mon gesecan,
fugol gefleogan,   ne ðon ma foldan neat.

around mount Gilboa and around Gadara in the north,
the halls of the Philistine's, the fortress of the Cretans,
the wood of the Egyptians, the waters of the Midians,
the cliffs of Horeb, the Chaldean kingdom,
the crafts of the Greeks, the Arabian people,   195
the teaching of Libya, the land of Syria,
Bythinia, Bashan,
Pamphilia, the border of Porus,
Macedonia, Mesopotamia,
Cappadocia, Christ's homeland: 200
Jericho, Galilee, Jerusalem . . .
    ". . . or I will be quiet,
thinking of something useful although I don't speak.
I know then, if you depart on the Mediterranean
past the river Chobar to seek your home,   205
that you will boast that you have overcome and shamed
the children of men. I know that the Chaldeans were
so boastful in war and so proud in gold,
so arrogant in their glories, that a warning came to them
in the south around Senaar field. Tell me about the land   210
where no one can set foot."
    Saturn said:
"The famous sailor was called
raging Wolf, known to the people
of the Philistines, Nimrod's friend.
He struck down twenty-five dragons   215
on that field at dawn, and then death cut him down;
therefore, no one can seek
that region, that borderland,
no more than any beast of the earth, nor bird fly there.

220 Đanon ater-cynn   ærest gewurdon
wide onwæcned,   ða ðe nu weallende
ðurh attres oroð   ingang rymað.
Git his sweord scineð   swiðe gescæned,
and ofer ða byrgenna   blicað ða hieltas."
    Salomon cwæð:
225 "Dol bið se ðe gæð   on deop wæter,
se ðe sund nafað   ne gesegled scip
ne fugles flyht,   ne he mid fotum ne mæg
grund geræcan;   huru se Godes cunnað
full dyslice,   Dryhtnes meahta."
    Saturnus cuæð:
230 "Ac hwæt is se dumba   se ðe on sumre dene resteð?
Swiðe snyttrað,   hafað seofon tungan;
hafað tungena gehwylc   twentig orda,
hafað orda gehwylc   engles snytro,
ðara ðe wile anra hwylc   uppe bringan,
235 ðæt ðu ðære gyldnan gesiehst   Hierusalem
weallas blican   and hiera win-rod lixan,
soð-fæstra segn.   Saga hwæt ic mæne."
    Salomon cuæð:
"Bec sindon breme,   bodiað geneahhe
weotodne willan   ðam ðe wiht hygeð.
240 Gestrangað hie and gestaðeliað   staðol-fæstne geðoht,
amyrgað mod-sefan   manna gehwylces
of ðreamedlan   ðisses lifes."
    Saturnus cwæð:
"Bald bið se ðe onbyregeð   boca cræftes;
symle bið ðe wisra   ðe hira geweald hafað."

From there the races of poisonous creatures were first   220
widely awakened, those surging ones that now
through poisonous breath open up the entrance.
His sword still shines, rendered very brilliant,
and the hilt gleams above the graves."
    Solomon said:
"Foolish is the one who goes into deep water,   225
who lacks the ability to swim or a sail-equipped ship
or the flight of a bird, or is unable to touch bottom
with his feet; indeed he tests God,
the power of the Lord very foolishly."
    Saturn said:
"But what is the dumb thing that rests in a certain valley?   230
It is very wise, has seven tongues;
each of the tongues has twenty tips,
each of the tips has the wisdom of an angel,
each of which will lead you up
so that you will see the golden walls   235
of Jerusalem gleaming and their blessed cross shining,
the sign of the righteous. Say what I mean."
    Solomon said:
"Books are renowned, often announcing
a sure will to the one who thinks at all.
They strengthen and make firm steadfast thought,   240
delight the heart of everyone
against the painful pressure of this life."
    Saturn said:
"Brave is the one who tastes grammar and rhetoric;
whoever has control of them will always be the wiser."

Salomon cuæð:

245 "Sige hie onsendað   soð-fæstra gehwam,
hælo hyðe,   ðam ðe hie lufað."

Saturnus cwæð:

"An wise is   on worold-rice
ymb ða me fyrwet bræc   fiftig wintra
dæges and niehtes   ðurh deop gesceaft;
250 geomrende gast   deð nu gena swa,
ærðon me geunne   ece Dryhten
ðæt me geseme   snoterra monn."

Salomon cwæð:

"Soð is ðæt ðu sagast;   seme ic ðe recene
ymb ða wrætlican wiht.   Wilt ðu ðæt ic ðe secgge?
255 An fugel siteð   on Filistina
middel-gemærum;   munt is hine ymbutan,
geap gylden weall.   Georne hine healdað
witan Filistina,   wenað ðæs ðe naht is,
ðæt hiene him scyle eall ðeod   on genæman
260 wæpna ecggum;   hie ðæs wære cunnon;
healdað hine niehta gehwylce   norðan and suðan
on twa healfa   tu hund wearda.
Se fugel hafað   feower heafdu
medumra manna,   and he is on middan hwælen;
265 geowes he hafað fiðeru   and griffus fet,
ligeð lonnum fæst,   locað unhiere,
swiðe swingeð   and his searo hringeð,
gilleð geomorlice   and his gyrn sefað,
wylleð hine on ðam wite,   wunað unlustum,
270 singgeð syllice;   seldum æfre
his leoma licggað.   Longað hine hearde,

Solomon said:
"They send victory to each of the righteous,   245
the harbor of salvation, to those who love them."
    Saturn said:
"There is one thing in the worldly kingdom
about which I have been curious for fifty winters
both day and night throughout deep creation;
a sorrowing spirit even now does the same,   250
until the eternal Lord should grant
that a wiser person should satisfy me."
    Solomon said:
"What you say is true; I will satisfy you immediately
about that wondrous creature. Do you want me to tell you?
A bird sits in the middle of the boundaries of   255
the Philistines; a mountain is around it,
a steep, golden wall. The wise men of the
Philistines guard it, expecting, which is not the case,
that the whole nation would steal it from them
with the edges of weapons; they knew how to be ready for   260
        that;
each night from north and south
two hundred sentries guard it on both sides.
The bird has four heads
of average human size, and it is like a whale in the middle;
it has the feathers of a vulture and the feet of a griffin,   265
lies fast in chains, gazes horribly,
beats its wings violently and clashes its armor,
cries out sorrowfully and laments its misfortune,
wallows in its pain, lives unhappily,
sings strangely; seldom ever do its   270
limbs lie still. It longs deeply,

ðynceð him ðæt sie ðria ðritig   ðusend wintra
ær he dom-dæges   dynn gehyre.
Nyste hine on ðære foldan   fira ænig
275   eorðan cynnes,   ærðon ic hine ana onfand
and hine ða gebendan het   ofer brad wæter,
ðæt hine se modega heht   Melotes bearn,
Filistina fruma,   fæste gebindan,
lonnum belucan   wið leod-gryre.
280   Ðone fugel hatað   feor-buende,
Filistina fruman,   *uasa mortis.*"
    Saturnus cwæð:
"Ac hwæt is ðæt wundor   ðe geond ðas worold færeð,
styrnenga gæð,   staðolas beateð,
aweceð wop-dropan,   winneð oft hider?
285   Ne mæg hit steorra ne stan   ne se steapa gimm,
wæter ne wildeor   wihte beswican,
ac him on hand gæð   heardes and hnesces,
micles and mætes;   him to mose sceall
gegangan geara gehwelce   grund-buendra,
290   lyft-fleogendra,   lagu-swemmendra,
ðria ðreoteno   ðusend-gerimes."
    Salomon cuæð:
"Yldo beoð on eorðan   æghwæs cræftig;
mid hiðendre   hilde-wræsne,
rumre racen-teage,   ræceð wide,
295   langre linan,   lisseð eall ðæt heo wile.
Beam heo abreoteð   and bebriceð telgum,
astyreð standendne   stefn on siðe,
afilleð hine on foldan;   friteð æfter ðam
wildne fugol.   Heo oferwigeð wulf,

it seems to it that it will be three times thirty thousand
winters before it hears the din of doomsday.
No one in the world of earthly kind
knew about it before I alone discovered it   275
and then had it bound over the broad water,
so that the brave son of Melot,
the leader of the Philistines, ordered it firmly bound,
locked in chains against the terror of his people.
The far-off dwelling leaders of the Philistines   280
call that bird *vasa mortis,* the instruments of death."
    Saturn said:
"But what is that wonder that travels through the world,
goes inexorably, beats the foundations,
awakens tears, often struggles its way here?
No star, nor stone, nor the bright gem,   285
no water, nor the wild beast can deceive it at all,
but into its hand goes the hard and the soft,
the great and small; every year
three times thirteen thousand of
of ground-dwelling, air-flying, sea-swimming   290
creatures must go as its food."
    Solomon said:
"Old age is all powerful on earth;
with ravaging fetters for captives,
extensive chains, a long rope,
it reaches widely, subduing all it wants to.   295
It destroys trees and breaks apart the branches,
uprooting the standing trunk as it does so,
fells it to the ground; after that, it eats
a wild bird. It overpowers the wolf,

300   hio oferbideð stanas,   heo oferstigeð style,
       hio abiteð iren mid ome,   deð usic swa."
       Saturnus cwæð:
       "Ac forhwon fealleð se snaw,   foldan behydeð,
       bewrihð wyrta cið,   wæstmas getigeð,
       geðyð hie and geðreatað,   ðæt hie ðrage beoð
305   cealde geclungne?   Full oft he gecostað eac
       wildeora worn,   wætum he oferbricgeð,
       gebryceð burga geat,   baldlice fereð,
       reafað . . ."
       (Salomon):
       " . . . swiðor micle   ðonne se swipra nið
310   se hine gelædeð   on ða laðan wic
       mid ða fræcnan   feonde to willan."
       Saturnus cwæð:
       "Nieht bið wedera ðiestrost,   ned bið wyrda heardost,
       sorg bið swarost byrðen,   slæp bið deaðe gelicost."
       Salomon cwæð:
       "Lytle hwile   leaf beoð grene;
315   ðonne hie eft fealewiað,   feallað on eorðan
       and forweorniað,   weorðað to duste.
       Swa ðonne gefeallað   ða ðe fyrena ær
       lange læstað,   lifiað him in mane,
       hydað heah-gestreon;   healdað georne
320   on fæstenne   feondum to willan,
       and wenað wan-hogan   ðæt hie wille wuldor-cining,
       ælmihtig God,   ece gehiran."
       Saturnus cwæð:
       "Sona bið gesiene,   siððan flowan mot
       yð ofer eall lond,   ne wile heo awa ðæs

it outlasts stones, it surpasses steel,   300
it bites iron with rust, does likewise to us."
    Saturn said:
"But why does the snow fall, covering the earth,
encircling the shoots of plants, tying up growth,
oppressing and attacking them so that for a while
they are withered by cold? Very often it also tries   305
many a wild beast with afflictions, it bridges the waters,
breaks the gates of the strongholds, boldly goes,
robs . . ."
    (Solomon):
". . . much stronger than the cunning evil
that leads him into the hateful abodes   310
with the dangerous ones as a joy to the enemy."
    Saturn said:
"Night is the darkest of weathers, need is the hardest of
      fates,
sorrow is the heaviest burden, sleep is most like death."
    Solomon said:
"For a little while, leaves are green;
then they yellow, fall to the ground   315
and decay, turn to dust.
Likewise then fall those who for a long time
before have been committing their crimes; they live in sin,
hide great treasures, holding them eagerly
in a strong place as a joy to the enemies,   320
and the fools expect that the king of glory,
almighty God, will listen to them eternally."
    Saturn said:
"Soon it will be seen, after the wave can
flow over all the land, it will never stop

325   siðes geswican,   sioððan hire se sæl cymeð,
    ðæt heo domes dæges   dyn gehiere."
        Salomon cwæð:
    "Wa bið ðonne ðissum modgum monnum,   ðam ðe her nu
                            mid mane lengest
    lifiað on ðisse lænan gesceafte.   Ieo ðæt ðine leode
                            gecyðdon;
    wunnon hie wið Dryhtnes miehtum,   forðon hie ðæt worc
                            ne gedegdon.
330   Ne sceall ic ðe hwæðre, broðor, abelgan;   ðu eart swiðe
                            bittres cynnes,
    eorre eormen-strynde.   Ne beyrn ðu in ða inwit-gecyndo!"
        Saturnus cwæð:
    "Saga ðu me, Salomon cyning,   sunu Dauides,
    hwæt beoð ða feowere   fægæs rapas?"
        Salomon cuæð:
    "Gewurdene wyrda,
335   ðæt beoð ða feowere   fæges rapas."
        Saturnus cwæð:
    "Ac hwa demeð ðonne   dryhtne Criste
    on domes dæge,   ðonne he demeð eallum gesceaftum?"
        Salomon cwæð:
    "Hwa dear ðonne Dryhtne deman,   ðe us of duste
                           geworhte,
    nergend of niehtes wunde?   Ac sæge me hwæt næren ðe
                            wæron."
        Saturnus cwæð:
340   "Ac forhwon ne mot seo sunne   side gesceafte
    scire geondscinan?   Forhwam besceadeð heo

its journey once its time has come   325
so that it hears the din of doomsday."
   Solomon said:
"Woe then to these proud people, those who with sin
live longest here in this transitory creation. Your nation
     showed that a long time ago;
they fought against the might of the Lord, therefore not
     completing that work.
I must not make you angry, however, brother; you are from   330
     a very bitter race,
a fierce and mighty generation. Don't you be involved in
     that evil nature!"
   Saturn said:
"Tell me, king Solomon, son of David,
what are the four ropes of the fated?"
   Solomon said:
"Fates that have come to pass,
those will be the four ropes of the fated."   335
   Saturn said:
"But who then will judge the lord Christ
on doomsday when he judges all creatures?"
   Solomon said:
"Who will then dare to judge the Lord, the Savior, who
     made us from dust,
from the wound of night? But tell me what were that were
     not."
   Saturn said:
"But why is the sun not allowed to shine brightly   340
     throughout
the broad creation? Why does it leave

muntas and moras   and monige ec
weste stowa?   Hu geweorðeð ðæt?"
        Salomon cuæð:
"Ac forhwam næron eorð-welan   ealle gedæled
345   leodum gelice?   Sum to lyt hafað,
godes grædig;   hine God seteð
ðurh geearnunga   eadgum to ræste."
        Saturnus cwæð:
"Ac forhwan beoð ða gesiðas   somod ætgædre,
wop and hleahtor?   Full oft hie weorð-geornra
350   sælða toslitað;   hu gesæleð ðæt?"
        Salomon cuæð:
"Unlæde bið and ormod   se ðe a wile
geomrian on gihðe;   se bið Gode fracoðast."
        Saturnus cwæð:
"Forhwon ne moton we ðonne ealle   mid onmedlan
gegnum gangan   in Godes rice?"
        Salomon cwæð:
355   "Ne mæg fyres feng   ne forstes cile,
snaw ne sunne   somod eardian,
aldor geæfnan,   ac hira sceal anra gehwylc
onlutan and onliðigan   ðe hafað læsse mægn."
        Saturnus cwæð:
"Ac forhwon ðonne leofað   se wyrsa leng?
360   Se wyrsa ne wat   in worold-rice
on his mæg-winum   maran are."
        Salomon cwæð:
"Ne mæg mon forildan   ænige hwile
ðone deoran sið,   ac he hine adreogan sceall."

mountains and moors and many other
desert places in shadow? How does that happen?"
    Solomon said:
"But why weren't all worldly goods dealt out
equally to people? A certain one, eager for good,   345
has too little; God will set him at rest
with the blessed because of his merits."
    Saturn said:
"But why are the companions
crying and laughing together? Very often they
destroy the happiness of the well intentioned; how does   350
      that come about?"
    Solomon said:
"Miserable and in despair is the one who always wants
to grieve in anxiety; he is most shameful to God."
    Saturn said:
"Why can't we all then go forward into
the kingdom of God with glory?"
    Solomon said:
"The grip of fire and the chill of frost,   355
snow and sun cannot live together,
sustain life, but one of them must
bend and yield, the one that has less might."
    Saturn said:
"But why then does the worse person live longer?
The worse one does not know greater honor   360
among kinsmen in the kingdom of this world."
    Solomon said:
"No one can put off for any time
the grievous journey, but he must endure it."

Saturnus cwæð:
"Ac hu gegangeð ðæt?   Gode oððe yfle,
365   ðonne hie beoð ðurh ane   idese acende,
twegen getwinnas,   ne bið hira tir gelic.
Oðer bið unlæde on eorðan,   oðer bið eadig,
     swiðe leof-tæle   mid leoda duguðum;
     oðer leofað   lytle hwile,
370   swiceð on ðisse sidan gesceafte,   and ðonne eft mid
                                        sorgum gewiteð.
Fricge ic ðec, hlaford Salomon,   hwæðres bið hira folgoð
                                        betra?"

     Salomon cuæð:
"Modor ne rædeð,   ðonne heo magan cenneð,
hu him weorðe geond worold   wid-sið sceapen.
Oft heo to bealwe   bearn afedeð,
375   seolfre to sorge,   siððan dreogeð
his earfoðu   orleg-stunde.
Heo ðæs afran sceall   oft and gelome
grimme greotan,   ðonne he geong færeð,
hafað wilde mod,   werige heortan,
380   sefan sorgfullne,   slideð geneahhe,
werig, wilna leas,   wuldres bedæled,
hwilum hige-geomor   healle weardað,
leofað leodum feor;   locað geneahhe
fram ðam unlædan   agen hlaford.
385   Forðan nah seo modor geweald,   ðonne heo magan
                                        cenneð,
bearnes blædes,   ac sceall on gebyrd faran
an æfter anum;   ðæt is eald gesceaft."

Saturn said:
"But how does that happen? For good or evil,
when they, two twins, are born   365
from one woman, their glory will not be alike.
One is accursed on earth, the other blessed,
very much beloved among hosts of people;
the other lives for a little while,
fails in this broad creation, and then departs again with   370
    sorrows.
I ask you, lord Solomon, which of their destinies is better?"
    Solomon said:
"When she bears a child, a mother does not have control
    over
how its wide journey through the world will be arranged.
Often she nurtures her child for destruction,
to her own sorrow, then endures   375
its miseries in the time of adversity.
She must constantly cry painfully
for her child when young he sets forth,
has a wild mind, a wicked heart,
a sorrowful spirit, slips frequently,   380
weary, lacking what it desires, bereft of glory,
sometimes sad in mind he occupies the hall,
lives far from people; his own lord
frequently looks away from the accursed one.
Therefore the mother does not have power, when she gives   385
    birth,
over the child's life, but one thing must go
after another in nature; that is the old dispensation."

Saturnus cwæð:
"Ac forhwan nele monn him on giogoðe   georne
                                             gewyrcan
deores dryhtscipes   and dæd-fruman,
390   wadan on wisdom,   winnan æfter snytro?"
       Salomon cwæð:
"Hwæt. Him mæg eadig eorl   eaðe geceosan
on his mod-sefan   mildne hlaford,
anne æðeling.   Ne mæg don unlæde swa."
       Saturnus cwæð:
"Ac forhwam winneð ðis wæter   geond worold-rice,
395   dreogeð deop gesceaft?   Ne mot on dæg restan,
neahtes neðyð,   neod-cræfte tyð,
cristnað and clænsað   cwicra manigo,
wuldre gewlitigað.   Ic wihte ne cann
forhwan se stream ne mot   stillan neahtes . . ."
       (Salomon):
400   ". . . his lifes fæðme.   Simle hit bið his lareowum hyrsum;
full oft hit eac ðæs deofles   dugoð gehnægeð,
ðær weotena bið   worn gesamnod.
Ðonne snottrum men   snæd oððglideð,
ða he be leohte gesihð,   luteð æfter,
405   gesegnað and gesyfleð   and him sylf friteð.
Swilc bið seo an snæd   æghwylcum men
selre micle,   gif heo gesegnod bið,
to ðycgganne,   gif he hit geðencan cann,
ðonne him sie seofon daga   symbel-gereordu.
410   Leoht hafað heow and had   Haliges Gastes,
Cristes gecyndo;   hit ðæt gecyðeð full oft.

164

Saturn said:
"But why does a young person not wish to work eagerly
for dear lordship and a leader,
walk in wisdom, struggle for prudence?"   390
  Solomon said:
"Yes. A blessed man can easily choose
in his mind a gentle lord,
a prince. The accursed cannot do so."
  Saturn said:
"But why does this water struggle through the kingdom of
     the world,
endure a profound destiny? It is not allowed to rest during   395
the day, it ventures on at night, pulls with might,
christens and cleanses many a living being,
beautifies with glory. I do not understand at all
why the stream cannot be still at night . . ."
  (Solomon):
". . . the expanse of his life. It is always obedient to its   400
     teachers;
very often it also vanquishes the devil's company,
where a number of the wise are gathered.
When a morsel of food slips away from a wise man,
he then sees it in the light, bends over for it,
blesses it and adds relish and eats it.   405
That one morsel likewise is much better
for anyone to receive if it is blessed,
if one can imagine it,
than would be seven days of banquets.
Light has the hue and character of the Holy Spirit,   410
the nature of Christ; it makes that known very often.

Gif hit unwitan   ænige hwile
healdað butan hæftum,   hit ðurh hrof wædeð,
bryceð and bærneð   bold-getimbru,
415   seomað steap and geap,   stigeð on lenge,
clymmeð on gecyndo,   cunnað hwænne mote
fyr on his frum-sceaft   on Fæder geardas,
eft to his eðle   ðanon hit æror cuom.
Hit bið eallenga   eorl to gesihðe,
420   ðam ðe gedælan can   Dryhtnes ðecelan,
forðon nis nænegu gecynd   cuic-lifigende
—ne fugel ne fisc   ne foldan stan,
ne wæteres wylm   ne wudu-telga,
ne munt ne mor   ne ðes middan-geard—
425   ðæt he forð ne sie   fyrenes cynnes."
    Saturnus cwæð:
"Full oft ic frode menn   fyrn gehyrde
secggan and swerian   ymb sume wisan,
hwæðer wære twegra   butan tweon strengra,
wyrd ðe warnung,   ðonne hie winnað oft
430   mid hira ðrea-medlan,   hwæðerne aðreoteð ær.
Ic to soðon wat;   sægdon me geara
Filistina witan,   ðonne we on geflitum sæton,
bocum tobræddon   and on bearm legdon,
meðel-cwidas mengdon,   moniges fengon,
435   ðæt nære nænig manna   middan-geardes
ðæt meahte ðara twega   tuion aspyrian."
    Salomon cwæð:
"Wyrd bið wended hearde,   wealleð swiðe geneahhe;
heo wop weceð,   heo wean hladeð,

If for any time at all the unwise
hold it without fetters, it moves through the roof,
breaks and burns the house timbers,
swings steep and lofty, ascends in height,   415
climbs by nature, explores when
fire may come back to its origin in the courts of the Father,
to its homeland from which it came before.
It is completely visible to any man
who knows how to share the Lord's lamp,   420
because there is no living species
—neither bird, nor fish, nor a stone on the ground,
neither the surging of water or a tree branch,
neither mountain or moor, nor this middle earth—
that does not continue to exist thanks to the nature of fire." 425
    Saturn said:
"Very often in the past I have heard wise people
speak and swear about a certain topic,
whether without doubt one of two things was stronger,
fate or foresight, when they often fight
with their mental oppressions to see who will become   430
        weary first.
I know in truth; the Philistine advisers
told me before when we sat in philosophical debate,
opened up books and set them on our lap,
exchanged formal speeches, took up many matters,
that there is no person in middle earth   435
who could settle by investigation the doubt about those
        two things."
    Solomon said:
"Fate is turned with difficulty, it wells up very often;
it brings forth weeping, it heaps up woe,

heo gast scyð,   heo ger byreð,

440 and hwæðre him mæg wis-sefa   wyrda gehwylce
gemetigian,   gif he bið modes gleaw
and to his freondum wile   fultum secan,
ðeh hwæðre god-cundes   gæstes brucan.”

Saturnus cwæð:
“Ac hwæt witeð us   wyrd seo swiðe,

445 eallra fyrena fruma,   fæhðo modor,
weana wyrt-wela,   wopes heafod,
frum-scylda gehwæs   fæder and modor,
deaðes dohtor?   Ac tohwan drohtað heo mid us?
Hwæt, hie wile lifigende   late aðreotan,

450 ðæt heo ðurh fyrena geflitu   fæhðo ne tydre.”

Salomon cwæð:
“Nolde gæd geador   in Godes rice
eadiges engles   and ðæs ofer-modan;
oðer his Dryhtne hierde,   oðer him ongan wyrcan ðurh
                               dierne cræftas
segn and side byrnan,   cwæð ðæt he mid his gesiðum wolde

455 hiðan eall heofona rice   and him ðonne on healfum sittan,
tydran him mid ðy teoðan dæle   oððæt he his tornes ne
                               cuðe
ende ðurh in-sceafte.   Ða wearð se æðelra ðeoden
gedrefed ðurh ðæs deofles gehygdo;   forlet hine ða of dune
                               gehreosan,

it injures the spirit, it carries the years,
and even so the one wise in heart   440
can govern each fate if he is shrewd in mind
and desires to seek support from friends
and moreover to keep a holy disposition."
   Saturn said:
"But why does fate the mighty,
the beginning of all crimes, the mother of feud,   445
the root of woes, the origin of weeping,
the father and mother of each first sin,
the daughter of death, afflict us? But to what end does it
     live among us?
Yes, at length while it is alive it will become weary,
so that through the conflict of crimes it will not propagate   450
     feud."
   Solomon said:
"There would be no fellowship together in God's kingdom
of the blessed angel and the proud one;
one obeyed his Lord, the other started making through
     secret crafts
a standard and broad mail shirt, said that he with his
     companions wanted
to plunder all the kingdom of heaven and place himself in   455
     one half,
breeding through internal generation with the tenth part of
     them
until he could know no end of his anger. Then the very
     noble prince became
troubled because of the devil's intention; he caused him to
     fall from the mountain,

afielde hine ða under foldan sceatas,
460 heht hine ðær fæste gebindan. Ðæt sindon ða usic
             feohtað on.
Forðon is witena gehwam wopes eaca.
Ða ðæt eadig onfand engla Dryhten,
ðæt heo leng mid hine lare ne namon,
aweorp hine ða of ðam wuldre and wide todraf,
465 and him bebead bearn heofon-wara
ðæt hie ec scoldon a ðenden hie lifdon
wunian in wylme, wop ðrowian,
heaf under hefonum. And him helle gescop,
wæl-cealde wic wintre beðeahte,
470 wæter in sende and wyrm-geardas,
atol deor monig irenum hornum,
blodige earnas and blace nædran,
ðurst and hungor and ðearle gewin,
egna egesan, unrotnesse;
475 and æghwylc him ðissa earfeða ece stondeð
butan edwende a ðenden hie lifigað."
  Saturnus cwæð:
"Is ðonne on ðisse foldan fira ænig
eorðan cynnes ðara ðe man age
ðe deað abæde ær se dæg cyme
480 ðæt sie his calend-cwide clæne arunnen
and hine mon annunga ut abanne?"
  Salomon cwæð:
"Æghwylcum men engel onsendeð
Dryhten heofona ðonne dæg cymeð;
se sceall behealdan hu his hyge wille

170

cast him under the surfaces of the earth,
ordered him to be bound fast there. These are those who   460
     fight against us.
Therefore for each of the wise, there is an increase of
     weeping.
When the blessed Lord of angels found
that they would no longer accept instruction from him,
he threw him out of glory and drove him far away,
and he commanded the children of heaven dwellers   465
that they, too, always while they lived
must dwell in the surging flame, endure weeping,
lamentation under the heavens. And he created hell for
     them,
a slaughter-cold dwelling covered by winter,
sent in water and snake pits,   470
many horrible beasts with iron horns,
bloody eagles and black adders,
thirst and hunger and fierce strife,
the terror of terrors, sadness;
and each of these miseries stands eternally   475
without change for them forever while they live."
     Saturn said:
"Is there anyone of earthly kind then
on this earth who may have acted sinfully
whom death may demand before the day comes
when the allotted time will have run out   480
and he may be summoned forth immediately?"
     Solomon said:
"The Lord of the heavens sends an angel
to every person when day breaks;
he must consider how his mind desires

485 grædig growan in Godes willan,
   murnan metodes ðrym, mid ðy ðe hit dæg bið.
  Ðonne hine ymbegangað gastas twegen;
 oðer bið golde glædra, oðer bið grundum sweartra;
   oðer cymeð . . .
490   . . . ofer ðære stylenan helle;
   oðer hine læreð ðæt he lufan healde,
   metodes miltse and his mæga ræd;
   oðer hine tyhteð and on tæso læreð,
   yweð him and yppeð earmra manna
495 misgemynda, and ðurh ðæt his mod hweteð,
   lædeð hine and læceð and hine geond land spaneð
   oððæt his ege bið æfðancum full,
   ðurh earmra scyld yrre geworden.
   Swa ðonne feohteð se feond on feower gecynd,
500 oððæt he gewendeð on ða wyrsan hand
   deofles dædum dæg-longne fyrst,
   and ðæs willan wyrcð ðe hine on woh spaneð.
   Gewiteð ðonne wepende on weg faran
   engel to his earde and ðæt eall sagað:
505 'Ne meahte ic of ðære heortan heardne aðringan
   stylenne stan; sticað him tomiddes.'"

to grow zealous in God's will,   485
be fearful of the creator's power when the day arrives.
Then two spirits circle around;
one is shinier than gold, the other blacker than the abyss;
the one comes . . .
     . . . over hell, hard as steel;   490
the one teaches that one should keep the love,
the mercy of the creator and his powerful counsel;
the other tempts and guides to ruin,
reveals and makes clear the evil memories
of wretched people, and through that, entices the mind,   495
leads and captures it and allures it throughout the land
until its eye, full of envy, has become fierce
through the crime of the wretched ones.
So, then, the enemy fights in four ways
until he turns to the worse side   500
because of the deeds of the devil that last all day long,
and he does the will of the one who allures him into woe.
Weeping, then, the angel goes on his way
home and says all this:
'I could not dislodge the hard, steel stone   505
from the heart; it sticks in his midsection.'"

Maxims II

Cyning sceal rice healdan. Ceastra beoð feorran gesyne,
or-ðanc enta geweorc, þa þe on þysse eorðan syndon,
wrætlic weallstana geweorc. Wind byð on lyfte swiftust,
þunar byð þragum hludast. Þrymmas syndan Cristes
                                                      myccle,
5   wyrd byð swiðost. Winter byð cealdost,
       lencten hrimigost (he byð lengest ceald),
       sumor sun-wlitegost (swegel byð hatost),
       hærfest hreð-eadegost, hæleðum bringeð
       geres wæstmas, þa þe him God sendeð.
10   Soð bið swicolost, sinc byð deorost,
       gold gumena gehwam, and gomol snoterost,
       fyrn-gearum frod, se þe ær feala gebideð.
       Wea bið wundrum clibbor; wolcnu scriðað.
       Geongne æþeling sceolan gode gesiðas
15   byldan to beaduwe and to beah-gife.
       Ellen sceal on eorle, ecg sceal wið hellme
       hilde gebidan. Hafuc sceal on glofe
       wilde gewunian, wulf sceal on bearowe,
       earm anhaga; eofor sceal on holte,
20   toð-mægenes trum. Til sceal on eðle
       domes wyrcean. Daroð sceal on handa,
       gar golde fah. Gim sceal on hringe
       standan steap and geap. Stream sceal on yðum

Maxims II

A king must rule a kingdom. Cities are seen from afar,
the ingenious work of giants, those that are on this earth,
the wondrous work of wall stones. Wind is swiftest in the
    air,
thunder is at times loudest. The powers of Christ are great,
fate is most mighty. Winter is coldest,   5
spring frostiest (it is cold longest),
summer most fair with sunshine (the sky is hottest),
autumn most glorious, bringing to men
the year's produce, which God sends them.
Truth is most deceiving, treasure most dear,   10
gold to every man, and an old one is wisest,
prudent from bygone years, who experienced much before.
Woe is wondrously clinging; clouds glide.
Good companions must encourage a young noble
in war and in ring giving.   15
Courage must be in a man, blade against helmet
must experience battle. The hawk must stand
wild on the glove, the wolf must be in the woods,
a wretched lone dweller; the boar must be in the forest,
secure in the strength of its tusks. A good person must   20
    achieve glory in his native land.
The javelin must be in the hand,
the spear decorated with gold. The gem must be in the ring
standing lofty and wide. The current must mingle

mencgan mere-flode.   Mæst sceal on ceole,
25 segel-gyrd seomian.   Sweord sceal on bearme,
drihtlic isern.   Draca sceal on hlæwe,
frod, frætwum wlanc.   Fisc sceal on wætere
cynren cennan.   Cyning sceal on healle
beagas dælan.   Bera sceal on hæðe,
30 eald and egesfull.   Ea of dune sceal
flod-græg feran.   Fyrd sceal ætsomne,
tir-fæstra getrum.   Treow sceal on eorle,
wisdom on were.   Wudu sceal on foldan
blædum blowan.   Beorh sceal on eorþan
35 grene standan.   God sceal on heofenum,
dæda demend.   Duru sceal on healle,
rum recedes muð.   Rand sceal on scylde,
fæst fingra gebeorh.   Fugel uppe sceal
lacan on lyfte.   Leax sceal on wæle
40 mid sceote scriðan.   Scur sceal of heofenum,
winde geblanden,   in þas woruld cuman.
Þeof sceal gangan þystrum wederum.   Þyrs sceal on fenne
                                            gewunian
ana innan lande.   Ides sceal dyrne cræfte,
fæmne hire freond gesecean   gif heo nelle on folce geþeon
45 þæt hi man beagum gebicge.   Brim sceal sealte weallan,
lyft-helm and lagu-flod   ymb ealra landa gehwylc,
flowan firgen-streamas.   Feoh sceal on eorðan

in the waves with the sea. A mast must sway
a sailyard on a ship. A sword must be in the lap,   25
a lordly iron. A dragon must be in its barrow,
wise, proud in its treasures. A fish must spawn
its kind in the water. A king must deal out rings
in the hall. A bear must be in the heath,
old and terrible. A river must flow off the hill,   30
gray as the sea. An army must be together,
a band of glorious men. Faith must be in an earl,
wisdom in a man. The wood must flourish with fruits
on the land. A hill on the earth must
stand green. God, the judge of deeds,   35
must be in heaven. A door, the spacious mouth of the
      building,
must be on the hall. The boss must be on the shield,
a sure defense for fingers. A bird must be playing
up in the air. A salmon must glide in a pool
with the trout. A shower must be from the heavens,   40
mixed with wind, coming into this world.
A thief must walk in dark weather. A giant must dwell in the
      fen
alone inside the land. A woman, a maiden, must by secret
      skill
seek her friend if she does not want it to happen among the
      people
that someone should buy her with rings. The sea must surge   45
      with salt,
covering cloud and ocean around every land,
the mountain streams must flow. Cattle must be on the
      earth,

tydran and tyman.　Tungol sceal on heofenum
beorhte scinan　swa him bebead meotud.
50　God sceal wið yfele,　geogoð sceal wið yldo,
lif sceal wið deaþe,　leoht sceal wið þystrum,
fyrd wið fyrde,　feond wið oðrum,
lað wið laþe　ymb land sacan,
synne stælan.　A sceal snotor hycgean
55　ymb þysse worulde gewinn,　wearh hangian,
fægere ongildan　þæt he ær facen dyde
manna cynne.　Meotod ana wat
hwyder seo sawul sceal　syððan hweorfan,
and ealle þa gastas　þe for Gode hweorfað
60　æfter deað-dæge,　domes bidað
on Fæder fæðme.　Is seo forð-gesceaft
digol and dyrne;　Drihten ana wat,
nergende Fæder.　Næni eft cymeð
hider under hrofas　þe þæt her for soð
65　mannum secge　hwylc sy meotodes gesceaft,
sige-folca gesetu,　þær he sylfa wunað.

bringing forth and multiplying. A star must shine brightly
in the heavens as the ruler ordered it.
Good must be against evil, youth against age,   50
life against death, light must be against darkness,
army against army, one enemy against another,
foe against foe fighting for land,
entering a conflict. The wise one must always think
about this world's strife, the criminal must hang,   55
fairly repaying the crime that he did before
to human kind. The ruler alone knows
where the soul must turn afterward,
and all the spirits who turn before God
after the day of death await judgment   60
in the Father's embrace. The shape of the future is
dark and hidden; the Lord alone knows,
the saving Father. No one comes here again
under the roofs who can say truthfully to people
what the nature of the ruler might be, what seats of the   65
victorious peoples might be like, where he himself dwells.

A Proverb from Winfrid's Time

Oft daed-lata   domę foręldit,
sigi-sitha gahuem,   suuyltit thi ana.

A Proverb from Winfrid's Time

The laggard's often slow to glory,
to every successful venture, so he dies alone.

Bede's Death Song: West Saxon Version

For þam ned-fere   næni wyrþeþ
þances snotera,   þonne him þearf sy
to gehicgenne,   ær his heonen-gange,
hwæt his gaste   godes oþþe yfeles
5   æfter deaþe heonon   demed weorþe.

Bede's Death Song: West Saxon Version

Before the compulsory journey, before his departure
from here, no one becomes wiser of thought
than when it is necessary to consider
what of good or evil in his soul
will be judged henceforth after death.   5

Latin-English Proverbs

Ardor frigesscit,   nitor squalescit,
amor abolescit,   lux obtenebrescit.
Hat acolað,   hwit asolað,
leof alaðaþ,   leoht aðystrað.
Senescunt omnia   que æterna non sunt.
Æghwæt forealdað   þæs þe ece ne byð.

Latin-English Proverbs

Ardor frigesscit,   nitor squalescit,
amor abolescit,   lux obtenebrescit.
Hot grows cold, white gets dirty,
what is dear turns hateful, light darkens.
Senescunt omnia   que æterna non sunt.   5
Everything grows old if it is not eternal.

Metrical Charm 1

For Unfruitful Land

Her ys seo bot, hu ðu meaht þine æceras betan gif hi nellaþ
wel wexan oþþe þær hwilc ungedefe þing on gedon bið on
dry oððe on lyb-lace. Genim þonne on niht, ær hyt dagige,
feower tyrf on feower healfa þæs landes, and gemearca hu hy
5 ær stodon. Nim þonne ele and hunig and beorman, and æl-
ces feos meolc þe on þæm lande sy, and ælces treow-cynnes
dæl þe on þæm lande sy gewexen, butan heardan beaman,
and ælcre nam-cuþre wyrte dæl, butan glappan anon, and do
þonne halig-wæter ðær on, and drype þonne þriwa on þone
staðol þara turfa, and cweþe ðonne ðas word: "*Crescite*, wexe,
et multiplicamini, and gemænig-fealda, *et replete*, and gefylle,
terre, þas eorðan. *In nomine Patris et Filii et Spiritus Sancti sit*
13 *benedicti*." And "Pater Noster" swa oft swa þæt oðer. And
bere siþþan ða turf to circean, and mæsse-preost asinge feo-
wer mæssan ofer þan turfon, and wende man þæt grene to
ðan weofode, and siþþan gebringe man þa turf þær hi ær
wæron ær sunnan setl-gange. And hæbbe him gæworht of
cwic-beame feower Cristes mælo and awrite on ælcon ende:

Metrical Charm 1

For Unfruitful Land

Here is the remedy, how you can improve your fields if they will not grow well, or if some troublesome thing is done there through sorcery or witchcraft. At night, before it dawns, take four pieces of sod from the four sides of the land and mark where they had been before. Then take oil   5
and honey and yeast, and the milk of each cow that is on the land, and a portion of each kind of tree that has grown on the land, except hard trees, and a portion of each well-known herb, except buckbean alone, and then pour holy water on it, and then drip it three times on the underside of those pieces of sod, and then say these words: "*Crescite,* grow, *et multiplicamini,* and multiply, *et replete,* and fill, *terre,* this earth. In the name of the Father and the Son and the Holy Spirit, may you be blessed." And as many times as you say it,   13
say the Pater Noster. And afterward carry those pieces of turf to church, and the mass priest should sing four masses over the sod, with the green side turned to the altar, and then before sunset the pieces of sod should be brought back to where they were before. And have four crosses of Christ made of wood from the rowan tree and write on each end:

19 *Matheus* and *Marcus, Lucas* and *Iohannes*. Lege þæt Cristes
mæl on þone pyt neoþeweardne, cweðe ðonne: "*Crux
Matheus, crux Marcus, crux Lucas, crux Sanctus Iohannes.*" Nim
ðonne þa turf and sete ðær ufon on and cweþe ðonne nigon
siþon þas word, "*Crescite,*" and swa oft "Pater Noster," and
wende þe þonne eastweard and onlut nigon siðon ead--
25 modlice, and cweð þonne þas word:

"Eastweard ic stande,   arena ic me bidde,
bidde ic þone mæran *domine,*   bidde ðone miclan
                                                                Drihten,
bidde ic ðone haligan   heofon-rices weard,
eorðan ic bidde   and up-heofon
30 and ða soþan   sancta Marian
and heofones meaht   and heah-reced,
þæt ic mote þis gealdor   mid gife Drihtnes
toðum ontynan   þurh trumne geþanc,
aweccan þas wæstmas   us to woruld-nytte,
35 gefyllan þas foldan   mid fæste geleafan,
wlitigigan þas wancg-turf,   swa se witega cwæð
þæt se hæfde are on eorþ-rice,   se þe ælmyssan
dælde domlice   Drihtnes þances."

Wende þe þonne ðrie sun-ganges, astrece þonne on and-
lang and arim þær letanias and cweð þonne: "*Sanctus, sanctus,*
41 *sanctus*" oþ ende. Sing þonne *Benedicite* aþenedon earmon
and *Magnificat* and "Pater Noster" ðrie and bebeod hit
Criste and sancta Marian and þære halgan rode to lofe and
to weorþinga and to are þam þe þæt land age and eallon þam
45 þe him underðeodde synt. Ðonne þæt eall sie gedon, þonne
nime man uncuþ sæd æt ælmes-mannum and selle him
twa swylc, swylce man æt him nime, and gegaderie ealle his

Matthew and Mark, Luke and John. Lay the cross of Christ   19
in the nethermost pit, then say: "Cross Matthew, cross
Mark, cross Luke, cross Saint John." Then take the pieces of
sod and set them on top and then say nine times these
words, "*Crescite* . . . ," and the Pater Noster as many times,
and then turn eastward and bow humbly nine times, and
then say these words: 25

> "Eastward I stand, I pray for mercies for myself,
> I pray the famous Lord, pray the great Lord,
> I pray the holy guardian of the heavenly kingdom,
> I pray the earth and the sky
> and the true Saint Mary   30
> and the might and high hall of heaven
> that I may by the gift of the Lord
> open this charm for the grassland through firm thought,
> awaken these crops for our worldly use,
> fill this ground by a fast belief,   35
> beautify this grassland, as the psalmist said
> that he had mercy in the earthly kingdom, who
> gave alms judiciously by the grace of the Lord."

Then turn three times with the sun, then stretch out
lengthwise and recite litanies there and then say: "*Sanctus,
sanctus, sanctus*" until the end. Then sing *Benedicite* with arms   41
extended and *Magnificat* and the Pater Noster three times
and commend it to Christ and Saint Mary and the holy cross
in praise and to the honor and glory of the one who owns
the land and to all those who are subject to him. When that   45
is all done, then someone should take unknown seed from
beggars and give them twice as much as was taken from
them, and gather all his plowing implements together; then

sulh-geteogo togædere; borige þonne on þam beame stor
and finol and gehalgode sapan and gehalgod sealt. Nim
50 þonne þæt sæd, sete on þæs sules bodig, cweð þonne:

"Erce, Erce, Erce,   eorþan modor,
geunne þe se al-walda,   ece Drihten,
æcera wexendra   and wridendra,
eacniendra   and elniendra,
55 sceafta hehra,   scirra wæstma,
and þæra bradan   bere-wæstma,
and þæra hwitan   hwæte-wæstma,
and ealra   eorþan wæstma.
Geunne him   ece Drihten
60 and his halige,   þe on heofonum synt,
þæt hys yrþ si gefriþod   wið ealra feonda gehwæne,
and heo si geborgen   wið ealra bealwa gehwylc,
þara lyb-laca   geond land sawen.
Nu ic bidde ðone waldend   se ðe ðas woruld gesceop
65 þæt ne sy nan to þæs cwidol wif   ne to þæs cræftig
man
þæt awendan ne mæge   word þus gecwedene."

Þonne man þa sulh forð drife and þa forman furh on-
sceote, cweð þonne:

"Hal wes þu, folde,   fira modor!
70 Beo þu growende   on Godes fæþme,
fodre gefylld   firum to nytte."

Nim þonne ælces cynnes melo and abacæ man inne-
werdre handa bradnæ hlaf and gecned hine mid meolce and
mid halig-wætere and lecge under þa forman furh. Cweþe
75 þonne:

bore and insert frankincense and fennel and hallowed salve
and hallowed salt into the wood. Then take that seed, set it
on the body of the plow, and say: 50

"Erce, Erce, Erce, earth's mother,
may the ruler of all, the eternal Lord, grant you
fields waxing and putting forth shoots,
being in labor and gaining strength,
higher shafts, bright crops   55
and the broad barley crops
and the white wheat crops
and all the crops of the earth.
May the eternal Lord and his saints,
who are in heaven, grant him   60
that his land be protected against each enemy
and that it be fortified against each harm
from witchcrafts sown throughout the land.
Now I pray the ruler who created this world
that there not be any woman so talkative nor person so   65
     cunning
to change the words thus spoken."

Then someone should drive forth the plow and cut the
first furrow, then say:

"Be in good health, earth, the mother of men!
Be fruitful in the embrace of God,   70
filled with food for the use of men."

Then take each kind of flour and have someone bake a
loaf as broad as the inside of a hand and knead it with milk
and with holy water and lay it under the first furrow. Then
say: 75

"Ful æcer fodres   fira cinne,
beorht-blowende,   þu gebletsod weorþ
þæs haligan noman   þe ðas heofon gesceop
and ðas eorþan   þe we on lifiaþ.
80   Se God, se þas grundas geworhte,   geunne us
                         growende gife,
þæt us corna gehwylc   cume to nytte."

Cweð þonne ðrie "*Crescite in nomine Patris, sit benedicti.*"
"Amen" and "Pater Noster" þriwa.

"Field full of food for human kind,
brightly blooming, be blessed
in the holy name of the one who created the heaven
and the earth on which we live.
May God, who made these foundations, grant us growing 80
    gifts
so that each grain comes to use."

Then say three times, "Grow in the name of the Father,
may you be blessed." Say "Amen" and the Pater Noster three
times.

Metrical Charm 2

The Nine Herbs Charm

"Gemyne ðu, mucg-wyrt,   hwæt þu ameldodest,
hwæt þu renadest   æt Regenmelde.
Una þu hattest,   yldost wyrta.
Ðu miht wið ðrie   and wið ðritig,
þu miht wiþ attre   and wið onflyge,
þu miht wiþ þam laþan   ðe geond lond færð.
Ond þu, weg-brade,   wyrta modor,
eastan openo,   innan mihtigu;
ofer ðe crætu curran,   ofer ðe cwene reodan,
ofer ðe bryde bryodedon,   ofer þe fearras fnærdon.
Eallum þu þon wiðstode   and wiðstunedest;
swa ðu wiðstonde   attre and onflyge
and þæm laðan   þe geond lond fereð.
Stune hætte þeos wyrt,   heo on stane geweox;
stond heo wið attre,   stunað heo wærce.

5

10

15

194

Metrical Charm 2

The Nine Herbs Charm

"Remember, mugwort, what you disclosed,
what you arranged at Regenmeld.
You were called Una, the oldest of herbs,
you have power against three and against thirty,
you have power against poison and against infectious   5
    disease,
you have power against the trouble that travels across the
    land.
And you, plantain, mother of herbs,
open from the east, mighty within;
over you carts creaked, over you women rode,
over you brides cried out, over you oxen snorted.   10
You withstood and dashed against all these;
thus you withstand poison and infectious disease
and the trouble that travels across the land.
This herb is called stune; it grew on stone;
it stands against poison, it dashes pain.   15

Stiðe heo hatte,   wiðstunað heo attre,
wreceð heo wraðan,   weorpeð ut attor.
Þis is seo wyrt   seo wiþ wyrm gefeaht,
þeos mæg wið attre,   heo mæg wið onflyge,
20 heo mæg wið ðam laþan   ðe geond lond fereþ.
Fleoh þu nu, attor-laðe,   seo læsse ða maran,
seo mare þa læssan,   oððæt him beigra bot sy.
Gemyne þu, mægðe,   hwæt þu ameldodest,
hwæt ðu geændadest   æt Alorforda;
25 þæt næfre for gefloge   feorh ne gesealde
syþðan him mon mægðan   to mete gegyrede.
Þis is seo wyrt   ðe wergulu hatte;
ðas onsænde seolh   ofer sæs hrygc
ondan attres   oþres to bote.
30 Ðas nigon magon   wið nygon attrum.
Wyrm com snican,   toslat he man;
ða genam Woden   nigon wuldor-tanas,
sloh ða þa næddran,   þæt heo on nigon tofleah.
Þær geændade   æppel and attor,
35 þæt heo næfre ne wolde   on hus bugan.
Fille and finule,   fela-mihtigu twa,
þa wyrte gesceop   witig Drihten,
halig on heofonum,   þa he hongode;
sette and sænde   on siofon worulde
40 earmum and eadigum   eallum to bote.
Stond heo wið wærce,   stunað heo wið attre,
seo mæg wið ðrie   and wið ðritig,

It is called stiff, it withstands poison,
forces the grievous to move, throws out poison.
This is the herb that fought against the snake,
this strength against poison, the strength against infectious
    disease,
the strength against the trouble that travels across the land.   20
Put now to flight, root of fumitory, the lesser the greater,
the greater the lesser, until there is a remedy for him for
    both.
Remember, chamomile, what you disclosed,
what you accomplished at Alorford;
no one ever yielded his life to infectious disease   25
after chamomile was prepared as a food for him.
This is the herb called crab apple;
the seal sent it over the sea's back
as a remedy for the evil of another poison.
These nine have power against nine poisons.   30
A serpent came crawling, it tore apart a person;
then Woden took nine glory twigs,
then struck the adder so that it fled away in nine.
There apple and poison brought it about
that it never wanted to enter a house.   35
Chervil and fennel, two very effective ones,
the wise Lord, holy in the heavens,
made when he hung;
he established and sent them into seven worlds
as a remedy for all the wretched and blessed.   40
It stands against pain, dashes against poison,
it has power against three and against thirty,

wið feondes hond   and wið fær-bregde,
wið malscrunge   manra wihta.
45   "Nu magon þas nigon wyrta   wið nygon wuldor-
                                    geflogenum,
wið nigon attrum   and wið nygon onflygnum,
wið ðy readan attre,   wið ðy runlan attre,
wið ðy hwitan attre,   wið ðy wedenan attre,
wið ðy geolwan attre,   wið ðy grenan attre,
50   wið ðy wonnan attre,   wið ðy wedenan attre,
wið ðy brunan attre,   wið ðy basewan attre,
wið wyrm-geblæd,   wið wæter-geblæd,
wið þorn-geblæd,   wið þystel-geblæd,
wið ys-geblæd,   wið attor-geblæd,
55   gif ænig attor cume   eastan fleogan
oððe ænig norðan cume
oððe ænig westan   ofer wer-ðeode.
Crist stod ofer adle   ængan cundes.
Ic ana wat   ea rinnende
60   þær þa nygon nædran   nean behealdað;
motan ealle weoda nu   wyrtum aspringan,
sæs toslupan,   eal sealt wæter,
ðonne ic þis attor   of ðe geblawe."

Mugc-wyrt, weg-brade þe eastan open sy, lombes cyrse,
attor-laðan, mageðan, netelan, wudu-sur-æppel, fille and fi-
66   nul, ealde sapan. Gewyrc ða wyrta to duste, mængc wiþ þa
sapan and wiþ þæs æpples gor. Wyrc slypan of wætere and of

against the enemy's hand and against sudden deceits,
against the bewitching of wicked beings.
   "Now these nine herbs are against nine fugitives from   45
     glory,
against nine poisons and against nine infectious diseases,
against the red poison, against the running poison,
against the white poison, against the purple poison,
against the yellow poison, against the green poison,
against the black poison, against the blue poison,   50
against the brown poison, against the crimson poison,
against the blister from a snake bite, against the water
     blister,
against the thorn blister, against the thistle blister,
against the ice blister, against the poison blister,
if any poison should come flying from the east   55
or any should come from the north
or any from the west over the people.
Christ stood over disease of any kind.
I alone know the running stream
where the nine adders behold it close;   60
may all the weeds now spring up as herbs,
seas slip away, all salt water,
when I blow this poison off you."

   Mugwort, plantain that is open from the east, lamb's
cress, fumitory, chamomile, nettle, crab apple, chervil and
fennel, old soap. Grind the herbs to dust, mix them with the   66
salve and with the juice of the apple. Make a paste of water

69   axsan, genim finol, wyl on þære slyppan and beþe mid æg-
gemongc, þonne he þa sealfe on do, ge ær ge æfter. Sing þæt
galdor on ælcre þara wyrta, ðrie ær he hy wyrce and on þone
æppel ealswa; ond singe þon men in þone muð and in þa
earan buta and on ða wunde þæt ilce gealdor, ær he þa sealfe
on do.

and of ash, take fennel, boil it in the paste and bathe it with
an egg mixture when he puts the salve on both before and
after. Sing that charm on each of the herbs, three times be-
fore he prepares them, and on the apple as well; and sing
that same charm into the mouth and into both ears of the
person and onto his wound before he applies the salve.

69

Metrical Charm 3

Against a Dwarf

Wið dweorh man sceal niman seofon lytle oflætan, swylce man mid ofrað, and writan þas naman on ælcre oflætan: *Maximianus, Malchus, Iohannes, Martimianus, Dionisius, Constantinus, Serafion.* Þænne eft þæt galdor, þæt her æfter cweð, man sceal singan, ærest on þæt wynstre eare, þænne on þæt
6 swiðre eare, þænne bufan þæs mannes moldan. And ga þænne an mæden-man to and ho hit on his sweoran, and do man swa þry dagas; him bið sona sel.

"Her com in gangan   in spider-wiht,
10 hæfde him his haman on handa,   cwæð þæt þu his
                              hæncgest wære,
legde þe his teage an sweoran.   Ongunnan him of
                              þæm lande liþan;
sona swa hy of þæm lande coman,   þa ongunnan him
                              ða liþu colian.
Þa com in gangan   dweores sweostar;
þa geændade heo   and aðas swor
15 ðæt næfre þis ðæm adlegan   derian ne moste,
ne þæm þe þis galdor   begytan mihte,
oððe þe þis galdor   ongalan cuþe.
Amen. Fiað."

202

Metrical Charm 3

Against a Dwarf

Against a dwarf, one must take seven little wafers such as the ones used in the sacrament and write these names on each wafer: *Maximianus, Malchus, Johannes, Martimianus, Dionisius, Constantinus, Serafion.* Then one must sing the charm that is quoted below, first in the left ear, then in the right ear, then on top of the person's head. And then a maiden should go and hang it on his neck, and one does that for three days; it will immediately be better for him.   6

"A spider came walking inside here
with coat in hand, saying that you were his horse,   10
laying his cords on your neck. They began to sail from the
    land;
as soon as they came away from the land, their limbs
    began to cool.
Then the dwarf's sister came walking in;
then she ended it and swore oaths
that this may never harm the sick,   15
nor the one who might gain this charm,
or who knew how to chant this charm.
Amen. Let it be done."

Metrical Charm 4

For a Stabbing Pain

Wið fær-stice fefer-fuige and seo reade netele ðe þurh ærn
inwyxð, and weg-brade; wyll in buteran.

"Hlude wæran hy, la, hlude,   ða hy ofer þone hlæw
                                         ridan,
    wæran an-mode   ða hy ofer land ridan.
5   Scyld ðu ðe nu; þu ðysne nið   genesan mote.
    Ut, lytel spere,   gif her inne sie!
    Stod under linde,   under leohtum scylde,
    þær ða mihtigan wif   hyra mægen beræddon
    and hy gyllende   garas sændan;
10   ic him oðerne   eft wille sændan,
    fleogende flane   forane togeanes.
    Ut, lytel spere,   gif hit her inne sy!
    Sæt smið,   sloh seax lytel,
    . . . iserna   wundrum swiðe.
15   Ut, lytel spere,   gif her inne sy!
    Syx smiðas sætan,   wæl-spera worhtan.
    Ut, spere,   næs in, spere!
    Gif her inne sy   isernes dæl,
    hægtessan geweorc,   hit sceal gemyltan.

Metrical Charm 4

For a Stabbing Pain

For a stabbing pain, feverfew, and the red nettle that grows
through a house, and plantain; boil in butter.

    "Loud were they, yes, loud, when they rode over the
mound, they were resolute when they rode over the land.
Shield yourself now; you may survive this attack.   5
Out, little spear, if you are in here!
I stood under a linden tree, under a light shield,
where the mighty women deliberated about their
    strength,
and they hurled their whistling spears;
I want to send another back to them,   10
a flying arrow in return.
Out, little spear, if it is in here!
A smith sat, forging a little knife,
. . . very wondrously of irons.
Out, little spear, if you are in here!   15
Six smiths sat, making deadly spears.
Out, spear, not in, spear!
If a portion of iron is here,
a witch's work, it must melt.

20 Gif ðu wære on fell scoten oððe wære on flæsc

                   scoten

   oððe wære on blod scoten

   oððe wære on lið scoten, næfre ne sy ðin lif atæsed;

   gif hit wære esa gescot oððe hit wære ylfa gescot

   oððe hit wære hægtessan gescot, nu ic wille ðin

                   helpan.

25 Þis ðe to bote esa gescotes; ðis ðe to bote ylfa

                  gescotes;

   ðis ðe to bote hægtessan gescotes; ic ðin wille helpan.

   Fleoh þær . . . on fyrgen-heafde.

   Hal westu, helpe ðin Drihten!"

  Nim þonne þæt seax; ado on wætan.

If you were shot in the skin or shot in the flesh   20
or were shot in the blood
or were shot in a limb, may your life never be injured;
if it were a shot of the æsir or it were a shot of elves
or it were a shot of witches, now I will help you.
This as your remedy for æsir shot; this as your remedy for   25
    elf shot;
this as your remedy for witch shot; I will help you.
Fly there . . . to the mountain headland.
Be well; may the Lord help you."

Take then that knife; put it in the liquid.

Metrical Charm 5

For Loss of Cattle

Þonne þe mon ærest secge þæt þin ceap sy losod, þonne
cweð þu ærest ær þu elles hwæt cweþe:

    "Bæðleem hatte seo buruh   þe Crist on acænned wæs,
    seo is gemærsod   geond ealne middan-geard;
5   swa þyos dæd for monnum   mære gewurþe
    þurh þa haligan   Cristes rode!
    Amen."

    Gebide þe þonne þriwa east and cweþ þonne þriwa:
9 *"Crux Christi ab oriente reducað."* Gebide þe þonne þriwa west
and cweð þonne þriwa: *"Crux Christi ab occidente reducat."*
Gebide þe þonne þriwa suð and cweþ þriwa: *"Crux Christi ab
austro reducat."* Gebide þonne þriwa norð and cweð þriwa:
*"Crux Christi ab aquilone reducað, crux Christi abscondita est et
14 inuenta est.* Iudeas Crist ahengon, dydon dæda þa wyrrestan,
hælon þæt hy forhelan ne mihtan. Swa þeos dæd nænige
þinga forholen ne wurþe þurh þa haligan Cristes rode.
Amen."

Metrical Charm 5

For Loss of Cattle

When someone first tells you that your livestock is lost, you should first say before you say anything else:

"Bethlehem is the name of the city where Christ was
    born,
it is famed throughout the world;
so let this deed be known among men   5
by the holy cross of Christ!
Amen."

Then pray three times to the east and say then three times: "Let the cross of Christ bring it back from the east." Then pray three times to the west and then say three times: 9 "Let the cross of Christ bring it back from the west." Then pray three times to the south and say three times: "Let the cross of Christ bring it back from the south." Then pray three times to the north and say three times: "Let the cross of Christ bring it back from the north, the cross was hidden and was found. Jews crucified Christ, did the worst things to   14 him, concealed what they could not hide. So, too, through the holy cross of Christ may this deed not remain hidden in any way. Amen."

Metrical Charm 6

For Delayed Birth

Se wif-man se hire cild afedan ne mæg gange to gewitenes
mannes birgenne and stæppe þonne þriwa ofer þa byrgenne
and cweþe þonne þriwa þas word:

> "Þis me to bote   þære laþan læt-byrde,
> ₅ þis me to bote   þære swæran swær-byrde,
> þis me to bote   þære laðan lam-byrde."

And þonne þæt wif seo mid bearne and heo to hyre hla-
forde on reste ga, þonne cweþe heo:

> "Up ic gonge,   ofer þe stæppe
> ₁₀ mid cwican cilde,   nalæs mid cwellendum,
> mid ful-borenum,   nalæs mid fægan."

And þonne seo modor gefele þæt þæt bearn si cwic, ga
þonne to cyrican, and þonne heo toforan þan weofode
cume, cweþe þonne:

> ₁₅ "Criste, ic sæde,   þis gecyþed!"

Se wif-mon se hyre bearn afedan ne mæge genime heo
sylf hyre agenes cildes gebyrgenne dæl, wry æfter þonne on
blace wulle and bebicge to cepe-mannum and cweþe þonne:

Metrical Charm 6

For Delayed Birth

Let the woman who cannot bring forth her child from the womb go to the grave of a dead person and step over that grave three times then say these words three times:

> "This as a remedy for me against the hateful slow birth,
> this as a remedy for me against the oppressive painful
>   birth,
> this as a remedy for me against the hateful lame birth."   5

And when the woman is with child and she goes to her lord in bed, then she should say:

> "Up I go, step over you
> with a live child, not at all with a dying, one   10
> with a full-born, not at all with one doomed to die."

And when the mother feels that the baby is alive, she should then go to church, and when she comes before the altar, she should say:

> "By Christ, I said, this has been made known."   15

Let the woman who cannot bring her baby to full term take part of her own child's grave, then wrap it in black wool and sell it to merchants and then say:

"Ic hit bebicge,   ge hit bebicgan,
20   þas sweartan wulle   and þysse sorge corn."

Se wif-man se ne mæge bearn afedan nime þonne anes
bleos cu meoluc on hyre handæ and gesupe þonne mid hyre
muþe and gange þonne to yrnendum wætere and spiwe þær
in þa meolc and hlade þonne mid þære ylcan hand þæs
25   wæteres muð fulne and forswelge. Cweþe þonne þas word:

"Gehwer ferde ic me þone mæran   maga þihtan,
mid þysse mæran   mete þihtan;
þonne ic me wille habban   and ham gan."

Þonne heo to þan broce ga, þonne ne beseo heo, no ne eft
30   þonne heo þanan ga, and þonne ga heo in oþer hus oþer heo
ut ofeode and þær gebyrge metes.

"I sell it, you should buy it,
this dark wool and seed of this sorrow." 20

Let the woman who cannot bring forth her baby then take the milk of a cow of one color in her hand and then sip it with her mouth and then go to running water and spit the milk in it and then with the same hand take a mouth full of water and swallow it. She should then say these words: 25

"Everywhere I carried with me that excellent, strong son,
strong with this excellent food;
then I wish to have control of my own body and go
home."

When she goes to the brook, then she should not look around nor when she goes away from there, and then she 30 should go into a house other than the one she exited from and there she should eat food.

Metrical Charm 7

For the Water-Elf Disease

Gif mon biþ on wæter-ælf-adle, þonne beoþ him þa hand-
næglas wonne and þa eagan tearige and wile locian niþer. Do
him þis to læcedome: eofor-þrote, cassuc, fone nioþoweard,
eow-berge, elehtre, eolone, mersc-mealwan crop, fen-minte,
dile, lilie, attor-laþe, polleie, marubie, docce, ellen, felt-erre,
6 wermod, streaw-bergean leaf, consolde. Ofgeot mid ealaþ,
do hælig-wæter to, sing þis gealdor ofer þriwa:

"Ic benne awrat   betest beado-wræda
swa benne ne burnon   ne burston
10 ne fundian   ne feologan
ne hoppettan,   ne wund waxsian
ne dolh diopian;   ac him self healde hale-wæge,
ne ace þe þon ma   þe eorþan on eare ace."

Sing þis manegum siþum: "Eorþe þe onbere eallum hire
15 mihtum and mægenum." Þas galdor mon mæg singan on
wunde.

214

Metrical Charm 7

For the Water-Elf Disease

If someone has the water-elf disease, then his fingernails will be livid and his eyes watery and he will want to look down. Give him this medicine: carline thistle, sedge, the lower part of fane, yew berry, lupine, elecampane, marshmallow sprout, water mint, dill, lily, fumitory, pennyroyal, marrubium, dock, elder tree, centaury, wormwood, strawberry leaves, daisy. Moisten with ale, add holy water, sing this charm three times:

"I have written out the best of troops for fighting disease
so wounds would not burn nor burst
nor worsen nor putrefy
nor throb, nor the wounds grow
nor the gash deepen; but let him hold the holy cup
    himself,
let it ache for you no more than with earth it aches in an
    ear."

Sing this many times: "May earth destroy you with all its strength and might." You can sing this charm on a wound.

215

Metrical Charm 8

For a Swarm of Bees

Wið ymbe nim eorþan, oferweorp mid þinre swiþran handa
under þinum swiþran fet, and cwet:

> "Fo ic under fot,   funde ic hit.
> Hwæt, eorðe mæg   wið ealra wihta gehwilce
> and wið andan   and wið æminde
> and wið þa micelan   mannes tungan."

And wið ðon forweorp ofer greot þonne hi swirman, and
cweð:

> "Sitte ge, sige-wif,   sigað to eorþan!
> Næfre ge wilde   to wuda fleogan.
> Beo ge swa gemindige   mines godes,
> swa bið manna gehwilc   metes and eþeles."

5

10

Metrical Charm 8

For a Swarm of Bees

For a swarm of bees, take some earth, throw it with your right hand under your right foot and say:

> "I take under foot, I have found it.
> Yes, earth can work against every creature
> and against malice and against envy   5
> and against the great human tongue."

And to counter them throw gravel over them when they swarm and say:

> "Sit down, victory women, sink to the earth!
> May you never fly wild to the woods.   10
> Be as mindful of my good
> as every person is of food and homeland."

Metrical Charm 9

For Loss of Cattle

Ne forstolen ne forholen nanuht þæs ðe ic age þe ma ðe
mihte Herod urne Drihten. Ic geþohte Sancte Eadelenan
and ic geþohte Crist on rode ahangen; swa ic þence þis feoh
to findanne, næs to oðfeorrganne, and to witanne, næs to
5 oðwyrceanne, and to lufianne, næs to oðlædanne.

    Garmund,   Godes ðegen,
    find þæt feoh   and fere þæt feoh
    and hafa þæt feoh   and heald þæt feoh
    and fere ham þæt feoh.
10   Þæt he næfre næbbe landes   þæt he hit oðlæde,
    ne foldan   þæt hit oðferie,
    ne husa   þæt he hit oðhealde.
    Gif hyt hwa gedo,   ne gedige hit him næfre!
    Binnan þrym nihtum   cunne ic his mihta,
15   his mægen and his mihta   and his mund-cræftas.
    Eall he weornige   swa syre wudu weornie,
    swa breðel seo   swa þystel,
    se ðe ðis feoh   oðfergean þence
    oððe ðis orf   oðehtian ðence.
20   Amen.

Metrical Charm 9

For Loss of Cattle

May nothing of what I own be stolen or hidden any more than Herod could our Lord. I thought of Saint Helena and I thought of Christ hanged on the cross; so I think to find this cattle, not take it away, and to keep it, not to harm it, and to hold it dear, not to carry it away. 5

Garmund, servant of God,
find the cattle and convey the cattle
and have the cattle and hold the cattle
and convey the cattle home.
May he never have land that he might carry it to, 10
nor earth that he might take it to,
nor houses so that he might hold it.
If anyone does it, may it never do him any good!
Within three nights, I will know his might,
his strength and his might and his protecting powers. 15
May he completely fade away as dry wood fades away,
be as weak as thistle,
he who thinks of carrying off this cattle
or of driving this livestock away.
Amen. 20

Metrical Charm 10

For Loss of Cattle

Ðis man sceal cweðan ðonne his ceapa hwilcne man forsto-
lenne. Cwyð ær he ænyg oþer word cweðe:

"Bethlem hattæ seo burh   ðe Crist on geboren wes,
seo is gemærsod   ofer ealne middan-geard;
swa ðeos dæd wyrþe   for monnum mære,
per crucem Christi!"

5

And gebide þe ðonne þriwa east and cweð þriwa: "*Crux
Christi ab oriente reducat.*" And þriwa west and cweð: "*Crux
Christi ab occidente reducat.*" And þriwa suð and cweð: "*Crux
Christi a meridie reducant.*" And þriwa norð and cweð: "*Crux
Christi abscondita sunt et inuenta est.* Iudeas Crist ahengon, ge-
didon him dæda þa wyrstan; hælon þæt hi forhelan ne mih-
ton. Swa næfre ðeos dæd forholen ne wyrðe *per crucem
Christi.*"

10

Metrical Charm 10

For Loss of Cattle

One should say this when someone has stolen one of his cattle. He should say before saying anything else:

> "Bethlehem is the name of the city where Christ was
>   born,
> it is famed throughout the world;
> so let this deed become known among the people,   5
> by the cross of Christ!"

And then pray to the east and say three times: "Let the cross of Christ bring it back from the east." And three times to the west: "Let the cross of Christ bring it back from the west." And three times to the south: "Let the cross of Christ bring it back from the south." And three times to the north   10 and say: "The cross of Christ was hidden and was found. Jews crucified Christ, did the worst things to him, concealed what they could not hide. So may this deed, by the Cross of Christ, never be hidden."

Metrical Charm 11

A Journey Charm

Ic me on þisse gyrde beluce   and on Godes helde
                                                bebeode
wið þane sara stice,   wið þane sara slege,
wið þane grymma gryre,
wið ðane micela egsa   þe bið eghwam lað,
5 and wið eal þæt lað   þe in to land fare.
Syge-gealdor ic begale,   sige-gyrd ic me wege,
word-sige and worc-sige.   Se me dege;
ne me mere ne gemyrre,   ne me maga ne geswence,
ne me næfre minum feore   forht ne gewurþe,
10 ac gehæle me Ælmihtig and Sunu   and frofre Gast,
ealles wuldres   wyrðig Dryhten,
swa swa ic gehyrde   heofna scyppende.
Abrame   and Isace
and swilce men,   Moyses and Iacob,
15 and Dauit and Iosep
and Evan and Annan   and Elizabet,
Saharie and ec Marie,   modur Cristes,
and eac þæ gebroþru,   Petrus and Paulus,

222

Metrical Charm 11

A Journey Charm

I make myself secure with this staff and commit myself into
     God's keeping
against the painful stitch, against the painful blow,
against the fierce terror,
against the great fear that is hateful to everyone,
and against all the misfortune that I encounter abroad.   5
A victory-bringing charm I chant, a victory-bringing rod I
     bear,
success in words, success in work. May this be good for me;
may no lake obstruct me nor a man afflict me
nor a fearful thing ever happen to me in my life,
but save me, Almighty, Son, and Spirit of consolation,   10
Lord worthy of all glory,
creator of the heavens, just as I have heard.
Abraham and Isaac
and such people, Moses and Jacob,
and David and Joseph   15
and Eve and Anna and Elizabeth,
Zacharias and also Mary, the mother of Christ,
and also the brothers, Peter and Paul,

and eac þusend   þinra engla
20 clipige ic me to are   wið eallum feondum.
Hi me ferion and friþion   and mine fore nerion,
eal me gehealdon,   me gewealdon,
worces stirende;   si me wuldres hyht
hand ofer heafod,   haligra rof,
25 sige-rofra sceolu,   soð-fæstra engla.
Biddu ealle   bliðu mode
þæt me beo Matheus helm,   Marcus byrne,
leoht lifes rof,   Lucos min swurd,
scearp and scir-ecg,   scyld Iohannes,
30 wuldre gewlitegod   wæl-gar Serafhin.
    Forð ic gefare,   frind ic gemete,
eal engla blæd,   eadiges lare.
Bidde ic nu sigeres God   Godes miltse,
sið-fæt godne,   smylte and lihte
35 windas on waroþum.   Windas gefran,
circinde wæter.   Simble gehælede
wið eallum feondum,   freond ic gemete wið,
þæt ic on þæs ælmihtgian frið   wunian mote,
belocun wið þam laþan   se me lyfes eht,
40 on engla blæd   gestaþelod,
and inna halre hand   heofna rices,
þa hwile þe ic on þis life   wunian mote.
Amen.

and also thousands of your angels
I call to me as a help against all enemies. 20
May they convey and keep me and protect my journey,
completely hold me and direct me,
protecting me from pain; let the hope of glory be for me
a sheltering hand, an array of the saints,
a host of the triumphant, righteous angels. 25
With an entirely happy heart, I pray
that Matthew be my helmet, Mark my mail shirt,
strong light of my life, Luke my sword,
sharp and bright edged, John my shield,
the Seraph my gloriously adorned deadly spear. 30
    Forth I go, I will find friends,
all the glory of the angels, the teaching of the blessed.
I ask now the God of victory for the mercy of God,
for a good journey, for calm and light
winds on the shores. I have heard of winds, 35
roaring waters. Always saved
against all enemies, may I meet with friends
so that I may dwell in the peace of the almighty,
protected from the hostile one who afflicts my life,
established in the glory of angels 40
and in the holy hand of the kingdom of heaven,
while I may dwell in this life.
Amen.

Metrical Charm 12

Against a Wen

Wenne, wenne,   wen-chichenne,
her ne scealt þu timbrien,   ne nenne tun habben,
ac þu scealt north eonene   to þan nihgan berhge,
þer þu hauest, ermig,   enne broþer.
5   He þe sceal legge   leaf et heafde.
Under fot wolues,   under ueþer earnes,
under earnes clea,   a þu geweornie.
Clinge þu alswa   col on heorþe,
scring þu alswa   scerne awage,
10   and weorne alswa   weter on anbre.
Swa litel þu gewurþe   alswa linset-corn

and miccli lesse alswa anes hand-wurmes hupe-ban, and
alswa litel þu gewurþe þet þu nawiht gewurþe.

Metrical Charm 12

Against a Wen

Wen, wen, little wen,
here you must not build nor have any dwelling,
but you must go from here to the nearby hill,
where you, poor wretch, have a brother.
He shall lay a leaf at your head.   5
Under the foot of the wolf, under the eagle's feather,
under the eagle's claw, you always will fade.
Wither like coal on the hearth,
shrink like filth on the wall,
and fade away like water in a pail.   10
You will become as little as a grain of linseed

and much smaller than the hip bone of a hand-worm, and
will you become so little that you will become nothing.

Note on the Texts

The texts of the Old English poems reproduced for this volume are presented in the order in which they are found in volumes III *(The Exeter Book)* and VI *(The Anglo-Saxon Minor Poems)* of the Anglo-Saxon Poetic Records (ASPR). Those volumes should be consulted for complete information about emendations, only the most important of which are mentioned here along with emendations suggested by other editions of the poems published after ASPR, especially Muir's *The Exeter Anthology.* Additional editions consulted for specific poems are referred to in the Notes to the Texts. Manuscript abbreviations are silently expanded; only emendations are noted.

Abbreviations

ASPR = The Anglo-Saxon Poetic Records: A Collective Edition. New York, 1931–1953. (See individual editions under Dobbie and under Krapp in the Bibliography.)

Bosworth-Toller = Joseph Bosworth, T. Northcote Toller, and A. Campbell. *An Anglo-Saxon Dictionary, Based on the Manuscript Collections of Joseph Bosworth. Supplement, by T. Northcote Toller, with Revised and Enlarged Addenda, by Alistair Campbell.* Oxford, 1992.

DOE = Antonette diPaolo Healey, ed., *Dictionary of Old English.* CD-ROM. Toronto, 2009.

Notes to the Texts

The reading adopted in the text is followed by the manuscript reading. Each of the poems has been edited in the ASPR: those in the first part, from *The Wanderer* to *The Ruin,* edited by Krapp and Dobbie in *The Exeter Book;* those in the second part, beginning with *Durham,* edited by Dobbie in *The Anglo-Saxon Minor Poems.* These two volumes provide manuscript information. Other editions consulted are noted separately under each title.

The Wanderer

See editions by Pope and Fulk, *Eight Old English Poems;* Mitchell and Robinson, *Guide;* and Klinck, *Old English Elegies.*

7 hryres: hryre   14 healde: healdne   22 minne: mine   24 waþuma: waþena   28 freond-leasne: freond lease   53 eft: oft   57 waþuma: waþema   59 mod-sefa min ne: modsefan minne   77 eall: ealle   78 weorniað: w oriað   89 deorce: deornce   102 hrusan: hruse

The Gifts of Mortals

13 oþþe: ond   30 sumum: sum   53 on: *not in MS*   66 gefeged: gefegan   70 wicg-cræfta: wic cræfta   76 hebbanne: habbenne   78 þearfe: þearf   87 est: eft   106a sumum: summum   109 þeaw-fæstne: þeaw fæf ne

Precepts

See edition by Shippey, *Poems of Wisdom*.

2 mon: *not in MS*   31 weorðe: weorð   53 geongum: geogum   73 forð
fyrn-gewritu: fyrn forð gewri tu

The Seafarer

See editions by Gordon, *Seafarer;* Pope and Fulk, *Eight Old English Poems;*
Mitchell and Robinson, *Guide;* and Klinck, *Old English Elegies*.

9 fruron: wæron   26 frefran: feran   52 gewitan: gewitað   56 seft-
eadig: eft eadig   63 hwæl-weg: wælweg   67 stondað: stondeð   69 ge-
gang: ge   72 bið: *not in MS*   75 fremum: fremman   79 blæd: blæð
82 nearon: næron   109 mon: mod   112 lufan: *not in MS*   115 swiþre:
swire   117 hwær we: hwær se

Vainglory

Ssee edition by Shippey, *Poems of Wisdom*.

3 onwreah: onwearh   8 witan: witon   10 ne: *not in MS*   12 druncen:
drucen   24 þringeð: þringe   36 feoð: feoh   39 sceolde: scealde
52 Se þe: seþe   60 wid-ledan: wid lædan

Widsith

See edition by Hill, *Minor Heroic Poems*.

2 monna: *not in MS*   mægþa: mærþa   on: *not in MS*   4 Him: hine
11 þeodna: þeoda   21 Holm-rygum: holm rycum   Heoden: henden
43 bi Fifeldore: bifi fel dore   62 mid Sycgum: Sycgum   65 geþah:
geþeah   78 wiolena: wiolane   101 swegle: swegl   103 Ðonne: don

THE FORTUNES OF MORTALS

See edition by Shippey, *Poems of Wisdom*.

21 beame: beane   43 Sumne: sum   brond aswencan: brondas þencan
44 lig: lif   63 forð: forh   73 weorþað: weorþeð   83 sceacol: gearo
84 neomegende: neome cende   93 weroda nergend: werod anes god

MAXIMS I

See edition by Shippey, *Poems of Wisdom*.

38 nyde: nyd   40 hi: hine   54 sund: wind   61 eorod: worod
85 leof: lof   89 æþelinga: æþelinge   100 belihð: behlið   101 fyrwet-
geornra: fyrwet geonra   109 alyfed: alyfeð   139 lofes: leofes   175 eo-
rles: eorle   179 mon tomælde: mon to mon to mælde   196 broðor:
bro   197 serede: nerede

THE ORDER OF THE WORLD

6 dogra: wundra   19 bewritan: bewriten   38 on: *not in MS*   42 hal-
gan: halge   46 gecynd: gemynd   77 witan: witeð   86 hi: *not in MS*
87 stondað: stondeð   91 heorð-werud: eorðwerud

THE RHYMING POEM

See editions by Macrae-Gibson, *Riming Poem;* and Klinck, *Old English
Elegies*.

6 wægon: wægum   7 wicg: wic   18 in: *not in MS*   22 steold: steald
24 gomen: gomel   45 in: *not in MS*   feore: feor   53 linnið: linnað
62 borg-sorg: burg sorg   65 singryn: singrynd   searo-fearo: sæcra
fearo   66 græf hæft hafað: græft hafað   70 gehwyrft: gehwyrt
71 græf: scræf   73 neaht: neah   74 ofonn: on fonn   eardes: heardes
79 gehloten: ge hlotene

Deor

See editions by Pope and Fulk, *Eight Old English Poems;* Klinck, *Old English Elegies;* and Hill, *Minor Heroic Poems.*

25 wenum: wenan   30 earfoða: earfoda

Wulf and Eadwacer

See editions by Mitchell and Robinson, *Guide;* Baker, "Classroom Edition"; and Klinck, *Old English Elegies.*

16 earmne: earne

The Wife's Lament

See editions by Leslie, *Three Old English Elegies;* Cassidy and Ringler, *Bright's Grammar;* Pope and Fulk, *Eight Old English Poems;* Mitchell and Robinson, *Guide;* and Klinck, *Old English Elegies.*

3 aweox: weox   15 hired: heard   20 -hycgendne: hycgende   24 seo neawest: *not in MS*   25 Sceal: seal   37 sittan: sittam

Resignation B: An Exile's Lament

See edition by Klinck, *Old English Elegies.*

3 forð-weg: ferðweg   12 martirdom: mart dom   30 *the line is defective*   44 gewunian: unian   46 gecweme: gecwe   48 selast: *not in MS*

Pharaoh

3 ongunnon: ongunn   6 siex hundred godra: siex hun a   7 yþa færgripe: yþ

The Husband's Message

See editions by Leslie, *Three Old English Elegies;* and Klinck, *Old English Elegies.*

8 hafu: hofu   21 læran: læram   30 gelimpan: *not in MS*   45 ne
meodo-dreama: nemeodo dreama

The Ruin

See editions by Leslie, *Three Old English Elegies;* Klinck, *Old English Elegies;*
and Orchard, "Reconstructing."

4 hring-geat: hrim geat torras   12 weal-steall: *not in MS*   wæpnum:
num   fel on foldan forð-gesceaft bærst: fel on   14 grund eall for-
swealg: *not in MS*   17 gebeag: beag   18 monade myne: mo yne
26 secg-rofa: secg rof   31 hrof: rof   33 gefrætwed: gefræt weð
41 þing: *not in MS*   45 oþþæt: þþæt

Durham

Text from MS Ff. i. 27, University Library, Cambridge (C); variants from
Hickes (H).

2 steppa: Steopa *H*   3 ymbeornad: ymb eornað *H*   4 ea: Ean *H*
stronge: strong *H*   5 feola fisca: fcola fisca *C;* Fisca feola *H*   kyn:
kinn *H*   gemonge: gemong *H*   6 ðær: ðere *H*   is: *not in H*
wudafæstern: Wuda festern *H*   micel: mycel *H*   7 wuniad: Wuniað *H*
wycum: wicum *H*   8 deope: deopa *H*   in: im *H*   gecyðed: geciðed *H*
10 Cudberch: Cuðbercht *H*   11 clene: clæne *H*   cyninges: *H;* cyniuges
C   heafud: heofud *H*   12 Osuualdes: Osualdes *H*   Engle: Engla *H*
biscop: bisceop *H*   13 Eadberch: Ædbercht *H*   Eadfrið: Ædfrid *H*
14 midd: mid *H*   Æðelwold: *H;* Æðelwold *C*   biscop: bisceop *H*
15 Beda: *H;* beba *C*   abbot: abbet *H*   16 clene: clæne *H*   Cudberte:
Cuðberchte *H*   gecheðe: gicheðe *H*   17 his: *H;* wis *C*   18 Eardiæð:
Eardiað *H*   minstre: mynstre *H*   20 ðær: *H;* ðe *C*   monia: monige *H*
ðes: *not in H*   writ: writa *H*   21 midd: Mid *H*   drihnes: drihtnes *H*

The Rune Poem

See editions by Shippey, *Poems of Wisdom;* and Halsall, *Rune Poem.*

23 sorge: forge   31 geworuht: ge worulit   41 secg eard: seccard
53 heah: þeah   56 hæleþas: hæleþe   60 oðrum: odrum   66 gymeð:
gym   68 eft: est   72 rihtes: rihter   73 bolde: blode   86 fyrd-
geatewa: fyrd geacewa   87 eafix: ea fixa   88 foldan: faldan

Solomon and Saturn

Based on MS 442 (A) and 41 (B), Corpus Christi College, Cambridge; see
editions by Shippey, *Poems of Wisdom;* and Anlezark, *Dialogues.*

9 samnode: samode *B*   11 oððe: *not in B but in A*   13 Sille: Wille *in B*
16 gebryrded: gebrydded *in B*   18 fare: fa   25 worað: *A;* warað *B*
he: *not in B but in A*   31 seolfres: *A;* silofres *B*   35 hwearfað: *A;* hwarfað
B eaðost: *A;* eaðusð *B*   37 heofona: *A;* heofna *B*   38 getæl-rime: *A;* ge
tales rime *B*   39 gepalmtwigede: *A;* ge palm twigude *B*   40 heofonas
A; heofnas *B*   halige: *A;* ha lie *B*   41 gefylleð: gesylleð *A;* gefilleð *B*
43 Swylce: *A;* Swilce *B*   44 dros: dream *A;* dry *B*   45 seofan: *A;* sefan *B*
46 egesfullicran: *A;* eges fullicra *B*   ðonne: *A;* þane *B*   gripu: *A;* gripo *B*
47 ðonne: *A;* þon *B* heo: *not in B*   48 gifrust: *A;* gifrost *B*   wealleð: *A;*
weallað *B*   49 Forðon: *A;* forðan *B*   51 steoreð: *A;* stefeð *B*   52 heo-
fona rices: *A;* heofonrices *B*   here-geatewa: *A;* heregea towe *B*   wigeð:
A; wegeð *B*   53 organ: *A;* organan *B*   54 begonganne: *A;* be gangen ne *B*
ðam ðe: *A;* þa þe *B*   gast: *A;* gæst *B*   55 meltan: *A;* miltan *B*   mergan:
A; merian *B*   56 scyldum: scyldigu *A;* scyldu *B*   scippend: *A;* scep
pend *B*   58 fyrwit: *A;* fyrwet *B*   59 gemengeð: *A;* geond mengeð *B*
60 hefenum: *A;* heofnum *B*   dreoseð: *A;* dreogeð *B*   61 bysig: *A;* bisi *B*
62 neah: *not in B*   hædre: *A;* hearde *B*   63 gimmum: *A;* gym mum *B*
64 sylfren: *A;* seolofren *B*   leaf: *not in B*   65 god-spel secgan: *A;* god
spellian *B*   66 seofan: *A;* sefan *B*   snytro: *A;* snytero *B*   saule: *A;*
sawle *B*   67 *entire line omitted from A*   68 saule: *A;* sawle *B*   sien-nihte:
A; syn nihte *B*   69 gefeccan: *A;* gefetian *B*   hie: *A;* hi *B*   70 hie: *A;*
hi *B*   71 clusum: *A;* clausum *B*   73 he ahieðeð: *A;* hege hege hideð *B*

74 toweorpeð: *A;* to worpeð *B*   getimbreð: *A;* getym breð *B*
75 middan-gearde: *A;* middan geardes *B*   76 staðole strengra: *A;* staðole
he is strengra *B*   ealra: *A;* ealle *B*   77 Lamena: *A;* lamana *B*   78 he is:
A; he his *B*   dumbra: *A;* deadra *B*   79 scyld: *A;* scild *B*   scyp-
pendes: *A;* scippendes *B*   80 ferigend: *A;* feriend *B*   nerigend: *A;* ne
riend *B*   81 earmra fisca: *A;* earma fixa *B*   82 welm: [.:elm *A;* wlenco *B*
83 on westenne: *A;* westenes *B*   84 ðone: *A;* þono *B*   85 soðlice: *A;*
smealice *B*   siemle: *A;* symle *B*   85–86 wile lufian: *A;* luian wile *B*
86 gæst: *A;* gesið *B*   87 feohtende: *A;* feohterne *B*   gebrengan: *A;*
gebringan *B*   88 on: *not in B*   ierne:A; yorn *B*   gebrengest: *A;* gebri
ngeð *B*   89 prologa prima: *A;* Plogo prim. *B*   *B omits the runes from
this line and the following*   90 guð-mæcga: *A;* guð maga *B*   gierde: *A;*
gyrde *B*   91 a: *not in B*   grymman: g [. . .: man *A;* grymman *B*
92 sweopað: *A;* swapeð *B*   him: *not in B*   fylgeð: *A;* læteð *underdotted for
deletion with* filgið *written above in B*   93 ofslihð: *A;* ofslehð *B*   94 T: *B
ends here*   106 ængestan: engestan *A*   108 O: *not in A*   110 bermur-
nað: be murneð *A*   123 I and: *not in A*   126 hæftling: hæft lig *A*
180 ræswan: ræswum *A*   194 cludas: claudas *A*   200 eðell: *not in A*
201 Hierusalem: hierusa   205 secean: seccan *A*   216 deað: of deað *A*
223 scineð: scinað *A*   255 Filistina: filitina *A*   261 healdað: healdeð
276 gebendan: gebemdan or gebeindan *A*   281 fruman: fruma *A*
288 and: *not in A*   294 ræceð: receð *A*   297 standendne: stan dene *A*
305 he: hie *A*   308 *a leaf is missing from the MS here*   327 Wa: swa
339 næren ðe: nærende *A*   344 gedæled: gode led *A*   358 mægn:
mægnn *A*   362 forildan: for ildo *A*   384 agen: ængan   387 gesceaft:
ge seaft *A*   396 neod-cræfte: cræfte *A*   399 *a leaf is missing from the MS
here*   428 strengra: strenra *A*   453 dierne: diere *A*   478 man: man
man *A*   479 ðe: *not in A*   480 clæne: *not in A*   482 Æghwylcum men:
Æghwylc *A*   483 dæg cymeð: eð

MAXIMS II

See edition by Shippey, *Poems of Wisdom.*

19 earm: earn   24 mencgan: mecgan   40 of: on

BEDE'S DEATH SONG

There are twenty-nine manuscripts of this poem, eleven in the Northumbrian dialect, seventeen in the West Saxon, and one in between. See *The Anglo-Saxon Minor Poems,* pp. c–cvii and p. 108, for detailed discussion. Only the West Saxon version is translated here, and the text is from MS Digby 211, with variants from the other MSS.

LATIN-ENGLISH PROVERBS

Text from MS Cotton Faustina A.x (F) with variants from Royal MS 2B. v (R).

1 frigesscit: refriescit *R*   squalescit: quualescit *R*   4 alaðaþ: alaþað *R* aðystrað: aþeostrað *R*   5 omnia: *not in R*   6 forealdað: ealdað *R*

METRICAL CHARM 1: FOR UNFRUITFUL LAND

35 gefyllan: gefylle   44 to are þam: þa are   55 hehra: hen se   scirra: scire   56 þæra: þære   57 þæra: þære   60 heofonum: eofonum   66 word: woru d   72 innewerdre: Innewerdne

METRICAL CHARM 2: THE NINE HERBS CHARM

6 þam: þa   8 openo: opone   9a ðe: ðy   crætu: cræte   9b ðe: ðy   10a ðe: ðy   10b þe: þy   20 ðam: ða   30 magon: ongan   31 he man: henan   43 wið fær-bregde: wið þæs hond wið frea begde   44 manra: minra   47b ðy: ða   53 þystel-geblæd: þysgeblæd   58 adle: alde   60 þær: and   nean: *not in MS*   68 æg-gemongc: aagemogc   69 on do: onde   73 on do: onde

METRICAL CHARM 3: AGAINST A DWARF

2 writan: writ tan   6 bufan: hufan   9 spider-wiht: spiden with   11 legde þe: legeþe   13 dweores: deores

METRICAL CHARM 4: FOR A STABBING PAIN

11 flane: flan   12 lytel: lyte   14 wundrum: wund   18 isernes: isenes   27 Fleoh: fled   fyrgen-heafde: fyrgen hæfde

METRICAL CHARM 5: FOR LOSS OF CATTLE

4 gemærsod: ge mærsad

METRICAL CHARM 6: FOR DELAYED BIRTH

17 wry: þry   21 Se wif-man se ne mæge: Seman seþemæge

METRICAL CHARM 7: FOR THE WATER-ELF DISEASE

8 benne: binne

METRICAL CHARM 8: FOR A SWARM OF BEES

7 wiððon: wið on

METRICAL CHARM 9: FOR LOSS OF CATTLE

12 he hit oðhealde: hehit oðhit healde   16 syre: syer   17 seo: þeo

METRICAL CHARM 10: FOR LOSS OF CATTLE

1 forstolenne: forstelenne   2 Cwyð: cyð   8 þriwa: in   9 þriwa: in   10 þriwa: in

METRICAL CHARM 11: A JOURNEY CHARM

2 stice: sice   8 mere: mer   10a ælmihtig: ælmihti gi   10b and: *not in MS*   11 wyrðig: wyrdig   19 þinra: þira   22b me: men   25 sceolu: sceote   27a me beo Matheus: me beo hand ofer heaford mathe us   29 scearp: scerp   30 wæl-gar: wega   35 windas on waroþum: wind wereþum   36 simble gehælede: simbli gehaleþe   38 þæs ælmihtgian frið: þis ælmih gian on his frið   39 þam: þa   40 blæd: bla blæd   41 heofna: hofna   rices: rices blæd

METRICAL CHARM 12: AGAINST A WEN

6 wolues: uolmes   9 scerne: scesne

Notes to the Translations

The Wanderer

For Germanic and Celtic analogues for the Old English elegies generally, see Calder et al., *Sources and Analogues II*, 23–64. For Latin analogues, see Allen and Calder, *Sources and Analogues*, 133–53.

1   *an-haga* (lone dweller): See *Beowulf,* line 2368.

5   *Wyrd bið ful aræd* (Fate is fully fixed): *Wyrd* in Old English, which comes from the verb *weorðan* (to become), means something like "that which happens." The modern English word "fate" contains more determinism in it than does the Old English word, but I use it here and throughout the following translations because it is the closest one-word equivalent available to us.

22, 35   *gold-wine* (gold friend): In a lord-retainer relationship, the lord dealt out treasure in return for service and loyalty.

24, 57   *waþuma gebind* (the binding of the waves): This phrase occurs only in *The Wanderer,* and it is unclear what it means. *The Rune Poem,* lines 63–64, may partially elucidate it, however: "Water seems endless to people if they have to venture out on the tilting ship."

27   *mine wise* (understand my feeling): The translation of this phrase is by Pope and Fulk, *Eight Old English Poems.*

55   *Fleotendra ferð no þær fela bringeð cuðra cwide-giedda* (The spirit of the floating ones does not bring many known utterances there): An instance of litotes. The birds ("the floating ones") do not make any utterances at all that are meaningful to humans. See *The Seafarer,* lines 19–21.

241

61   *flett* (floor): Synecdoche for "mead hall."

65   *Wita sceal geþyldig* (The wise man must be patient): Note the gnomic wisdom from here to line 72.

80   *Sume* (some): This begins a series of four instances of this word, an iterative device used also in *The Gifts of Mortals,* lines 30ff., and *The Fortunes of Mortals,* lines 10ff., and elsewhere in Old English poetry.

87   *enta geweorc* (works of giants): See *The Ruin,* line 2, and *Maxims II,* line 2. This term refers to the Romans, who built with stone instead of wood.

88   *þisne weal-steal* (this foundation): For a similar meditation on a ruined building, see *The Ruin.*

92   *Hwær cwom mearg* (Where has the horse gone): The theme of past glory and prosperity expressed here is linked to the *ubi sunt* (where are) theme in Latin religious literature by Cross, "'Ubi Sunt' Passages."

96   *swa heo no wære* (as if it hadn't been): See *The Wife's Lament,* line 24.

98   *wyrmlicum* (with serpents): These are probably decorative motifs left by the Roman "giants."

100   *wyrd seo mære* (fate the mighty): See *The Seafarer,* line 115; *Maxims I,* line 5; *The Ruin,* line 24; and *Solomon and Saturn,* line 444.

THE GIFTS OF MORTALS

For Germanic and Celtic analogues for Old English wisdom poetry generally, see Calder et al., *Sources and Analogues II,* 71–100. For an Old English analogue for this poem, see Cynewulf's *Christ II,* lines 659–91, in Bjork, *Old English Poems of Cynewulf;* for an Old Norse analogue, see Calder et al., *Sources and Analogues II,* 70; and for a Latin analogue, see Allen and Calder, *Sources and Analogues,* 154–55.

51   *rynig* (good in counsel): The meaning of this word is debated. If the vowel *y* is short, the word would relate to running, meaning something like "good at running." If the vowel is long, which is more likely, the word probably derives from *run* (counsel).

73   *tæfle* (tables): This could be a dice game or a board game such as chess. See *The Fortunes of Mortals* , line 70.

80–81   *Sum bið fugel-bona, hafeces cræftig* (One is a fowler, skilled with the hawk): See *The Fortunes of Mortals,* lines 85–92; *Maxims II,* lines 17–18; and Oggins, "Falconry."

Precepts

6–7   *feond þam oþrum wyrsan gewyrhta* (an enemy to others in worse deeds): I take *feond* in apposition to *God* in this translation, but *feond* could also refer to the devil and the phrase translated as an elliptical construction: "the devil [a lord] to others in worse deeds."

9   *Fæder ond modor freo þu mid heortan* (Love your father and your mother with your heart): See the Fourth Commandment, *Exodus* 20:12.

19–20   *He þe mid wite gieldeð, swylce þam oþrum mid ead-welan* (He will repay you with punishment, as he will repay others with prosperity): See *Deor,* lines 31–34.

31   *þu næfre fæcne weorðe freonde þinum* (you should never be deceitful to your friend): See *Maxims I,* line 144.

46   *toscead simle* (always distinguish): See *Beowulf,* lines 287–89.

The Seafarer

19–22   *hwilum ylfete song dyde ic me to gomene, ganetes hleoþor ond huilpan sweg fore hleahtor wera, mæw singende fore medo-drince* (at times taking the song of the wild swan as my entertainment, the cry of the gannet and the sound of the curlew instead of the laughter of men, the singing seagull instead of mead): See *The Wanderer,* line 55.

29   *wlonc ond wingal* (proud and flushed with wine): See *The Ruin,* line 34.

31   *Nap nihtscua* (The night shadow grew dark): See *The Wanderer,* line 104.

32   *corna caldost* (coldest of grains): See *The Rune Poem,* line 25.

38   *el-þeodigra eard* (land of strangers): This can refer to foreign lands or kingdoms or to heaven. See note in Muir, *Exeter Anthology*.

43   *to hwon hine dryhten gedon wille* (as to what purpose the Lord might have in store): The "sea voyage" seems pretty clearly a metaphor for life. See *An Exhortation to Christian Living*, line 61, where this sentiment, similarly phrased, also appears, as Muir notes in *Exeter Anthology*.

53   *Swylce geac monað geomran reorde* (The cuckoo likewise urges with a sad voice): The cuckoo can be a harbinger of summer, as in *Guthlac A*, line 744, or a sign of sorrow, sickness, and death. See the note to this line in Leslie, *Three Old English Elegies*. Here and in *The Husband's Message*, line 23, the cuckoo is sad.

62   *an-floga* (lone flyer): This could be the cuckoo in line 53 or a metaphorical expression of the speaker's heart or soul developed in lines 58–64. See note in Muir, *Exeter Anthology*.

65   *þis deade life* (this dead life): Note the oxymoron: earthly life is temporary and will end; eternal life will not.

70   *adl oþþe yldo* (disease or old age): See *Maxims I*, line 10.

89   *wið ælda* (among people): Bosworth-Toller translates this as "against the age" in the entry for *ældu* and as here in the entry for *wið* (III.13). In context, the latter makes more sense to me.

106   *Dol biþ se þe him his Dryhten ne ondrædeþ; cymeð him se deað unþinged* (Foolish is the one who does not dread his Lord; death comes on him unexpected): See *Maxims I*, line 35.

111–15   *scyle monna gehwylc mid gemete healdan wiþ leofne lufan ond wið laþne bealo, þeah þe he hine wille fyres fulne habban oþþe on bæle for-bærnedne his geworhtne wine* (everyone should hold in moderation love of friend and spite for foe even if the foe may want him steeped in fire or the fast friend consumed on a funeral pyre): This translation is indebted to Pope and Fulk, *Eight Old English Poems*, 110.

115   *Wyrd* (Fate): See note to *The Wanderer*, line 5.

VAINGLORY

3   *Word-hord* (Word hoard): See the Introduction, note 2.

6   *Godes agen bearn* (God's own son): This could refer to a human

	being or to Christ. See the discussion in Shippey, *Poems of Wisdom,* 7–8.
7	*þone wacran* (the weaker one): This could refer to a human being or to Satan. See the discussion in Shippey, *Poems of Wisdom,* 7–8.
16	*wordum wrixlað* (exchanging words): See *Beowulf,* lines 366 and 874, and *Riddle 60,* line 10.
49	*gode orfeormne* (destitute of good): This phrase may also be translated as "destitute of God."
51	*þæt gyd* (this song): Huppé, *Web of Words,* 20, asserts that lines 55 to 66 are based on Psalms 36:12, where David asks God not to allow the proud to trample on him or the evil to drive him away.
80	*Godes agen bearn* (God's own son): See line 6.
81	*wilsum in worlde* (delightful in the world): See line 7.

Widsith

For Celtic analogues for this poem, see Calder et al., *Sources and Analogues II,* 101–5. For full discussions of the names that follow, consult Hill, *Minor Heroic Poems,* from which most of the information for the notes on *Widsith* derives.

1	*Widsith:* "Far Traveler," perhaps a real name but more likely a fictitious one that describes the "far-traveling" mind of any poet. *Word-hord* (Word hoard): See the Introduction, note 2.
3	*flette* (floor): Synechdoche for "mead hall."
4	*Myrgingum* (Myrgings): Widsith's tribe. Identity unknown.
5	*Ealhhilde* (Ealhhild): The wife of either Eadgils, Widsith's lord and lord of the Myrgings, or of Eormanric.
6	*freoþu-webban* (peace weaver): A woman married to a man from another tribe with which her tribe has been feuding. The marriage could create peace between those tribes. See Frantzen, *Keywords,* 209–13.
8	*Ongle* (Anglen): District in Schleswig. *Eormanrices* (of Eormanric): King of the Ostrogoths and mentioned pejoratively in *Deor,* line 21.
14	*Hwala:* Identity unknown.
19	*Becca Baningum* (Becca the Banings): Identities of the king and his tribe are unknown.

Burgendum Gifica (Gifica the Burgundians): Gifica was a fifth-century king, father of Guthhere in line 66, below.

20 *Casere weold Creacum* (Ceasar ruled the Greeks): Caesar here would be the emperor of Constantinople.

Celic (Celic): Identity unknown.

21 *Hagena Holmrygum* (Hagena the Rugas): Father of Hild in the Scandinavian and German traditions. See note to *Deor,* line 39.

Heoden Glommum (Heoden the Glommas): Heoden is the abductor of Hild in the Scandinavian legend.

22 *Witta weold Swæfum* (Witta ruled the Swæfe): Identities unknown. The tribe seems to belong to the Swabian group, however.

Wada Hælsingum (Wada the Hælsings): In the German and Scandinavian traditions, Wada is either a great warrior or a supernatural being linked to the sea. The Hælsings, apparently a Baltic tribe, are unknown except perhaps in the Swedish and Danish names for towns on the opposite sides of the Kattegat sound, Helsingborg and Helsingør.

23 *Meaca* (Meaca): Identity unknown.

Mearchealf Hundingum (Mearchealf the Hundings): Identities unknown.

24 *Þeodric weold Froncum* (Theodoric ruled the Franks): Theodoric I, who was the son of Clovis and ruled the Franks 511–534. The Franks, according to Frantzen, *Keywords,* 106–10, were a group of peoples who expanded as their territory expanded.

Rondingum (Rondings): Identity unknown.

25 *Breoca Brondingum* (Breoca the Brondings): Breoca or Breca is Beowulf's opponent in a swimming contest in his youth (see *Beowulf,* ll. 506–606.) The identity of the Brondings is unknown.

Billing Wernum (Billing the Wernas): Identity of Billing is unknown. The Wernas may have been neighbors of the Angles.

26 *Oswine weold Eowum* (Oswine ruled the Eowan): Identity of Oswine is unknown. The Eowan could be a tribe either on Öland in the Baltic or on one of the islands in the Kattegat strait between Sweden and Denmark.

Gefwulf: Identity unknown.

27   *Fin:* See the Finnsburg episode in *Beowulf,* lines 1063–1159.

28   *Sigehere:* Identity unknown, although Saxo and Snorri mention a king Sigarus or Sigarr of the Danes, or Siklingar.

29   *Hnæf Hocingum* (Hnæf the people of Hoc): Hnæf is the son of Hoc and brother of Hildeburh in the Finnsburg episode in *Beowulf,* where he is chief of the Half-Danes.

Helm Wulfingum (Helm the Wulfings): Identity of Helm is unknown. The Wulfings are a Scandinavian tribe that the *Beowulf* poet locates near the Geats and the Danes.

30   *Wald Woingum* (Wald the Woingas): Identities unknown.

Wod Þyringum (Wod the Thuringians): Identity of Wod is unknown. The Thuringians were a tribe from east of the Rhine.

31   *Sæferð Sycgum* (Sæferth the Secgan): Identity of Sæferth is unknown. The Secgan is a Germanic coastal tribe mentioned in *The Fight at Finnsburg,* line 24.

Ongendþeow (Ongendtheow): In the English tradition, a late fifth-century king of the Swedes mentioned in several places in *Beowulf.*

32   *Sceafthere Ymbrum* (Sceafthere the Ymbras): Identities unknown.

Sceafa Longbeardum (Sceafa the Lombards): Sceafa is the probable father of Scyld in the Danish royal genealogy at the beginning of *Beowulf* (Scyld Scefing). Only in *Widsith* is he identified as the ruler of the fierce Lombards.

33   *Hun Hætwerum* (Hun the Hætwere): The identity of Hun is unknown. The Hætwere are mentioned in *Beowulf* (with the spelling Hetware) as partnering with the Franks to resist Hygelac's raid on Frisia.

Holen Wrosnum (Holen the Wrosnan): Identities unknown.

34   *Hringweald:* Identity unknown.

Herefarena: Identity unknown.

35   *Offa weold Ongle* (Offa ruled the Angles): Offa flourished during the second half of the fourth century.

Alewih: Identity unknown.

43   *Fifeldore:* The Lower Eider.

45   *Hroþwulf ond Hroðgar* (Hrothwulf and Hrothgar): Hrothwulf is

25

the nephew of Hrothgar, the Danish king in *Beowulf* whose hall, Heorot, is attacked constantly by the monster Grendel.

48 *Ingeldes* (of Ingeld): Ingeld was the son-in-law of Hrothgar, whose daughter he married in order to make peace between his tribe and Hrothgar's. The peace did not hold, however.

49 *Heorote:* The legendary mead hall of Danish kings that seems to have stood at Lejre near Roskilde in Denmark.

   Heaðobeardna (Heathobard): Ingeld's tribe, the Heathobards, is unknown outside of *Widsith* and *Beowulf,* where it is defeated when it attacks Heorot.

59 *Wenlum* (Wenlas): Mentioned in *Beowulf,* line 348. They inhabited either Vendel in Uppland, Sweden, or Vendill (modern Vendsyssel) in northern Jutland, Denmark.

   Wærnum (Wernas): Tacitus mentions this tribe (the Varini), apparently a neighbor of the Angles, in his *Germania,* chapter 40.

60 *Gefþum* (Gepidae): An East Germanic tribe also mentioned in *Beowulf,* line 2494.

   Winedum (Wends): A Slavonic tribe mentioned by Tacitus as the Veneti in *Germania,* chapter 46.

   Gefflegum (Gefflegas): Identity unknown.

62 *Sycgum* (Secgan): The Secgan is a Germanic coastal tribe mentioned in *The Fight at Finnsburg,* line 24.

   Sweordwerum (Swordsmen): Identity unknown.

63 *Hronum* (Hronas): Identity unknown.

   Heaþoreamum (Heathoremes): The Raumarici according to Jordanes; this tribe flourished at the head of the Oslo fjord in Norway.

64 *Þyringum* (Thuringians): A tribe from east of the Rhine.

   Þrowendum (Throwendas): Probably the inhabitants of the Trondheim area in Norway.

66 *Guðhere* (Guthhere): Fifth-century king of the Burgundians.

68 *Frumtingum* (Frumtings): Malone identifies these as the followers of Framta, a fifth-century king in what is now Spain. Hill, *Minor Heroic Poems,* 104, points out that the name could also mean "the original people" or "chief people."

69   *Rugum* (Rugas): The Rugii that Tacitus talks of in *Germania,* chapter 44.

     Glommum (Glommas): Perhaps the Lemovii of Tacitus's *Germania,* chapter 44.

70   *Ælfwine:* Alboin, king of the Lombards (565–572).

74   *Eadwine:* Audoin, king of the Lombards (ca. 546–565).

75   *Seringum* (Serings): A tribe from the East? See the note in Hill, *Minor Heroic Poems,* 122–23.

79   *Scridefinnum* (the Scride-Finns): Lapplanders.

80   *Lidwicingum* (Lidwicings): Either the Armoricans of Brittany or the Letavici mentioned in the *Anglo-Saxon Chronicle* under the year 855.

     Leonum (Leonas): Probably a Scandinavian tribe that Ptolemy refers to as the Leuoni.

81   *Hundingum* (Hundings): A people perhaps from the south Baltic coast.

85   *Mofdingum* (Mofdings): Perhaps the Moabites.

86   *Amothingum* (Amothings): Identity unknown. Perhaps the Ammonites.

     East-Þyringum (East Thuringians): We do not know if this is the same as the Thuringians in lines 30 and 64 or another Germanic tribe east of them or a tribe from Asia.

87   *Eolum* (Eolas): Identity unknown. Both Germanic and oriental possibilities have been suggested.

     Istum (Istas): Identity unknown. It could be either a Germanic or an oriental tribal name.

     Idumingum (Idumings): Perhaps the Idumeans or the Edomites from the Bible.

93   *Eadgils:* Lord of the Myrgings and therefore Widsith's lord.

97   *Ealhhild:* The wife of either Eadgils, Widsith's lord, or of Eormanric.

98   *Eadwine:* Audoin, king of the Lombards (ca. 546–565).

103   *Scilling:* Perhaps a fellow poet or perhaps Widsith's harp.

112   *Heðcan* (Hethca): Identity unknown.

     Beadecan (Beadeca): Identity unknown.

249

Herelingas (the Harlungs): Nephews of Eormanric.

113   *Emercan* (Emerca), *Fridlan* (Fridla): Perhaps the Harlungs of the previous line; perhaps aligned with Ostrogotha.

         Eastgotan (Ostrogotha): Ruler of the Ostrogoths, who flourished 218–250.

115   *Seccan* (Secca): Identity unknown.

         Beccan (Becca): King of the Baningas, line 19.

         Seafolan (Seafola): Sabene in some Middle High German epics. It is not clear which of the three characters is referred to here.

         Þeodric (Theodoric): Probably Theodoric the Ostrogoth who ruled Italy 493–526 and is probably mentioned in line 18 of *Deor.*

116   *Heaþoric* (Heathoric): This could be the fierce king of the Goths, Heiðrekr, in *Hervarar saga.*

         Sifecan (Sifeca): Usually regarded as the evil counselor Sifka in *Þiðriks saga.*

         Hliþe (Hlithe): Possibly the equivalent of the Old Norse Hlǫðr, the half brother of Angantýr in *Hervarar saga.*

         Incgenþeow (Incgentheow): Usually interpreted as equivalent to the Old Norse Angantýr from *Hervarar saga.*

117   *Eadwine:* Audoin, king of the Lombards (ca. 546–565).

         Elsan (Elsa): Identity unknown.

         Ægelmund: The first king of the Lombards, who flourished ca. 175.

         Hungar: Identity unknown.

118   *Wiþmyrginga* (Withmyrgings): This could be a subgroup of the Myrgings.

119   *Wulfhere:* Identity unknown.

         Wyrmhere: Ormarr in the Old Norse *Hervarar saga,* chapter 10.

123   *Rædhere:* Identity unknown.

         Rondhere: Identity unknown.

         Rumstan: Identity unknown.

         Gislhere: Perhaps an early king of the Burgundians.

124   *Wiþergield* (Withergield): Identity unknown.

         Freoþeric (Frederick): Identity unknown.

         Wudgan (Wudga): Son of Weland.

Haman (Hama): Companion of Wudga. He is mentioned in *Beowulf,* line 1198.

129   *wundnan golde* (twisted gold): A reference to the interlace and braided patterning of gold rings, bracelets, and necklaces during the period.

THE FORTUNES OF MORTALS

For an Old English analogue for this poem, see Cynewulf's *Juliana,* lines 468–505, in Bjork, *Old English Poems of Cynewulf.*

21–26   *Sum sceal on holte of hean beame fiþerleas feallan: bið on flihte seþeah, laceð on lyfte, oþþæt lengre ne bið westem wudu-beames. Þonne he on wyrt-ruman sigeð sworcen-ferð, sawle bireafod, fealleþ on foldan; feorð biþ on siþe* (One will fall from a high tree in the forest, featherless: that one is flying anyway, playing in the air, until no longer a fruit hanging from the tree. Then to the foot of it, dark minded, bereft of soul, he plummets, falls to the earth; the spirit journeys on): See *Christ II,* lines 78–79, in Bjork, *Old English Poems of Cynewulf* ("one can ascend the tall, steep tree"). Tree climbing was evidently an important part of Anglo-Saxon life and may have had its origin in shamanistic practices. See Neil D. Isaacs, "Up a Tree: To See *The Fates of Men,*" in *Anglo-Saxon Poetry: Essays in Appreciation,* ed. Lewis E. Nicholson and Dolores Warwick Frese (Notre Dame, 1975), 363–75. The sardonic humor in this passage comes from the implicit comparison of the featherless human being described here with the feathered and flying falcon described in lines 88–89, below.

41   *wyrde* (fate): See note to *The Wanderer,* line 5. In a Christian interpretation, *wyrd* here could mean the Last Judgment. See Weber, *Wyrd,* 134.

58–59   *Sum sceal on geoguþe mid Godes meahtum his earfoð-siþ ealne forspildan* (One during youth through God's might will waste the whole time of hardship): See *Beowulf,* 2183ff., where Beowulf is described as not showing much promise in his youth. The Cinderella or Ash Lad motif is a common folk motif.

70   *tæfle* (tables): This could be a dice game or a board game such as chess.

77–79   *Sum sceal on heape hæleþum cweman, blissian æt beore benc-sittendum; þær biþ drincendra dream se micla* (One in the troop will please the people, gladden the bench sitters through beer; there will be great joy among the drinkers): This passage is ambiguous and could refer to a person entertaining the troop in some fashion while people drink beer. Or it could, as translated here, refer to the cupbearer (see line 51, above) who brings the beer to the troop.

84   *neod* (delight): Eric G. Stanley, citing *Beowulf,* line 2116, translates the word thus, instead of as "need" or "necessity." See "Old English *The Fortunes of Men,* lines 80–84," *Notes & Queries* 50 (2003): 268.

86   *heoro-swealwe* (falcon): See *The Gifts of Mortals,* lines 80–81; *Maxims II,* lines 17–18; and Oggins, "Falconry."

Maxims I

9   *wyrda* (fates): See note to *The Wanderer,* line 5.

24–25   *sceal wif ond wer in woruld cennan bearn mid gebyrdum* (a woman and man must bring forth in the world a child through birth): See *The Fortunes of Mortals,* lines 2–3.

30   *se cwealm* (the death): Perhaps a reference to deadly disease or plague.

31   *Umbor yceð, þa ær-adl nimeð* (He adds infants, early disease takes them): Because of the uncertain grammatical function of *umbor* (singular subject or plural object) and *þa* (plural object or adverb), this line could also be translated as "The child adds when premature disease takes" or "He adds infants when premature disease takes." I take *umbor* and *þa* to be parallel, plural objects.

35   *Dol biþ se þe his Dryhten nat, to þæs oft cymeð deað unþinged* (Foolish is the one who does not know his Lord, because death often comes unexpected): See *The Seafarer,* line 106.

50   *Styran sceal mon strongum mode* (One must steer with a strong mind): See *The Seafarer,* line 109.

64   *oft hy mon wommum biliþð* (often she is blamed for wrongs).
      This may also be translated "she often blames someone for her
      faults." Line 99 has similar phrasing.

66   *hond sceal heofod inwyrcan* (the head must work the hand): The
      meaning of this line is uncertain. Shippey, *Poems of Wisdom*, 131,
      reads it as a reference to the lord-retainer relationship, where
      the hand of the lord is put on the retainer's head during gift
      giving.

94   *Frysan wife* (Frisian wife): Ernst A. Kock postulates that the spe-
      cific reference to Frisia here may come from parts of the poem
      perhaps having Frisian origin ("Interpretations and Emenda-
      tions of Early English Texts V," *Anglia* 43 [1919]: 309).

105   *mægð-egsan wyn* (the maiden's own joy): That is, her lover or
      sailor. The translation is Carl Berkhout's, cited in Muir's note to
      this line in *Exeter Anthology.*

106–7 *Ceap-eadig mon cyning-wic þonne leodon cypeþ þonne liþan cymeð*
      (The rich merchant will then buy a kingly dwelling for his peo-
      ple when he comes sailing home): The meaning of this line is
      uncertain. Shippey, *Poems of Wisdom*, 69, translates "The rich
      merchant then buys his men quarters from the king, when he
      comes sailing in." See his note on the line, 132–33.

137   *rune writan* (write down mysteries): This may also be translated
      as "carve runes." Knowledge of runes and how to inscribe them
      were associated with mystery.

139   *dæges onettan* (hasten while it is day): There is a possible echo
      here of John 9:4, where Christ tells his disciples that we have to
      do the bidding of the one who sent him while the day lasts, for
      the night is coming when no one can work.

143   *Wel mon sceal wine healdan on wega gehwylcum* (One must be true
      to a friend on each path): See *Precepts,* line 31.

157   *Licgende beam læsest groweð* (The tree lying down grows least):
      Note the litotes in this gnomic utterance.

158   *Treo sceolon brædan ond treow weaxan* (Trees must broaden and
      faith be fruitful): Note the play on *treo* and *treow* in the Old Eng-
      lish.

184–85 *ful oft mon wearnum tihð eargne, þæt he elne forleose* (very often the sluggish man attracts reproaches that he lacks courage): See *A Proverb from Winfrid's Time.*

187   *stan* (stone): This word could refer either to a gem stone or to a game piece in chess, for example.

191   *fæhþo* (a state of feud): The description of feud here to line 200 offers an important backdrop for understanding the whole of *Beowulf* and specifically the Cain and Abel material relating to Grendel, lines 102–14.

The Order of the World

22   *þæt he wislice woruld fulgonge* (of engaging wholly and wisely in the world): The meaning of this clause is not clear. Bosworth-Toller translates, "that he wisely perfect the world"; the DOE translates, "in completing wisely his worldly ways."

The Rhyming Poem

On the multiple difficulties this poem presents in almost every line, see the Introduction. Note also that wherever possible in the translation, I have tried to replicate the effect of the rhyme in the Old English without doing violence to the sense—as I perceive it—of the original. Rhyme, therefore, appears only sporadically in the translation. For a successful attempt to replicate all the rhyme in modern English, see Earl, "Hisperic Style," 188.

2   *ond þæt torhte geteoh* (and brought forth that brightness): This could also be translated, for example, as "and that bright doctrine" or "firmament" or "matter." See the note on this line and the notes on subsequent lines in Muir, *Exeter Anthology.*

8   *lisse mid long leoma gehongum* (gently past trees with long branches): It seems that the horses carry the speaker across plains and through forests. As noted in Muir, *Exeter Anthology,* Eric G. Stanley translates this line as "gently with long contacts with branches."

46   *brond-hord* (burning thought): There is much debate about what this word actually means. See Macrae-Gibson, *Riming Poem,*

48–50. Lockett, *Anglo-Saxon Psychologies,* 85–86, interprets the word, which is literally "fire hoard," to mean "burning thought" or "fire thought."

59   *wyrde* (fate): See note to *The Wanderer,* line 5.

67   *searo-hwit solaþ, sumur-hat colað* (brilliant whiteness gets defiled, summer heat cools): See *Latin-English Proverbs,* line 3.

78–79   *ond æt nyhstan nan nefne se neda tan balawun her gehloten* (and at the last none except the inescapable lot appointed for men): The translation is Klinck's, *Old English Elegies,* 158.

Deor

For Germanic analogues for this poem, see Calder et al., *Sources and Analogues II,* 65–69.

1   *Welund:* Weland, the legendary Germanic smith whose metalwork was unparalleled and who was coveted for it by a king Nithhad. His story is told in the ninth-century (?) Old Norse poem *Vǫlundarkviða* (Lay of Weland) in the poetic Edda and in the twelfth- or thirteenth-century Norwegian *Þiðreks saga* (Saga of Thidrek) by Dietrich von Bern. Prompted by his evil wife, the king has Weland's hamstrings cut so he cannot flee and then puts him on an isolated island where he will produce weapons, armor, and adornments for the king alone. The loss of freedom, mobility, and one of his prize swords enrages Weland, so he bides his time until he can have his revenge. The king's two sons visit the island to see the precious treasure Weland has wrought. He urges them to come again, alone; they do, and he beheads them both. He then skillfully encases their skulls in silver and gives them to the king as cups, makes jewels out of their eyes for the queen, and forges a necklace out of their teeth for the king's daughter, Beadohild, whom he later rapes and impregnates (see the following stanza). When the horror of the skull gift is revealed to the stunned and inconsolable king, a laughing Weland raises himself aloft and out of captivity with the help of a coat of feathers he and his brother, Egill, have made.

him be wurman (among his damascened work): The meaning of

wurma is unknown but has been taken to refer to "snakes" or "swords" or "rings" or, metaphorically, the damascened patterning on swords. See discussions in Pope and Fulk, *Eight Old English Poems,* 114; and Hill, *Minor Heroic Poems,* 18–19.

7   *Þæs ofereode; þisses swa mæg* (That passed away; so can this): Literally, "It passed over from that; it can from this, too." This line is one of the most perplexing and discussed of Old English verse because of the unclear references for "that" and "this." The line also seems to shift meaning from one stanza to the next.

8   *Beadohilde:* See note to line 1, above.

14   *Mæðhild:* There is no known source for this tale. *Mange* (moans) occurs uniquely here and is of uncertain meaning. It has been thought to mean "moans," "affairs," or "many." See Hill, *Minor Heroic Poems,* 48.

18   *Ðeodric:* Probably Theodoric the Ostrogoth, who ruled Italy from 493–526. See *Widsith,* line 115.

19   *Mæringa burg* (fortress of the Goths): Ravenna, Italy.

21   *Eormanrices* (Eormanric): See *Widsith,* lines 8, 18, 88, and 111, and *Beowulf,* line 1201.

36   *Heodeninga* (Heodeningas): The name of a Germanic tribe.

37   *Deor:* The name of this poem's poet. As an adjective, it means "brave" or "bold"; as a noun, it means "animal."

39   *Heorrenda:* Deor's successor and the poet or singer Horant in the Middle High German poem, *Kudrun.* Horant's talents help his king (Heoden in Old English) secure the love of a beautiful maiden name Hild, daughter of Hagen (Hagena in Old English). For summaries of the story, see Pope and Fulk, *Eight Old English Poems,* 119–20; and Hill, *Minor Heroic Poems,* 20–21, 108.

WULF AND EADWACER

2, 7   *willað hy hine aþecgan* (they want to kill him): The verb *aþecgan* according to the DOE means "to serve with food" or "feed" but contextually here "to kill." Since the context is so unclear, the verb has also been taken to mean "receive" or "welcome."

9   *Wulfes ic mines wid-lastum wenum dogode* (I dogged my Wolf with

far-wandering expectations): The meaning of the verb *dogian* is unknown, but given the lupine or animal imagery throughout the poem, "dogged" seems a good choice for a modern English equivalent of its past tense. For a full discussion of this hypothesized verb, see Osborn, *"Dogode* in *Wulf and Eadwacer"*; see also Sarah L. Higley, "Finding the Man Under the Skin: Identity, Monstrosity, Expulsion, and the Werewolf," in *The Shadow-Walkers: Jacob Grimm's Mythology of the Monstrous,* ed. Tom Shippey (Tempe, Arizona, 2006), 369–75. Some editors have emended the word to *hogode* (thought about).

10   *reotugu* (mournful): That the speaker of the poem is female is indicated by the feminine form of this adjective.

11   *bogum bilegde* (embraced me): *bogum* can mean upper arms, boughs, or the forequarters of an animal. The whole phrase has been taken to mean sexual intercourse. See entry in DOE.

16   *Eadwacer* (Eadwacer, vigilant one): Since this word can be either a proper name or a common noun, I translate using both senses of it.

    Uncerne earmne hwelp (our wretched whelp): The enigmatic whelp has been interpreted as a wolf cub, a child, a metaphor for the lovers' relationship, a reference to Wolf, a reference to Eadwacer, a reference to the poem itself, and a reference to the consequences of outlawry within the context of Old Norse law and literature.

The Wife's Lament

1   *ful geomorre* (very sad): The adjective has a feminine ending, which indicates that the speaker is female.

6   *hlaford* (husband): This begins the pattern of imagery in the poem that implicitly likens the husband-wife relationship to the lord-retainer relationship.

21   *bliþe gebæro* (with joyful demeanor): This is a squinting modifier that can qualify "the man" in the preceding clause or "we" in the following clause. With Pope and Fulk, *Eight Old English Poems,* I opt for the latter. See the note on this phrase in their edition.

24   *swa hit no wære* (as if it hadn't been): See *The Wanderer,* line 96.

25   *freondscipe* (friendship): See *The Husband's Message,* line 19.

26   *fæhðu dreogan* (endure the hostility): The word *fæhðu* usually means "feud." Its use here could be a continuation of the lord-retainer imagery begun in line 6. See the note in Pope and Fulk, *Eight Old English Poems.*

28   *under ac-treo in þam eorð-scræfe* (under an oak tree in the earth cave): This obscure line remains obscure despite many attempts to clarify it. See the notes in Cassidy and Ringler, *Bright's Old English Grammar;* and Pope and Fulk, *Eight Old English Poems.* The importance of the oak in Anglo-Saxon society is attested in *The Rune Poem,* lines 77–80: "The oak is the nourishment of pork for human beings; it often fares over the gannet's bath; the ocean tests whether the oak has noble faith."

37   *sumor-langne dæg* (summer-long day): See *Juliana,* line 495.

40–53 The ambiguity of these lines has given rise to a number of inter-pretations that affect one's view of the whole poem. Is this passage a curse or a gnomic meditation, for instance? See the Intro-duction.

49   *wætre beflowen* (conveyed by water): Thus Pope and Fulk, *Eight Old English Poems,* instead of "surrounded by water."

RESIGNATION (B): AN EXILE'S LAMENT

For an edition and translation of *Resignation (A),* see Christopher A. Jones, ed. and trans., *Old English Shorter Poems,* vol. 1, *Religious and Didactic,* DOML 15 (Cambridge, Mass., 2012), 110–15. On the relationship of this poem to *Resignation (A),* see the Introduction to this volume and Jones, *Old English Shorter Poems,* 354–55. Line numbers in other editions are con-tinuous from *Resignation (A),* so that *Resignation (B)* begins with line 70, a practice that has no authority if the two are fragments of separate poems. Accordingly, the edition here begins with line 1.

6   *bliþe mode; nu ic gebunden eom* (with a blithe spirit; now I am firmly bound): The full clause has been regarded by others, such as Bradley, *Anglo-Saxon Poetry,* as subordinate and *gebunden* as

metaphorical ("now that I am firmly chastened," p. 389). Bliss and Frantzen, "Integrity," translate, "now that I am in firm control," but note that their interpretation is conjectural. See Klinck, *Old English Elegies,* 194.

48–49   *Giet biþ þæt selast, þonne mon him sylf ne mæg wyrd onwendan, þæt he þonne wel þolige* (Still it is always best when one cannot avoid fate that he should then endure it well): See *Guthlac B,* lines 1348–51, and *Maxims I,* line 80, for parallel constructions for this gnomic wisdom.

49   *wyrd* (fate): See note to *The Wanderer,* line 5.

PHARAOH

6   *siex hundra godra searo-hæbbendra* (six hundred chariots full of good warriors): See *Exodus* 14:7.

7   *þæt eal fornam yþa fær-gripe* (the sudden grip of waves took all that): See *Exodus* 14:28.

THE HUSBAND'S MESSAGE

13   *beam* (tree): This could refer to a rune stick on which a message is written, as many scholars have assumed, or to the mast of the ship, as Niles, "Trick of the Runes," 203–4, has cogently argued.

19   *freondscype* (friendship): See *The Wife's Lament,* line 25.

23   *geomorne geac* (sad cuckoo): See *The Seafarer,* line 53, and note.

32   *alwaldend God* (all-ruling God): Leslie, *Three Old English Elegies,* regards this as the only overtly Christian reference in the poem.

49–50   *gehyre ic ætsomne* ᛋᚱ *geador* ᛖᚪᚹᛗ *aþe benemnan* (I hear S R together EA W and M declare an oath): How the runes function in this passage is a matter of dispute. If they stand for letters of the alphabet, no one knows what they spell, although "sword" has been suggested (see Leslie, *Three Old English Elegies,* 15); if they stand for words, several scholars have offered interpretations. Leslie, for example, translates, "I hear heaven, earth and the man declare together by oath" (17), but that requires taking R and EA for something other than what *The Rune Poem* says they

259

stand for. (*The Rune Poem* describes the runes in the passage as follows: For S, "The sun is always a hope for seafarers when they convey the sea steed over the fish's bath until it brings them to land" [lines 45–47]; for R, "Riding is easy for each warrior in the hall, and very hard for the one who sits on the very strong mare on the milestoned paths" [lines 13–15]; for EA, "Eohl-sedge most often has its place in a fen, grows in the water, wounds fiercely, reddens with blood everyone who lays hold of it" [lines 41–44]; for W, "They experience joy who know few woes, pain, and sorrow, and who have dignity and happiness and also an abundance of fortified settlements" [lines 22–24]; and M, "A human being in delight is dear to his kin; nevertheless each one has to depart from the others because the Lord wants, by his decree, to cover the wretched flesh with earth" [lines 59–62]). For a lucid discussion of all the problems involved in interpreting this runic passage, see Niles, "Trick of the Runes."

THE RUIN

1   *weal-stan* (wall stone): See *Maxims II,* line 3.

2   *enta geweorc* (the work of giants): See *The Wanderer,* line 87, and *Maxims II,* line 2. The reference to the Romans, who built with stone and brick instead of wood.

21   *burn-sele monige* (many bathing halls): This and other details in the poem have led some scholars to conjecture that the poem refers to the Roman city of Bath, but the identification is not definite. Other sites suggested include Chester and Hadrian's Wall. See Leslie, *Three Old English Elegies,* 22–28, and Wentersdorf, "Observations."

24   *wyrd seo swiþe* (fate the mighty): See *The Seafarer,* line 115; *Maxims I,* line 5; and *Solomon and Saturn,* line 444. On *wyrd,* see note to *The Wanderer,* line 5.

34   *wlonc ond win-gal* (proud and flushed with wine): See *The Seafarer,* line 29.

41   *hat on hreþre* (hot to the core): See *Beowulf,* line 3148, and *Christ and Satan,* line 98.

45   *hring-mere* (circular pool): This word occurs no place else in Old English and may refer to a circular bath excavated in Bath in 1885. See Leslie, *Three Old English Elegies,* 76.

DURHAM

For a Latin analogue for this poem, see Allen and Calder, *Sources and Analogues,* 204–7.

2   *steppa gestaðolad* (steeply established): Durham is built on hills, and the cathedral sits on top of the highest of them.

3   *Weor* (Wear): The river that flows around the city on three sides, thus making the land on which it sits seem an island. The Old English name for Durham was appropriately Dunholm (hill + water). See entry in Bosworth-Toller.

10   *Cudberch* (Cuthbert): Saint Cuthbert, bishop of Lindisfarne, d. 687, memorialized in Bede's *Vita Sancti Cuthberti* (Life of Saint Cuthbert). See Lapidge et al., *Encyclopaedia,* 131–33, and Bertram Colgrave, ed. and trans., *Two Lives of Saint Cuthbert* (Cambridge, 1940).

12   *Osuualdes* (Oswald): Saint Oswald, king of Northumbria, d. 642, the first royal saint of the Anglo-Saxons. See Lapidge et al., *Encylopaedia,* 347–48.

        Engle leo (protector of the English): *leo* or "protector" could be a pun on *leo* or "lion." See Fred C. Robinson, "The Royal Epithet *Engle Leo* in the Old English *Durham* Poem," *Medium Ævum,* 37 (1968): 249–52.

        Aidan (Aidan): Saint Aidan, monk of Iona and bishop of Lindisfarne, d. 651. See Lapidge et al., *Encyclopaedia,* 23.

13   *Eadberch* (Eadbert): Saint Eadbert was Cuthbert's successor as bishop of Lindisfarne, d. 698. See entry in Farmer, *Dictionary of the Saints,* 117.

        Eadfrið (Eadfrith): Saint Eadfrith, bishop of Lindisfarne after Eadbert and illustrator of the Lindisfarne Gospels, d. 721. See Farmer, *Dictionary of the Saints,* 119.

14   *Æðelwold* (Æthelwold): bishop of Winchester, prominent

scholar and leader in the Benedictine reform, d. 984. See Lapidge et al., *Encyclopaedia, 19.*

15 *Beda* (Bede): the Venerable Bede was the most dominant intellectual force in Anglo-Saxon England, d. 735. See Lapidge et al., *Encyclopaedia, 57–59.*

Boisil (Boisil): prior of Melrose, d. 660 or 661. See Lapidge et al., *Encyclopaedia, 67–68.*

THE RUNE POEM

For Germanic analogues for this poem, see Calder et al., *Sources and Analogues II,* 166–68, and Halsall, *Rune Poem,* 181–87.

7 Þ (*þorn*, "the thorn"): The Scandinavian name for this rune is *þurs* (giant).

10 ᚠ (*os,* "the mouth"): The name for this rune in two of the Scandinavian analogues is *os* or *oss* (god). There may be an underlining reference in the Old English poem to Woden as the god of eloquence. See the note on this rune in Halsall, *Rune Poem,* 109–11.

36 *hyrde fyres* (a guardian of fire): Besides having magical and protective qualities and perhaps being Yggdrasil, the tree of life, the yew tree has its practical uses: it makes good firewood. See the note on this rune in Halsall, *Rune Poem,* 126–27.

38 ᚦ (*peorð,* "peorth"): The meaning of this word is unknown, but it is apparently a kind of game.

41 ᛉ (*eolhx-secg,* "eolh-sedge"): The DOE defines this as "some sort of sedge, reed or rush."

46 *fisces beþ* (fish's bath): Kenning for "sea."

47 *brim-hengest* (sea steed): Kenning for "ship."

48 ↑ (*Tir,* "Tir"): Name of a guiding planet or star or constellation, the equivalent of Latin Mars. Originally, Tiw was the supreme god for the Germanic peoples. See note on this rune in Halsall, *Rune Poem,* 135–37.

50 *næfre swiceþ* (never fails): In the geocentric, Ptolemaic system of the universe that would have been part of the Anglo-Saxon worldview, everything below the circle of the moon was mutable; everything above it was immutable.

54   *geloden leafum* (growing with leaves): See Cynewulf's *Elene,* line 1227.

55   ᛗ (*eh,* "the warhorse"): On the possible meaning of *eh* as "warhorse," see R. H. C. Davis, "Did the Anglo-Saxons Have Warhorses?" in *Weapons and Warfare in Anglo-Saxon England,* ed. S. Chadwick Hawkes, Oxford Univ. Committee for Archaeoline 21 (Oxford, 1989), 141–44.

66   *brim-hengest* (sea steed): Kenning for "ship."

67   ᛝ (*Ing,* "Ing"): The Anglo-Saxons' name for the Old Norse god Freyr. See the note on this rune in Halsall, *Rune Poem,* 146–47.

77–78   *elda bearnum flæsces fodor* (nourishment of pork for the sons of men): The oak tree provides acorns to feed the pigs, which in turn as pork feed human beings.

79   *ganotes bæð* (gannet's bath): Kenning for "sea."

83   *ðeah him feohtan on firas monige* (although many men fight against it): This line probably refers to the use of ash wood for making spears.

84   ᚣ (*yr,* "bow"): The precise meaning of this rune is unknown, but the context here suggests a bow to many scholars. "Saddle," "yew-wood saddlebow," "adornment," "female aurochs," "ax iron," and "gold buckle" have also been suggested as possible meanings. See the note on this rune in Halsall, *Rune Poem,* 155–57.

Solomon and Saturn

For an Old Norse analogue for this poem, see Calder et al., *Sources and Analogues II,* 168–72. For the gaps in the text, see the notes in ASPR 6, 160–70.

1–2   *Ic ig-landa eallra hæbbe boca onbyrged* (I have eaten the books of all islands): The islands are probably Africa, Europe, and Asia, and the image of eating books or words for acquiring knowledge has biblical precedent (*Revelations* 10:9–10; *Jeremiah* 15:16; *Ezekiel* 3:1–3) as pointed out by Jonathan Wilcox, "Eating Books: The Consumption of Learning in the Old English Poetic *Solomon and Saturn,*" *American Notes and Queries* ns 4 (1991): 116–17. See lines 243–44, below.

8–9   Translation from Katherine O'Brien O'Keeffe, *Visible Song: Transitional Literacy in Old English Verse* (Cambridge University Press, 2006), 49. Regarding the missing letters, Dobbie observes, "Here the scribe of B wrote the words *on þam micelan bec* and then left blank sufficient space for ten or twelve letters, in the middle of a line, before writing the next words *M ces heardum*" (*Anglo-Saxon Minor Poems,* 160). The half-line divisions printed here follow Dobbie, even though line 8a is metrically irregular.

12   *se gepalm-twigoda Pater Noster* (the palm-twigged Pater Noster): Anlezark, *Dialogues,* 100, points out that the palm "is a conventional symbol of victory."

17   *ðurh þæs cantices cwyde Cristes linan* (through the word of the canticle of Christ's line of letters): The meaning of "line of letters" has not been determined, but it seems to be the nineteen letters that combine to form the Pater Noster. See note to line 49, below.

20   *Cofer-flod* (the river Chobar): A tributary of the Tigris and Euphrates Rivers where the prophet's vision begins in the book of *Ezekiel.*

28   *irenum aplum* (iron apples): The apples here are usually interpreted as balls. The image of growth in the larger context of this passage, however, works better with "apples," which have the added advantage of bringing to mind the devil's treachery in the Garden of Eden.

29   *of edwittes iða heafdum* (from the heads of waves of disgrace): The meaning of this line is uncertain.

43–44   *Swylce ðu miht mid ðy beorhtan gebede blod onhætan, ðæs deofles dros, þæt him dropan stigað* (Likewise with bright prayer you may heat the blood, the devil's dross, so that the drops rise in him): The meaning of this sentence and nature of the torture inflicted on the devil are unclear. See the note on lines 43–48 in Anlezark, *Dialogues,* 102–3.

48   *twelf fyra tydernessum* (twelve weaknesses of human beings): Thomas D. Hill, "Two Notes on *Solomon and Saturn,*" *Medium Ae-*

vum 40 (1970): 217–21, argues that this is an allusion to the medieval concept of the twelve abuses of the world.

89   *prologa prima* (prologa prima, the prime first letter): See Anlezark, *Dialogues,* 50–51, for a discussion of this phrase. From here to line 145, the poet seems to want to describe the virtues of each of the nineteen letters used to write the Pater Noster, probably in the Vulgate (Matthew 6:9–13). Three are missing, however. See ASPR 6.

137   *stæf stræte neah* (letter near the street): Meaning unknown.

161–62   *awriteð he on his wæpne wæll-nota heap, bealwe boc-stafas, bill forscrifeð, meces mærðo* (he inscribes on his weapon a host of baleful inscriptions, deadly letters, blunts the sword, the glory of the blade): See *Beowulf,* lines 1687–98, which describes the inscribed hilt of a sword.

167   *palm-treow* (palm tree): See the note to line 12, above.

169   *folme* (limb): This word literally means "hand." The DOE defines it here as "power, ? strength, ? victory."

186   *east Corsias* (east Cossias): On the geographic list that begins with this line and ends at line 210, below, consult O'Brien O'Keeffe, "Geographic List." "Cossias" may be a people who bordered the land of the Medes ("Geographic List," 136).

188   *norð Predan* (Parthian): This identification is O'Brien O'Keeffe's, "Geographic List," 136.

189   *Marculfes eard* (the land of Marculf): Probably Turkey. See O'Brien O'Keeffe, "Geographic List," 137.

213   *weallende Wulf* (raging Wulf): Identity unknown.

214   *Nebrondes* (Nimrod): Traditionally considered responsible for the building of the Tower of Babel.

225   *Dol bið se ðe* (Foolish is the one who): See *The Seafarer,* line 106, and *Maxims I,* line 35.

277   *Melotes* (Melot): Perhaps Mellothi mentioned in 1 Chronicles 25:4, 26. See note on line 99b in Anlezark, *Dialogues,* 125.

281   *vasa mortis* (instruments of death): Identity unknown. Perhaps, according to J. A. Dane, "'a representation of the very curiosity that plagues Saturn'" (cited in Anlezark, *Dialogues,* 123). The

name comes from *Psalms* 7:14 in the Vulgate: *Et in ipso praeparavit vasa mortis* (and in it he has prepared the instruments of death). See note in Anlezark, *Dialogues,* 125.

329   *ðæt worc* (that work): The Tower of Babel.

334   *wyrda* (fates): See note to *The Wanderer,* line 5.

338   *niehtes wunde* (the wound of night): The meaning of this phrase is unknown.

425   *fyrenes cynnes* (the nature of fire): Fire and light exist in all living things according to medieval tradition. See the notes in Anlezark, *Dialogues,* 133–34.

429   *wyrd* (fate): See note to *The Wanderer,* line 5.

436   *ðæt meahte ðara twega tuion aspyrian* (who could settle by investigation the doubt about those two things): This translation is slightly adapted from that in the DOE under *aspyrian.*

437, 440   *wyrd* (fate): See note to *The Wanderer,* line 5.

444   *wyrd seo swiðe* (fate the mighty): See *The Seafarer,* line 115; *Maxims I,* line 5; and *The Ruin,* line 24.

456   *ðy teoðan dæle* (the tenth part): The fallen order of angels.

469   *wæl-cealde wic wintre beðeahte* (a slaughter-cold dwelling covered by winter): Removed from the light and warmth of God, hell was conceived of as a dark and extremely cold place.

478   *man age* (acted sinfully): This is an unresolved crux. The translation comes from the DOE under *agan,* definition IA13.

Maxims II

2   *enta geweorc* (work of giants): See *The Wanderer,* line 87, and *The Ruin,* line 2. This is a reference to the Romans, who built with masonry instead of wood.

3   *wrætlic weall-stana geweorc* (wondrous work of wall stones): See *The Ruin,* line 1.

5   *wyrd* (fate): See note to *The Wanderer,* line 5.

10   *Soð bið swicolost* (Truth is most deceiving): This enigmatic line has caused most editors to emend *swocolost* to *switolost* (most evident). But truth, as John Donne observes in his third *Satire* (lines 79–85) and as jesting Pilot does in Francis Bacon's essay

"On Truth," is not easily apprehended, and that may be the general sentiment articulated here.

13   *Wea bið wundrum clibbor; wolcnu scriðað* (Woe is wondrously clinging; clouds glide): Some editors emend *wea* to *weax* (wax). The unemended line, however, seems more insightful and instructive: human misery has no palpable effect on an indifferent universe.

17–18   *Hafuc sceal on glofe wilde gewunian* (The hawk must stand wild on the glove): See *The Gifts of Mortals,* lines 80–81; *The Fortunes of Mortals,* lines 85–92; and Oggins, "Falconry."

A Proverb from Winfrid's Time

Saint Boniface [ca. 675–754] was named Wynfrith at birth.

1–2   See *Maxims I,* lines 185–86: "Very often the sluggish man attracts reproaches that he lacks courage."

Bede's Death Song

This poem is contained in a letter from Saint Cuthbert on Bede's death, but there is no conclusive evidence for ascribing the poem definitely to Bede. See George Hardin Brown, *A Companion to Bede* (Woodbridge, 2009), 15, 93.

Latin-English Proverbs

3   *Hat acolað, hwit asolað* (Hot grows cold, white gets dirty): See *The Rhyming Poem,* line 67.

Metrical Charm 1: For Unfruitful Land

For Germanic and Celtic analogues for the Old English metrical charms, see Calder et al., *Sources and Analogues II,* 175–87. For a Latin analogue for this charm and charm 2, see Allen and Calder, *Sources and Analogues,* 214–15.

8   *glappan* (buckbean): The meaning is uncertain. The DOE notes that the word means "a plant, perhaps bogbean/buckbean."

9   *halig-water* (holy water): This could perhaps originally have re-

ferred to dew. See Schneider, "The Old English *Æcerbot*," 277–78.

18   *cwic-beam* (rowan tree): The quick-beam, or rowan tree, is related to the mountain ash in North America and was held to have protective, magical powers in pre-Christian Europe. See Rosenberg, "Meaning of *Æcerbot*," 429–30.

36   *se witega* (the psalmist): David, and the psalm alluded to, is 112 (111 in the Vulgate), where David extols the one who fears God and delights in his commandments. See ASPR 6, 208.

40–41   *Sanctus, sanctus, sanctus:* The Tersanctus, a liturgical hymn that is part of the Order of Mass.

41   *Benedicite:* Song of creation from the Liturgy of the Hours based on Daniel 3:56–88.

42   *Magnificat:* Song of Mary from the Liturgy of the Hours based on Luke 1:46–55.

51   *Erce:* Identity and etymology unknown. It is typically understood as the name of a Germanic fertility goddess (see ASPR 6, 208), but scholars have suggested other possibilities as well, e.g., "earth" (Rudolf Kögel, *Geschichte der deutschen Literatur bis zum Ausgange des Mittelalters.* Vol. 1, pt. 1 [Strassburg, 1894], 39–42); "dew" (Robert Boenig [*Erce* and Dew] *Names* 31 [1983]: 130–31); and "gibberish" (A. J. Wyatt, *An Anglo-Saxon Reader* [Cambridge, 1919], 255).

METRICAL CHARM 2: THE NINE HERBS CHARM

2   *Regenmelde* (Regenmeld): Generally accepted as the name of an unknown place.

21–22   *Fleoh þu nu, attor-laðe, seo læsse ða maran, seo mare þa læssan, oððæt him beigra bot sy* (Put now to flight, root of fumitory, the lesser the greater, the greater the lesser, until there is a remedy for him for both): The sense seems to be that the root of fumitory is less powerful than some afflictions and more powerful than others but still efficacious.

24   *Alorford:* Place unknown.

32–33   *ða genam Woden nigon wuldor-tanas, sloh ða þa næddran, þæt heo on nigon tofleah* (then Woden took nine glory twigs, then struck the adder so that it fled away in nine): The twigs are runic letters, each representing the first letter of each herbal name, according to Storms, *Anglo-Saxon Magic,* 195.

METRICAL CHARM 3: AGAINST A DWARF

1   *dweorh* (dwarf): A dwarf could harm a human being in various ways, including inducing nightmares and infecting with disease. It is unclear what malice is being described in this charm, however. See Grattan and Singer, *Anglo-Saxon Magic,* 61–62. Gay argues that the charm is against witch riding ("Anglo-Saxon Metrical Charm 3"). Hutcheson argues that it is against fever ("*Wið dweorh*").

3–4   *Maximianus, Malchus, Iohannes, Martimianus, Dionisius, Constantinus, Serafion:* The Seven Sleepers of Ephesus, Christians who escaped the Decian persecution by hiding in a cave, where they were walled up but rose from the dead during the reign of Emperor Theodosius. See entry in F. L. Cross, ed., *The Oxford Dictionary of the Christian Church,* 3rd ed. rev. by E. A. Livingstone (Oxford, 2005). The legend is retold in Ælfric's *Lives of the Saints.*

9   *Her com in gangan, in spider-wiht* (A spider came walking inside here): The association of dwarves and spiders is affirmed in a modern Swedish dialect, where *dvärg* (dwarf) refers to both, and the word for cobweb is *dvärgsnät* (dwarf's net). See Gratan and Singer, *Anglo-Saxon Magic,* 61. Hutcheson, "*Wið dweorh,*" 190, retains the manuscript reading *spiden* for *spider* and translates "fever-spirit."

10   *haman* (coat): Grattan and Singer, *Anglo-Saxon Magic,* 163, translate this as "bridle"; Grendon, *Anglo-Saxon Charms,* 167, as "harness"; and Storms, *Anglo-Saxon Magic,* 167, as "web."

12   *colian* (to cool): Glosecki, *Shamanism,* 186, observes that "the effect of dreamtime flight is felt as a rush of air chilling the sleeper's limbs."

13   *dweores sweostar* (the dwarf's sister): Because the MS has *deores sweostar,* this could also be translated as "the beast's [*deor*'s, or animal's] sister." The meaning is obscure either way.

18   *Fiað:* for Latin *fiat.*

METRICAL CHARM 4: FOR A STABBING PAIN

1   *ærn* (house): The DOE notes that *ærn* "has alternatively been taken as **ern* 'harvest' . . . , here in the transferred sense 'standing crop' [cf. *ernþ*] and the passage interpreted as 'the red nettle which grows into and through the harvest field [or crop]'; since red nettle commonly grows in fields and cultivated ground, the latter interpretation prob. represents the original sense of the word in this context, although it may have been misunderstood by the scribe."

3   *hy* (*they*): Like the pain they inflict, these malevolent entities are not identified in the charm. But see notes to lines 8 and 19.

5   *Scyld ðu ðe nu; þu ðysne nið genesan mote* (Shield yourself now; you may survive this attack): This line could also be translated with an understood subordinating conjunction between the clauses: "Shield yourself now so that you may survive this attack." See ASPR 6, 212.

8   *ða mihtigan wif* (the mighty women): Nora Chadwick argues that these women are the Valkyries, who are probably referred to in line 19 as *hægtessan.* See "The Monsters and Beowulf" in *The Anglo-Saxons,* ed. Peter Clemoes (London, 1959), 176. Greenfield and Calder, *Critical History,* 257, view the women as female spirits, perhaps witches.

13, 16   *smið, smiðas* (smith, smiths): Skemp, "Old English Charms," 290, identifies these as elf smiths, the first one benevolent and the remaining six, not. Minna Doskow views them all as hostile ("Poetic Structure and the Problem of the Smiths in 'Wið Færstice,'" *Papers on Language and Literature* 12 [1976]: 321–26).

19   *hægtessan* (witch's): Audrey L. Meaney maintains that this word "was originally applied to a tutelary goddess of a village or an

estate" ("Women, Witchcraft and Magic in Anglo-Saxon England," in *Superstitions and Popular Religion in Anglo-Saxon England*, ed. Donald G. Scragg, 17 [Manchester, 1989]).

23   *æsir:* The pagan gods.

METRICAL CHARM 5: FOR LOSS OF CATTLE

Thomas D. Hill points out that in this charm and Metrical Charm 10 an idea derived from Ephesians 3:18–19 about the nature of Christ's love is central. It has all areas of the world under its domain, and in these charms, the cross is its symbol. See "The Theme of the Cosmological Cross in Two Old English Cattle Theft Charms," *Notes and Queries* 223, ns 25 (1978): 488–90.

METRICAL CHARM 6: FOR DELAYED BIRTH

28   *þonne ic me wille habban and ham gan* (then I wish to have control of my own body and go home): The translation of this line is taken from Nelson, "A Woman's Charm," 5.

METRICAL CHARM 7: FOR THE WATER-ELF DISEASE

1   *wæter-ælf-adle* (water-elf disease): Storms, *Anglo-Saxon Magic*, 162, speculates that this is chicken pox.

3   *cassuc* (sedge): The DOE defines this word as "a plant, probably one of the grasses or sedges."

8   *Ic benne awrat betest beado-wræda* (I have written out the best of troops for fighting disease): The meaning of this sentence depends on whether *awrat* is the past tense of *awritan* (to write out) or *awriþan* (to wreathe). The speaker therefore either has written out "the best of troops," if *beado-wræda* is figurative, or has wreathed "the best of amulets around the wounds," if *beado-wræda* is literal. The figurative meaning seems best fit to context in this charm.

10   *ne fundian, ne feologan* (nor worsen nor putrefy): Both these verbs are of uncertain meaning. The DOE observes that *fundian*, the

base meaning of which is "to set out, depart, or hasten," may mean "to get worse" or "to spread (inwards)" when used of a wound. Of *feologan,* it states that the verb may have developed from the word *fealu,* "yellow, dusky," and therefore may mean "to become discolored, putrify," or (less likely) from *fela,* "many," and therefore may mean "to spread, multiply."

13   *eorþan* (with earth): "earth" may refer to a mud poultice applied to the ear. See ASPR 6, 214.

Metrical Charm 8: For a Swarm of Bees

For a Latin analogue for this charm, see Allen and Calder, *Sources and Analogues,* 215.

6   *and wið þa micelan mannes tungan* (and against the great human tongue): The meaning is obscure. It could refer to spells (see ASPR 6, 214–15) or simply the power of speech.

Metrical Charm 9: For Loss of Cattle

2   *Herod* (Herod): Herod Antipas (4 BCE–39 CE), the ruler in Judea by whom Christ was to be tried. Herod declined to do so, however, and sent Christ back to Pontius Pilate. See the Gospel of Luke.

    Sancte Eadelenan (Saint Helena): Saint Helena (d. ca. 330) was the mother of Constantine the Great, the first Christian Roman emperor (d. 337), who brought tolerance for and imperial favor to Christianity. She and her discovery of the cross of Christ are the subjects of a poem by Cynewulf, *Elene: The Finding of the True Cross.* For a translation, see Bjork, *Old English Poems of Cynewulf,* 141–235.

6   *Garmund* (Garmund): Identity unknown.

Metrical Charm 10: For Loss of Cattle

See headnote to Metrical Charm 5.

METRICAL CHARM 11: A JOURNEY CHARM

For a Latin analogues for this charm, see Allen and Calder, *Sources and Analogues*, 215–17.

1 *gyrde* (staff): The kind of staff is unspecified, but Frederick Klaeber suggests it is a stick inscribed with the sign of the cross ("Belucan in dem altenglischen Reisesegen," *Anglia Beiblatt* 40 [1929]: 283–84); Ferdinand Holthausen, responding to Klaeber, postulates that it is a walking stick ("Nochmals der altgenglische Reisesegen," *Anglia Beiblatt* 41 [1930]: 255); and Meaney, *Anglo-Saxon Amulets*, 18–19, argues that it could be a rune stave.

16 *Annan* (Anna): A prophetess and widow who adored Christ. See Luke 2:36–38.
  Elisabet (Elizabeth): Mother of John the Baptist and cousin to the Virgin Mary. See Luke 1:5.

17 *Saharie* (Zacharias): Father of John the Baptist. See Luke 1:6.

18 *gebroþru, Petrus and Paulus* (brothers, Peter and Paul): A reference to the two apostles, although they were not brothers except in a spiritual sense.

30 *Serafhin* (the Seraph): The Seraphims, or "burning ones" (singular in the Old English), sitting above the throne of the Lord in Isaiah 6:2.

METRICAL CHARM 12: AGAINST A WEN

1 *wenne* (wen): A cyst or blemish. The word is still used in modern English for a sebaceous cyst.

5 *leaf* (leaf): Perhaps a reference to a poultice. Meaney, *Anglo-Saxon Amulets*, 19, suggests that the leaf could be a sheet of vellum or a tree leaf on which the charm is written.

6–7 *Under fot wolues, under ueþer earnes, under earnes clea* (Under the foot of the wolf, under the eagle's feather, under the eagle's claw): Perhaps "a compound amulet which had the property of making the wen wither away" (Meaney, *Anglo-Saxon Amulets*, 19), or perhaps references to tokens of the shaman's power (Niles, "Pagan Survivals," 136).

12   *hand-wurmes hupe-ban* (hip bone of a hand-worm): The hand-worm was an insect thought to cause a disease of the hand. See entry in Bosworth-Toller.

Bibliography

This is a selected bibliography. For complete coverage, consult Stanley B. Greenfield and Fred C. Robinson, eds., *A Bibliography of Publications on Old English Literature to the End of 1972* (Toronto, 1980); Bernard Muir, ed., *The Exeter Book: A Bibliography* (Exeter, 1992); and the bibliographies in the journals *Anglo-Saxon England* and *Old English Newsletter* (accessible online as OEN Bibliography database). For an annotated bibliography on wisdom poetry alone, see Russell Poole, ed., *Old English Wisdom Poetry* (Cambridge, 1998).

EDITIONS

Anlezark, Daniel, ed. *The Old English Dialogues of Solomon and Saturn.* Cambridge, 2009.

ASPR. See Dobbie, and Krapp and Dobbie.

Baker, Peter S. "A Classroom Edition of *Wulf and Eadwacer,*" *Old English Newsletter* 16.2 (1983): A1–8.

Cassidy, Frederic G., and Richard N. Ringler, eds., *Bright's Old English Grammar and Reader.* 3rd ed. New York, 1971.

Dobbie, Elliott van Kirk, ed. The Anglo-Saxon Poetic Records 6. *The Anglo-Saxon Minor Poems.* New York, 1942. Referred to in the text as ASPR 6.

Gordon, I. L., ed. *The Seafarer.* 1960. Reprint Exeter, 1979, and with bibliography by Mary Clayton, 1996.

Grattan, J. H. G., and Charles Singer. *Anglo-Saxon Magic and Medicine.* London, 1952.

Grendon, Felix, ed. and trans. *The Anglo-Saxon Charms.* New York, 1909.

Halsall, Maureen, ed. and trans. *The Old English Rune Poem: A Critical Edition.* Toronto, 1981.

Hickes, George. *Linguarum Veterum Septentrionalium Thesaurus.* 3 vols. Oxford, 1705.

Hill, Joyce, ed. *Old English Minor Heroic Poems.* 1983. 3rd ed. Toronto, 2009.

Klinck, Anne L., ed. *The Old English Elegies: A Critical Edition and Genre Study.* Montreal, 1992.

Krapp, George Phillip, and Elliott Van Kirk Dobbie, eds. The Anglo-Saxon Poetic Records 3. *The Exeter Book.* New York, 1936. Referred to in the text as ASPR 3.

Leslie, R. F., ed. *Three Old English Elegies: The Wife's Lament, The Husband's Message, and The Ruin.* 1961. Rev. ed. Exeter, 1988.

Macrae-Gibson, O. D., ed. *The Old English Riming Poem.* Cambridge, 1983.

Malone, Kemp, ed. *Widsith.* 1936. 2nd ed. Copenhagen, 1962.

Mitchell, Bruce, and Fred C. Robinson, eds. *A Guide to Old English.* 8th ed. Oxford, 2011.

Muir, Bernard, ed. *The Exeter Anthology of Old English Poetry.* 2 vols. Exeter, 1994. The Exeter DVD version 2006.

Orchard, Andy. "Reconstructing *The Ruin.*" In *Intertexts: Studies in Anglo-Saxon Culture Presented to Paul E. Szarmach,* ed. Virginia Blanton and Helene Scheck, 45–68. Tempe, Ariz., 2008.

Osborn, Marijane. "*Dogode* in *Wulf and Eadwacer* and King Alfred's Hunting Metaphors." *American Notes and Queries* 13.4 (2000): 3–9.

Pope, John C., ed. *Eight Old English Poems.* 3rd ed. rev. by R. D. Fulk. New York, 2001.

Shippey, T. A., ed. *Poems of Wisdom and Learning in Old English.* Cambridge, 1976.

Storms, Godfrid. *Anglo-Saxon Magic.* The Hague, 1948.

English Translations

Alexander, Michael, ed. and trans. *The Earliest English Poems: A Bilingual Edition.* Berkeley, 1970.

Bradley, S. A. J., ed. and trans. *Anglo-Saxon Poetry: An Anthology of Old Eng-*

lish Poems in Prose Translations with Introduction and Headnotes. London, 1982.

Gordon, R. K., ed. and trans. *Anglo-Saxon Poetry.* London, 1967.

Grendon, Felix, ed. and trans. *The Anglo-Saxon Charms.* New York, 1909.

Halsall, Maureen, ed. and trans. *The Old English Rune Poem: A Critical Edition.* Toronto, 1981.

Kennedy, Charles W., trans. *An Anthology of Old English Poetry.* New York, 1960.

McCully, Chris, trans. *Old English Poems and Riddles.* Manchester, 2008.

Rodrigues, Louis J. *Anglo-Saxon Verse Charms, Maxims & Heroic Legends.* Middlesex, 1993.

Storms, Godfrid. *Anglo-Saxon Magic.* The Hague, 1948.

Williamson, Craig, ed. and trans. *Beowulf and Other Old English Poems.* Philadelphia, 2011.

SECONDARY SOURCES

Abram, Christopher. "The Errors in *The Rhyming Poem.*" *The Review of English Studies* N.S. 58, no. 233 (2007): 1–9.

Allen, Michael J. B., and Daniel G. Calder, ed. and trans., *Sources and Analogues of Old English Poetry: The Major Latin Texts in Translation.* Cambridge, 1976.

Biggs, Frederick M. "*Deor*'s Threatened 'Blame Poem.'" *Studies in Philology* 94 (1997): 297–320.

Bjork, Robert E. "*Sundor æt rune:* The Voluntary Exile of the Wanderer." In Liuzza, *Old English Literature,* 315–27.

——, ed. and trans. *The Old English Poems of Cynewulf.* DOML 23. Cambridge, Mass., 2013.

Bliss, Alan, and Allen J. Frantzen. "The Integrity of *Resignation.*" *Review of English Studies* n. s. 27 (1976): 385–402.

Bosworth, Joseph, T. Northcote Toller, and A. Campbell. *An Anglo-Saxon Dictionary, Based on the Manuscript Collections of Joseph Bosworth. Supplement, by T. Northcote Toller, with Revised and Enlarged Addenda, by Alistair Campbell.* Oxford, 1992. (Cited as Bosworth-Toller)

Calder, Daniel G., Robert E. Bjork, Patrick K. Ford, and Daniel F. Melia, eds. and trans. *Sources and Analogues of Old English Poetry II: The Major Germanic and Celtic Texts in Translation.* Cambridge, 1983.

Cameron, M. L. *Anglo-Saxon Medicine.* Cambridge,1993.

Cavill, Paul. *Maxims in Old English Poetry.* Cambridge, 1999.

Champion, Margrét Gunnardóttir. "From Plaint to Praise: Language as Cure in "The Wanderer." In Liuzza, *Old English Literature,* 328–52.

Cross, James E. "'Ubi Sunt' Passages in Old English." *Vetenskaps-Societeten i Lund Årsbok 1956,* 23–44.

Deskis, Susan. *Beowulf and the Medieval Proverb Tradition.* Tempe, Ariz., 1996.

——. "Jonah and Genre in *Resignation B.*" *Medium Aevum* 67 (1998): 189–200. *Literature Resource Center.* Web. 21 Feb. 2013.

DiNapoli, Robert. "Wisdom Literature." In Lapidge et al., *Blackwell Encyclopedia,* 484–85.

DOE. See Healey.

Donoghue, Daniel. *Style in Old English Poetry: The Test of the Auxiliary.* New Haven, 1987.

Drout, Michael D. C. *How Tradition Works: A Meme-Based Cultural Poetics of the Anglo-Saxon Tenth Century.* Tempe, Ariz., 2006.

Earl, James W. "Hisperic Style in the Old English "Rhyming Poem." *PMLA* 102 (1987): 187–96.

Farmer, David Hugh, ed. *The Oxford Dictionary of the Saints.* 4th ed. Oxford, 1997.

Frank, Roberta. "Germanic Legend in Old English Literature." In *The Cambridge Companion to Old English Literature,* ed. Malcolm Godden and Michael Lapidge, 88–106. Cambridge, 1991.

Frantzen, Allen J. *Anglo-Saxon Keywords.* Oxford, 2012.

Fry, Donald K. "*Wulf and Eadwacer:* A Wen Charm." *Chaucer Review* 5 (1971): 247–63.

Fulk, R. D., and Christopher M. Cain. *A History of Old English Literature.* Oxford, 2003.

Garner, Lori Ann. "Anglo-Saxon Charms in Performance." *Oral Tradition* 19 (2004): 20–42.

Gay, David E. "Anglo-Saxon Metrical Charm 3 against a Dwarf: A Charm against Witch-Riding?" *Folklore* 99 (1988): 174–77.

Glosecki, Stephen O. *Shamanism and Old English Poetry.* New York, 1989.

Green, Martin, ed. *The Old English Elegies: New Essays in Criticism and Research.* Rutherford, N.J., 1983.

Greenfield, Stanley B. "The Old English Elegies." In *Continuations and Beginnings: Studies in Old English Literature,* ed. E. G. Stanley, 142–75. London, 1966.

Greenfield, Stanley B., and Daniel G. Calder. *A New Critical History of Old English Literature.* New York, 1986.

Hall, Alaric. *Elves in Anglo-Saxon England: Matters of Belief, Health, Gender and Identity.* Rochester, 2007.

Hansen, Elaine Tuttle. *The Solomon Complex: Reading Wisdom in Old English Poetry.* Toronto, 1988.

Harris, Joseph. "Elegy in Old English and Old Norse: A Problem in Literary History." In Green, *Old English Elegies,* 46–56.

Healey, Antonette diPaolo, ed. *Dictionary of Old English.* CD-ROM. Toronto, 2009. (Cited as DOE)

Hermann, John P. *Allegories of War: Language and Violence in Old English Poetry.* Ann Arbor, 1989.

Horner, Shari. "En/closed Subjects: *The Wife's Lament* and the Culture of Early Medieval Female Monasticism." In Liuzza, *Old English Literature,* 381–90.

Howe, Nicholas. *The Old English Catalogue Poems.* Copenhagen, 1985.

———. "The Cultural Construction of Reading in Anglo-Saxon England." In Liuzza, *Old English Literature,* 1–22.

Howlett, D. R. "*The Wife's Lament* and *The Husband's Message.*" *Neuphilologische Mitteilungen* 79 (1978): 7–10.

Huppé, Bernard F. *The Web of Words: Structural Analyses of the Old English Poems Vainglory, The Wonder of Creation, The Dream of the Rood, and Judith.* Albany, 1970.

Hutcheson, B. R. "*Wið dweorh:* An Anglo-Saxon Remedy for Fever in its Cultural and Manuscript Setting." *Amsterdamer Beiträge zur Älteren Germanistik* 69 (2012): 175–202.

Jolly, Karen Louise. *Popular Religion in Late Saxon England: Elf Charms in Context.* Chapel Hill, 1996.

Jurasinski, Stefan. "Caring for the Dead in *The Fortunes of Men.*" *Philological Quarterly* 86 (2007): 343–63.

Kendall, Calvin B. "Let Us Now Praise a Famous City: Wordplay in the OE

Durham and the Cult of St. Cuthbert." *Journal of English and Germanic Philology* 87 (1988): 507–21.

Lapidge, Michael, John Blair, Simon Keynes, and Donald Scragg, eds. *The Blackwell Encyclopaedia of Anglo-Saxon England.* Oxford, 1999.

Larrington, Carolyne. *A Store of Common Sense: Gnomic Theme and Style in Old Icelandic and Old English Wisdom Poetry.* Oxford, 1993.

Liuzza, Roy M., ed. *Old English Literature: Critical Essays.* New Haven, 2002.

Lockett, Leslie. *Anglo-Saxon Psychologies in the Vernacular and Latin Traditions.* Toronto, 2011.

McKinnell, John. "A Farewell to Old English Elegy: the Case of *Vainglory.*" *Parergon* n.s. 9.2 (1991): 67–89.

Meaney, Audrey L. *Anglo-Saxon Amulets and Curing Stones.* Oxford, 1981.

———. "Charms." In Lapidge et al., *Blackwell Encyclopedia,* 96–97.

Nelson, Marie. "A Woman's Charm." *Studia Neophilologica* 57 (1985): 3–8.

Niles, John D. "Pagan Survivals and Popular Beliefs." In *The Cambridge Companion to Old English Literature,* ed. Malcolm Godden and Michael Lapidge, 126–41. Cambridge, 1991.

———. "The Problem of the Ending of *The Wife's Lament.*" *Speculum* 78 (2003): 1107–50.

———. "The Trick of the Runes in *The Husband's Message.*" *Anglo-Saxon England* 32 (2003): 189–223.

O'Brien O'Keeffe, Katherine. "The Geographic List of *Solomon and Saturn II.*" *Anglo-Saxon England* 20 (1991): 123–41.

———, ed. *Old English Shorter Poems: Basic Readings.* New York, 1994.

Oggins, Robin S. "Falconry in Anglo-Saxon England." *Mediaevalia* 7 (1984 for 1981): 173–208.

Olsan, Lea. "The Inscription of Charms in Anglo-Saxon Manuscripts." *Oral Tradition* 14 (1999): 4–1–19.

Orchard, Andy. "Not What It Was: The World of Old English Elegy." In *The Oxford Handbook of the Elegy,* ed. Karen Weisman, 101–17. Oxford, 2010.

Orton, Peter. "The Form and Structure of *The Seafarer.*" In Liuzza, *Old English Literature,* 353–80.

Page, R. I. *An Introduction to Old English Runes.* 2nd ed. Woodbridge, 1999.

Pulsiano, Phillip, and Kirsten Wolf. "The 'Hwelp' in *Wulf and Eadwacer.*" *English Language Notes* 28.3 (1991): 1–9.

Renoir, Alain. "The Least Elegiac of the Elegies: A Contextual Glance at *The Husband's Message.*" *Studia Neophilologica* 53 (1981): 69–76.

Rohde, Eleanour Sinclair. *The Old English Herbals.* London, 1922.

Rosenberg, Bruce A. "The Meaning of Æcerbot." *Journal of American Folklore* 79 (1966): 428–36.

Schlauch. Margaret. "An Old English 'Encomium Urbis.'" *Journal of English and Germanic Philology* 40 (1941): 14–28.

Schneider, Karl. "The Old English *æcerbot*—an Analysis." In *Sophia Lectures on Beowulf,* ed. Shoichi Watanabe and Norio Tuschiya, 276–98. Tokyo, 1986.

Skemp, A. R. "The Old English Charms." *Modern Language Review* 6 (1911): 289–301.

Sorrell, Paul. "Oaks, Ships, and the Old English *Rune Poem.*" *Anglo-Saxon England* 19 (1990): 103–16.

Trahern, Joseph B., Jr. "Caesarius, Chrodegang, and the Old English *Vainglory.*" In *Gesellschaft, Kultur, Literatur: Rezeption und Originalität im Wachsen einer europäischen Literatur und Geistigkeit : Beiträge Luitpold Wallach gewidmet,* ed. Karl Bosl, 167–78. Stuttgart, 1975.

Weber, Gerd Wolfgang. *Wyrd: Studien zum Schicksalsbegriff der altenglischen und altnordischen Literatur.* Bad Hamburg, 1969.

Wentersdorf, Karl P. "Observations on *The Ruin.*" *Medium Ævum* 46 (1977): 171–80. n.s. 58 (2007): 1–9.

Williams, Blanche Colton. *Gnomic Poetry in Anglo-Saxon.* New York, 1914.

Index

Roman numerals refer to page numbers of the Introduction; Arabic numerals refer to the line numbers of the Old English poems. An *n* after an Arabic numeral (e.g., *Deor* 14n) refers to the Notes to the Translations; an hn after the title of a poem (e.g., *Deor* hn) refers to the relevant headnote in the Notes to the Translations; and a minus sign after a line number (e.g., 36−) refers to the preceding unnumbered line in *Solomon and Saturn* introducing a speaker. The poems are abbreviated here as follows:

BDS-WS = *Bede's Death Song*
  (*West-Saxon version*)
Deor = *Deor*
Dur = *Durham*
Fort = *The Fortunes of Mortals*
Gifts = *The Gifts of Mortals*
Husb = *The Husband's Message*
LEProv = *Latin-English*
  Proverbs
Max I = *Maxims I*
Max II = *Maxims II*
MCharm 1, 2, 3, etc. = *Metrical*
  Charm 1, 2, 3, etc.
MsRune = *The Rune Poem*

Pha = *Pharoah*
Prec = *Precepts*
ProvW = *A Proverb from*
  Winfrid's Time
Res = *Resignation B*
Rim = *The Rhyming Poem*
Ruin = *The Ruin*
Sea = *The Seafarer*
Sol = *Solomon and Saturn*
Vain = *Vainglory*
Wan = *The Wanderer*
Wid = *Widsith*
Wife = *The Wife's Lament*
Wulf = *Wulf and Eadwacer*